WORLD TRADE ISSUES

Regime, Structure, and Policy

by
Young Whan Kihl
and
James M. Lutz

PRAEGER SPECIAL STUDIES • PRAEGER SCIENTIFIC

New York • Philadelphia • Eastbourne, UK
Toronto • Hong Kong • Tokyo • Sydney

382
K47w

Library of Congress Cataloging in Publication Data

Kihl, Young W., 1932-
  World trade issues.

  Bibliography: p.
  Includes index.
  1. International economic relations. 2. Commerce.
I. Lutz, James M. II. Title.
HF1411.K478 1985   382   84-15986
ISBN 0-03-063057-6 (alk. paper)

Published and Distributed by the
Praeger Publishers Division
(ISBN Prefix 0-275)
of Greenwood Press, Inc.,
Westport, Connecticut

To

Mary, Ann, and Chip

and

K.R.F.

86-9899

Published in 1985 by Praeger Publishers
CBS Educational and Professional Publishing
a Division of CBS Inc.
521 Fifth Avenue, New York, NY 10175 USA

Printed in the United States of America
on acid-free paper

Preface

The present joint research project had its genesis a number of years ago as a result of our mutual academic interest in the pursuit of a study on the international political economy and policy issues relative to world trade. This interest perhaps became most apparent as a result of a shared journey to the University of Nebraska (Lincoln) from Iowa State University to attend the Hendricks Symposium on "U.S. International Economic Policy and Global Scarcity" in April 1980. From that shared experience in an aging, but largely functional, automobile, this research project grew slowly over time to reach the present stage of fruition. This particular work is truly a collaborative undertaking that has been improved as a result of our continuous, indeed incessant, interactions with each other for four years.

The material presented in this volume has both economic and political ramifications, and it is our earnest hope that the material will prove useful to both practitioners and scholars dealing with world trade issues and the international economy. We realize that the book does not begin to deal with all the complex policy issues that are manifest in the international economy, but hopefully it does shed some light on at least some of the difficult emerging transnational political and economic issues. We are the first to recognize that this volume hardly exhausts academic interests, including our own, in world trade issues and the international political economy. The book itself may have raised more questions than it has answered, but we take consolation from the fact that such is the process of ongoing academic research in almost any area of inquiry. The material in this volume hopefully will aid in answering some questions and may have raised some new questions that will prove to be important in the future.

We owe our special gratitude to a number of sources for aid received. Iowa State University and Indiana University–Purdue University at Fort Wayne, our respective universities, have provided the institutional support that is critical for any undertaking of this type of academic endeavor. The general support of colleagues and departments was immensely helpful, and the provision of departmental funds for travel to conventions where some of the ideas in the following pages were first tested was also invaluable. We profited greatly from the comments of colleagues on convention papers delivered at such meetings, particularly at a number of the annual meetings of the International Studies Association (Toronto, 1979; Philadelphia, 1980; Cincinnati, 1982; Mexico City, 1983; and Atlanta, 1984) and the Midwest Political Science Association (Cincinnati, 1981; and Chicago, 1983). The process of preparing and presenting these papers provided an indispensable opportunity to clarify our thoughts and to receive valuable insights and suggestions from individuals too numerous to mention.

Special acknowledgments by Dr. Kihl to a number of people are necessary. The encouragement and support of Dr. Victor Olorunsola, friend and colleague at Iowa State University, was very important. Dr. Kim Kihwan, past president of the Korea Development Institute in Seoul, and Dr. Charlotte Roderuck, director of the Iowa State University World Food Institute, also deserve special thanks for their aid in obtaining faculty research grants between 1979 and 1984. The students in political science courses at Iowa State University, particularly Political Science 453, International Organization, and Political Science 559, International Relations Theory, provided many useful comments, criticisms, and ideas over the years. Sammy Buo, Dean Kopechy, and S. S. Yoon, three graduate students, assisted in some phases of preparing materials for the present volume. Dr. Robert Evanson of the University of Missouri at Kansas City deserves special thanks for helping Dr. Lutz to familiarize himself with materials on Eastern Europe and the Soviet Union for another purpose. That assistance has proven to be quite valuable for parts of the present work.

Our editors at Praeger Publications also deserve our special thanks. John Lambert initially encouraged us to start this project and facilitated the initial steps. Betsy Brown, who later took charge of the project, was also extremely helpful and very understanding of some of the unavoidable delays that we encountered as a result of the distances between our two campuses that limited opportunities for face-to-face conferences. Barbara Leffel finished up the project with us. A most essential contributor to the final product was Mrs. Marci Irey in the College of Arts and Letters Office at Indiana University-Purdue University at Fort Wayne. She did a truly marvelous job of typing the final manuscript. Without her cheerful work, there could have been no final product. Finally, the efforts of the copy editor at Praeger are gratefully acknowledged.

Notwithstanding all of the above help, we remain responsible for the contents of this volume and any errors of omission or commission that it might contain.

Young Whan Kihl

James M. Lutz

Contents

Chapter   Page

List of Tables

List of Acronyms

ACP	African, Caribbean, and Pacific states
ASEAN	Association for South East Asian Nations
CACOM	Central American Common Market
CAP	Common Agricultural Policy (EC)
CIPEC	Intergovernmental Council of Copper Exporting Countries
CMEA	Council for Mutual Economic Assistance
COMECON	See CMEA
EC	European Community or Communities
EFTA	European Free Trade Association
GATT	General Agreement on Trade and Tariffs
GNP	Gross national product
GSP	General System of Preferences
IMF	International Monetary Fund
ITA	International Tin Agreement
JETRO	Japan's External Trade Organization
LAFTA	Latin American Free Trade Association
MITI	Ministry of International Trade and Industry (Japan)
NIC	Newly industrializing countries
NIEO	New International Economic Order

OMA	Orderly Marketing Arrangement
OPEC	Organization of Petroleum Exporting Countries
OPTAD	Organization of Pacific Trade and Development
PAFTA	Pacific Free Trade Area
SITC	Standard International Trade Classification
STABEX	Stabilization fund (Lomé Convention)
UNCTAD	UN Conference on Trade and Development
UNITAR	UN Institute for Training and Research
VER	Voluntary Export Restraint

1   Introduction

The present international economic system is a multifaceted phenomenon with many component parts, interactions, and subactor vagaries. It is also a complex system whose many parts affect others to greater or lesser extents in ways that are sometimes only dimly perceived. Economic exchanges that take place regularly and frequently across territorial boundaries of the nation-states are at the core of the system. The world trading system, as a subset of the international economic system, is clearly discernible as an autonomous structure of economic interactions between the nation-states that involve the exchange of goods and services.

What is peculiar in international economic interaction, as contrasted to domestic economic processes, is that it is not economics but politics that are given prominence and that the politics are more domestic than international. Although economic considerations generally underlie the process of international economic exchanges, noneconomic factors can also be very important and even critical in decision making on policy matters, thus making the analysis of international economic issues more difficult. Trade policy, for instance, seems to be a quintessential example of international economic policy as it involves decisions about diverting the income of some groups in a country (for example, consumers of automobiles) for the benefit of other groups in the same country (producers of automobiles). The trade policy may be carried out at the border by limiting access to a domestic market, but both its beneficiaries and its victims are often primarily domestic and only secondarily foreign (Wallis 1984, p. 1). For this reason world trade issues need to be examined from both political and economic perspectives, as well as both domestic and international perspectives.

The present volume seeks to specify certain interaction patterns in the world trading system, their important consequences, and the political and economic policy responses made by the various participating countries in world trade. These interactions are particularly worthy of study in a period when political demands for changes in the operation of the world economic system have appeared, often in the form of a need for a new international economic order. In particular, a subset of these interactions based on substantive issues in various types of commodity trade and regional patterns in international trade will be the focus of the subsequent chapters. Many of these interactions are at the core of the ongoing changes in the world trading system and constitute the issue areas where changes have been called for.

The twin perspectives of commodity trade and regional trends that form the core of the present study provide a slightly different view of world trade and its attendant institutions and structures compared to some previous studies of international trade. Some aspects of these two perspectives have already been studied in greater detail, and all of the various aspects have likewise been discussed in broader overviews of the international political economy. The theoretical framework for the present volume, however, will be able to provide more insight and detail by virtue of concentrating on the above two areas of investigation. As a result, it is hoped that the study will effectively supplement previous analyses and provide input for future work as well; it is not intended to serve as an alternative to other existing approaches. By choice of topics for emphasis and analysis, of course, the present work is bound to be normative, implicitly if not explicitly, but it is not designed to be directly prescriptive in terms of policy recommendations. The findings and conclusions that emerge from the subsequent discussions will generate sufficient data for more informed analysis, including normative suggestions that may result from the clarification of the nature of the prevailing issues in world trade.

COMMODITIES AND REGIONALISM

The two dominant analytical focuses used in the present study will thus constitute twin perspectives on the world trade regime. The specific issue areas related to trade in particular commodities will first be analyzed, and the regional trading blocs that have appeared in the world will be considered next. The focus on specific commodity trade issues, in relative isolation from the rest of the structures and practices of trade, must precede any attempts to enhance an understanding of the problems and difficulties existing in world trade. The emphasis on regional groupings is likewise more realistic because it is an accurate reflection of ongoing processes in world trade that have led to the formation of a trading bloc in Western Europe and similar trends elsewhere in the world.

The rationale for looking at world trade from the perspective of issue areas, rather than that of other conventional approaches, such as one of North-South differences or East-West interactions, is that not all conflict or cooperation lines are clearly drawn on the basis of level of economic development or type of political system. The developing countries are hardly a monolithic group of states in terms of shared interests or needs. Different subsets of states are more integrally involved in some types of world trade and not in others (Frey-Wouters 1980, pp. 160-67; Mahler 1981, p. 470; Monroe 1975, p. 51). Possibly greater variation prevails among the developing countries than among the developed ones simply because of the fact that industrialization and reliance on technology are likely to create similar problems and institutional patterns of response (Rothstein 1977, p. 48). The lack of homogeneity for the developing countries has been recognized by various international agencies (OECD 1979a, pp. 199-202). The United Nations, for example, has divided the developing countries into two groups—a smaller group consisting of the least developed countries and a larger group composed of all other countries not considered developed (cf. Rothstein 1977, p. 59n).

Similar to the differences that exist among the developing countries, there are likewise trade issues or issue areas that tend to divide the developed and industrialized states (Frey-Wouters 1980, p. 247; Mahler 1981, p. 490). Some industrialized nations, for example, are significant exporters of raw materials or agricultural commodities, items typically considered to be the principal exports of developing states. While such items do not normally constitute a majority of the exports of these developed countries in terms of overall value of trade, in many cases

they are an important proportion of the total world trade
in such products. Thus, simply focusing on the North-
South trade issues, issues among the developed countries,
or East-West concerns is likely to obscure the underlying
patterns that are more significant. Different reactions and
policy responses from various governments in the North,
South, or East are more likely to be present depending on
the nature of issues and circumstances.

The appearance of regional trading systems, an important trade issue in its own right, is the second perspective used in the present study. Regional trading systems or blocs have increasingly appeared in the post-World
War II era as much of international trade has come to be
trade among states within these groups rather than between
states in different trading systems (Bracewell-Milnes 1976,
p. 192; Calleo and Rowland 1973; Frey-Wouters 1980; Green
and Lutz 1978). The process first became noticeable with
the formation of the European Common Market,* a process
since accelerated by the enlargement of the membership as
well as by association agreements between the EC and a
large number of other states. Regional trading systems
have also appeared in other parts of the world. This
trend of regionalization in world trade is important because it is partially a response by various governments to
a particular set of trade and economic problems that have
emerged, including the differences that exist among the
developed states as well as differences between the developed and developing countries. These governments perceive
that differences exist among the developed countries as
well as among the developing states that are relative to
the specific regional trading systems. It is quite possible
that some relevant North-South trade issues, such as access
to raw materials, the pricing of raw materials, and preferential pricing arrangements for the developing countries,
would be perceived differently by countries in the various
trading blocs. Thus, greater insight can be gained from
analyzing the trading systems independently of other trade

---

*The European Economic Community, or Common Mar-
ket, is presently generally referred to as the European
Community or Communities (EC). The term EC will thus be
normally used to refer to this collection of nations, although EEC or Common Market will occasionally be used as
equivalent terms.

issues or divisions among countries such as one based on levels of economic development.

While the twin perspectives used in the chapters of this volume are distinctive and valuable, other theoretical approaches and political economy perspectives of world trade also remain important. At times some of these other political economy theories will be used to clarify the nature of key problems or policy issues, permitting a view of the world trade regime as an integral whole. In fact, the five composite perspectives on world trade that are summarized in Chapter 2 reflect the importance of alternative and competing perspectives in the analysis of world trade issues. The findings of the present volume combined with these theoretical perspectives can contribute to a greater understanding of trade issues and the changing world trade regime.

THE WORLD TRADE REGIME: CONCEPTUAL FOUNDATIONS

Reference to a world trade regime in describing the present international exchange of goods and services conveys an appropriate level of organization and structure that are visible in the trading relationships among nations. An international regime as defined by Krasner (1982, p. 186) is a set of

> implicit or explicit principles, norms, rules
> and decision-making procedures around
> which actors' expectations converge in a
> given area of international relations. Prin-
> ciples are beliefs of fact, causation, and
> rectitude. Norms are standards of behavior
> defined in terms of rights and obligations.
> Rules are specific prescriptions or proscrip-
> tions for action. Decision-making proce-
> dures are prevailing practices for making
> and implementing collective choice.

Such regimes will often serve as an intervening variable in specific issue areas between the capabilities of participating actors and transactions that occur among these actors (Lipson 1982, p. 417). Regimes also provide a context for international interactions and often lead to distinct patterns of events and outcomes (Keohane 1980, p. 134). The economic interactions involved in world trade will generally meet the criteria for a regime in broad outline. Many of the criticisms that have been made of the present global trading relationships also either implicitly or explicitly assume the presence of the appropriate set of relationships and interactions of an international regime (Keohane and Nye 1977, pp. 6-8, 19-22).

An amplified characteristic of the concept of a regime is that the participants are willing to give up some short-term interests on occasion in favor of the maintenance of the overall regime (Keohane 1980, p. 136; 1982, p. 342; Krasner 1982, p. 187). This facet of sacrifice has clearly been present in world trade in the immediate past. The United States, for example, forwent some existing advantages in the early post-World War II era, and more recently some of the oil-exporting states have also displayed their awareness of the needs of various international regimes by moderating the price increases for petroleum. The calls for a new international order are also implicitly based on the need to change the nature of the world regime. Although the idea of international regime has been criticized by some as conceptually vague (Strange 1982), the concept seems sufficiently clear to be useful in discussing political and related economic aspects of world trade.

As noted, a key for the idea of a regime is that some nations are willing to maintain the regime at some cost to themselves. For many years the country in this position was the United States, which clearly occupied a position of economic and political hegemony in the years after World War II. Beginning in the 1960s, however, the economic hegemony of the United States began to erode, and more recently the political hegemony of the United States has become much weaker (Keohane 1980; Krasner 1976, 1979; Lipson 1982; Ruggie 1982). Although Keohane (1980) has argued that the weakening U.S. hegemony has had fewer impacts on the trade regime than other world economic regimes, the weakening of this hegemony has been related to the calls for change in the system. It has also affected issues surrounding the trade in most commodities and has indirectly contributed to the formation of regional blocs since a logical hegemonic power would have circumscribed such blocs so as to maintain worldwide dominance.

WORLD TRADE DEVELOPMENT IN PERSPECTIVE

The world trade regime that has prevailed since World War II is a liberal one that was established under the auspices of the United States. This regime, sustained by the multilateral trade negotiations under the General Agreement on Trade and Tariffs (GATT) principle, encourages the trade practice of unimpeded free movement and exchange of commodities internationally by pledging to reduce and remove the artificial barriers to international trade, barriers that individual national governments may have imposed for the protection of domestic industries. As of 1983, GATT as a multilateral treaty was subscribed to by 88 countries that together accounted for more than four-fifths of world trade. Thus, GATT is both a code of rules and a forum in which countries can discuss their trade problems and negotiate to expand opportunities for world trade.

With the relative decline of U.S. hegemonic power internationally, however, this open and liberal trading regime has come under increasing challenge and criticism, first by the Soviet bloc countries and then by the developing countries. Most of the developing countries are newly independent, economically poor, and politically and militarily weak. As a result, these nations have pursued the strategy of collective action through international organizations vis-à-vis the developed countries in their demand for reform in the international economic system (Keohane and Nye 1977, pp. 35-36; Krasner 1982). The UN General Assembly Resolution of 1974 calling for the establishment of the New International Economic Order (NIEO) is a typical example of the attitudes of the developing countries that are dissatisfied with the prevailing liberal trade regime supported by the industrialized free market economy countries. The developing countries consider the free and open trade regime to operate to the advantage of the rich and powerful nations and therefore to be inherently unequal.

The resultant pattern of world trade in the 1980s is both complex and region-specific. Differences in perception between the rich and industrialized market-oriented economies and the economically poor developing countries regarding the trade regime need to be reconciled so that both parties can benefit from the opportunities for world trade. With the expansion of world trade and the presence of differing perceptions regarding the fairness of the existing norms and rules, new problems and policy issues have emerged. These issues, in terms of global, regional, and national levels and commodity-specific areas, need to be clarified and evaluated from the perspective of promoting world trade. Trade can be an infinitely better and civilized way of conducting international relations by providing an alternative instrument for political policies than war and conflict.

From a historic perspective, the trading system in the post-World War II era brought about rapid increase in the volume of trade and expansion of trade interactions among countries. The ninefold growth in the volume of international trade from the end of World War II to the early 1980s is perhaps evidence of GATT's success in its role as an international body concerned with promoting world trade and with negotiating the reduction of trade barriers. Trade has also been increasing at a faster rate since the 1950s than total world productive output (Anell and Nygren 1980, pp. 48-51; Lipson 1982, pp. 421-22). A larger proportion of all economic activity has thus come to be affected by such international exchanges, and more areas of the world are affected to greater degrees. This trade expansion ushered in an unprecedented degree of economic prosperity to countries participating in trade, thereby raising the standards of living of their populations. Trade has become an engine for economic growth and development for many countries. Both developed and developing countries have relied on the policy of export expansion as a means to bring about economic growth, as did Japan in the 1960s and the newly industrializing countries in the developing world in the 1970s. Likewise, the formation of the EC, which encouraged intraregional trade, has led to common prosperity and benefits for its member countries.

In light of the historic development of world trade in the post-World War II era, there is a need to know what patterns world trade has followed and what types of policy issues have emerged in the international economic system, particularly policies affecting different types of commodities and policies affecting regional trading patterns. The need to analyze these issues is also present because of the changing nature of the world economy. Not only has there been the decline of U.S. hegemony, but other changes in the environment in which the world trade regime operates have also occurred.

While the post-World War II period was generally one of spectacular economic growth and expansion, especially compared with other periods, a time of transition was entered in the early 1970s. It became necessary to adjust to a series of altered situations, such as inflation, the realignment of currencies following the collapse of the Bretton Woods system of fixed exchange rates in 1971, the 1972-74 world food crisis, the quadrupling and later increase in the price of oil, limited availability of energy supplies, the sharp recession of 1974-76 that is still being felt in the early 1980s, and, more recently, debt service problems for many developing countries and even a temporary decline in the prices for oil. The lack of hegemony, such as that exercised by the United States earlier, has undoubtedly contributed to this volatility in the world economy, and as a result economic shocks to the system are more likely to be the case in the future.

There has also been an intensification of competition among trading countries for the control of the same resources in the world. This competition has been a long-term trend that has been accentuated by a rapid increase in world population. Industrialization and economic advances by the developing countries, limited though they have been in many cases, have also been a factor. The increasing demand for raw materials and the products of an industrialized world by both developed and developing countries has exacerbated the pressures on the available resources. While greater demand will bring marginal sources into production through the tapping of lower grade resources, and technological advances may present the opportunity of utilizing entirely new material sources, such as would be possible with the mining of the seabeds, the pressure of demands will still be present in terms of access to supplies in general and control of the cheaper sources (Russet 1981-82). The problems of scarcity, in a relative sense at least, have thus appeared on the agendas of debates and dialogues at international forums on world trade issues and the world trade regime.

Associated with the relative scarcity of world resources, which is rapidly escalating, has been a sense of enhanced conflict over the distribution of the advantages to be expected and gained from the use of these resources domestically and their international exchange. The various international forums have been affected by such controversy, if not conflict, over the question of the equitable distribution or redistribution of benefits between the North and the South. Among the contentious issues, to be discussed in greater detail in subsequent chapters, have been differences in the levels of economic development and the mounting absolute gap in wealth between the advanced developed and many of the economically poor developing countries. Increasing conflicts are also evident in terms of trade disputes among the advanced industrialized countries of the West, dissent in the Soviet camp, and disagreements among the developing countries.

ORGANIZATION OF THE VOLUME

In Part I, Chapter 2 outlines five leading political economy perspectives on world trade that are readily identifiable in the literature. Each of these perspectives—classic free trade, neomercantilist, reformist, dependency-neocolonialist, and neo-Marxist—will be examined in terms of their descriptions of the existing world trade situation and its impacts and their prescriptions regarding the world trade regime. Chapter 3 examines the content of the demand for a NIEO that the developing countries have put forward. Both substantive issues and strategic calculations of the call for the NIEO will be assessed and evaluated.

Chapters 4 through 7 in Part II deal with world trade issues and issue areas important to many trading nations. Chapters 4 and 5 are concerned with trends in the trade of manufactures, first among the advanced industrialized nations and then in the trade of the developing countries. Manufactures have been increasingly important in world trade, and there has been contentious debate and even some incipient trade wars. The role of manufactures in the trade of the developing countries is dealt with separately in Chapter 5, given the distinctive nature of this type of trade for these states. Chapter 6 is concerned with trade in primary commodities, and Chapter 7 with trade in food and agricultural commodities.

Chapters 8 through 11 in Part III will focus on regionalism in world trade and the attendant problems faced by the member states in the specific trading systems. The trading systems are centered on the four principal markets and centers of world trade—the United States, Western Europe, Japan, and the Soviet Union. While these centers

have major interactions with each other, they are also important as the focuses of trade ties for many of the other
states in the world. The method used to assign countries
to particular trading systems is specified in Chapter 8,
which in turn also discusses the Western Hemisphere system
centered on the United States. Chapter 9 considers the
trading systems centered on the original six members of
the European Economic Community and the United Kingdom.
Chapter 10 looks at the trading system forming in the
Asia-Pacific Basin and the Japanese role in the system.
Finally, Chapter 11 deals with the trading system encompassing the Soviet Union and most of the other centrally
planned economies.

Chapter 12 in Part IV concludes the volume by high-
lighting some of the main findings of the study and by
speculating about the emerging world trade issues and the
future of the world trade regime. It will examine the
broader impacts of regionalism on the world trade regime
as well as the interaction of trade issues or concerns in
specific commodities with the appearance of the regional
trading systems that have begun to display a degree of
permanence. While it may not be possible to answer all
the questions surrounding trade issues, some implications
for the future of the world trade regime will be drawn.

PART I

Theory and
Politics of
Reform

2 Political Economy
   Views of World Trade

A variety of theories and theoretical explanations have been formulated to account for the operation of the present global economic system. Such theories are both descriptive and prescriptive and provide models of how the world economic system operates and how the trade regime can be seen to work. They also provide the criteria for interpreting a variety of effects, as well as for rendering a normative judgment. The present chapter will consider five competing political economy perspectives of the world economic system that have been abstracted from the literature: free trade, neomercantile, reformist, dependency-neocolonial, and neo-Marxist perspectives. Of these perspectives, the classic free trade theory is a prototype in the sense that it has served as a starting point for the other four, and that they are in part critiques of the free trade idea. Thus, the five theories could be arranged in two broad groups that separate the status quo-oriented free trade view from the other four. There are important differences, however, among the four remaining perspectives, even though they share one basic intellectual orientation, namely, the prescription of changes in the status quo.

These five political economy perspectives of world trade have practical importance and value in at least two significant respects. First, they provide conceptual frameworks or paradigms within which the activities and occurrences of the international economic system may be better analyzed and understood. Second, they are important because they have influenced decision makers' perceptions of the world problems and their possible solutions.

The extraction of these five competing perspectives is, admittedly, somewhat arbitrary. Others have advanced quite different typologies with fewer than five categories (for example, see Blake and Walters 1983; Spero 1977; and McGowan and Smith 1978), and the limitation of the present discussion to these five broader views may be criticized for simplifying the existing discussions of the structure of the international economic system. Given subtle, but important, distinctions among competing theorists or groups of theorists, a much larger number than five could have been extracted and presented. The joint notation for the fourth perspective of dependency-neocolonialism is a case in point that demonstrates the potential for more than the five categories adopted. (The rationale for the double notation is discussed below.) The selection and presentation of these perspectives in broad overview, however, was deemed most useful for the purposes of the present study, and their discussion will provide a theoretical background for many of the policy issues discussed in subsequent chapters.

THE COMPETING PERSPECTIVES ON WORLD TRADE

Theory of Free Trade

Free trade theory specifies an ideal wherein the international economic system is independent of all but minimal interference by governments. Adam Smith's "invisible hand" is simply transferred from the domestic economic setting to the world marketplace. Certain exceptions to the general law of free trade, such as the infant industry argument, have been somewhat reluctantly accepted (Kennedy and Dowling 1975, p. 75).* but the idea of unfettered trade has remained at the heart of the theory. The free trade idea has served as the norm for the world trade regime in many respects for much of the period after World War II. The general principles incorporated in 1947 into GATT, the most important trade agreement concluded in the years following the war, largely reflect this ideal of free trade.

-----

*The authors noted do not necessarily support the view being discussed. In some cases they are advocates, while in others they are providing descriptions or critiques.

The core of the free trade concept is the idea of comparative advantage. With comparative advantage, each country produces those items that it can produce most cheaply in relation to other countries and then exchanges them in international trade. Comparative advantage thus replaced the idea of absolute advantage, which held that countries should produce those goods that they could produce most cheaply without reference to production in other states. The end result of comparative advantage is that all countries are provided with the goods that they need at the cheapest prices. Production and trade based on comparative advantage will maximize the world economic product and will, therefore, lead to a more efficient allocation of world resources (Kennedy and Dowling 1975, p. 75; Monroe 1975, p. 30). The idea of comparative advantage implies, moreover, that all countries will receive economic gains from the specialization and division of labor involved in this production and trade. There is no specification as to how the resultant gains will be distributed to the participants in trade, although even weak states (in a political or economic sense) will gain from free trade since they have at least a residual veto power that they can use by threatening not to trade unless they receive at least some of the benefits from participation in trade (Mutti and Richardson 1979, p. 44).

The concept of the product life cycle can be considered an adjunct or modern variation of the classic free trade perspective. This concept, which provides for shifts in comparative advantage, assumes that most new manufactured products requiring technology inputs will appear in the industrialized countries, particularly in the United States with its large market (Vernon 1971, pp. 66–69). The result will be a competitive advantage in the world market for the products of these innovative firms, and a country's export position will reflect these new advantages. Firms introducing the product will lose these advantages over time, as the technology becomes more readily available and imitated abroad. An expanding world market will lead to new competitors that utilize large–scale production techniques, resulting in the standardization of the technology involved (Adler 1970; Gruber, Mehta, and Vernon 1967; Lall 1980, pp. 110–20; Lowinger 1975; Vernon 1971, p. 66). As a consequence, the initial comparative advantage to the country of the initial innovator will disappear. Standardization will ultimately permit the displacement of production to other countries that have lower labor costs or other advantages (Walker 1979, p. 15). As individual firms or multinational corporations invest abroad and relocate industrial production to developing countries, the life cycle of the manufactures will be prolonged internationally. Comparative advantage will also have shifted to new countries through a quasi-automatic process. The industrialized countries that lost their initial advantages should be introducing new innovative manufactures to the world market with the concomitant initial advantage for their export positions (Adler 1970; Gruber, Mehta, and Vernon 1967; Ozawa 1968; Walker 1979, p. 22). The product life cycle concept has thus added a dynamic element to the traditional concept of comparative advantage.

Since free trade, in principle, leads to gains by all participating nations, it can also act as a valuable stimulus for domestic growth (Kennedy and Dowling 1975, pp. 71-77; McGowan and Smith 1978, p. 208; Morton and Tulloch 1977, p. 15). Involvement in trade exchanges, including both exports and imports, will serve to improve economic efficiency in individual countries (Kennedy and Dowling 1975, p. 75). Likewise, interference with the flow of free trade will limit the economic potential of countries undertaking such actions since the automatic workings of the world marketplace will no longer be operative (Makler, Martinelli, and Smelser 1982, p. 6). In fact, it has been argued that the failure of many of the developing countries to grow more quickly is in part a consequence of the "perverse effects" of the domestic and international policies of these states, rather than the inapplicability of the free trade theory (Meier 1974, p. 13).

Neomercantilism

Neomercantilists suggest that an economic policy that will further the interests of an individual state and the welfare of its citizens should be the central focus of its trade policies and practices. State economic activity in the world marketplace should be integrated into overall national economic policies to provide advantages for the state. Maximization of world economic output is not the sole goal that the state seeks; rather, state gains and interests should be maximized. In cases of conflict between these goals, the state interests should receive priority. A neomercantilist view, in effect, advocates a "creative" redistribution of the benefits that accrue from participation in trade. The benefits to be gained are not necessarily restricted to higher prices for exports and lower prices for imports for a particular state. They may include other policy goals, such as stable prices for products that are traded, even if they are higher for needed imports or lower for exports, as well as security of supply (Krasner 1978, p. 39). Among the other policy goals pursued by states with a neomercantilistic orientation are the expansion of exports and the capture of markets, a reduction in imports, the stimulation of domestic production, and the creation of a balance of payments surplus (Blake and Walters 1983, p. 18).

The neomercantilists do not necessarily disagree with the idea of strengthening the world economic order, whether or not it is based on free trade. They are more concerned with the maintenance of stability in the trade regime and with a particular set of national values (Gourevitch 1978, p. 895). A neomercantilist could accept, for example, national sacrifices to preserve a world trade regime, if the regime were to the overall advantage of the state in question. A neomercantile view does not necessarily have to include a Hobbesian concept of the world economic system, "a war of all against all," although if every state followed neomercantile practices, such a situation could be the result.

The prevalence of neomercantile ideas can be seen in the increased calls in many countries for protection of domestic industries from foreign competition. In fact, "[i]nternational economic relationships constantly tend to verge on neo-mercantilism." The national interests of various states, usually narrowly defined, inevitably call for a policy that will yield some temporary advantage (Fishlow 1978, p. 46). This tendency for neomercantile ideas to permeate the trade regime has had important implications for trade between and within the regional trading systems.

The Reformist Perspective

Adherents of the reformist perspective, like the neomercantilists, are unwilling to accept the idea of an automatic adjustment process in the world economy, as suggested by free trade theory, or that the market plays the role of a benign governor for the world trade regime. Reformists argue that certain conditions have arisen over time in the operation of the trade regime, for whatever reasons, that present major economic problems, particularly for the developing countries. As a result, reformists advocate that politics change and adapt the existing structure of the international economic system to correct the imbalances and to compensate the developing states by providing greater equity for them.

According to the reformist school, the bulk of the benefits of international trade accrue to the Western industrialized countries, primarily due to the fact that Western Europe and North America, as well as Japan, entered the industrial stage of development earlier than the rest of the world. These industrialized countries now naturally have a comparative advantage in manufactures and other goods requiring skill and capital inputs, while the developing countries are left to provide raw materials and other commodities of lesser value. With the partial exception of petroleum, the same volume of traditional exports from the developing countries is seen as being exchanged for fewer and fewer manufactured goods in return, as the price of manufactured products has been rising much faster than the price of traditional commodity exports (Anell and Nygren 1980, pp. 132–35; Prebisch 1959). As a consequence, the present distribution of benefits in the world trade regime is seen to be increasingly more unfair. In fact, this perception of the existence of declining terms of trade for the developing countries led Raul Prebisch, then head of the secretariat of the Economic Commission for Latin America, to emerge as one of the first to suggest reforms in the structures of the world trade regime (Monroe 1975, pp. 31–33).

Proposed solutions by reformists have included a number of measures, such as the improvement of prices for exports from the developing countries, changes in trade patterns to facilitate new nontraditional exports from these countries, preferential trade arrangements, and nonreciprocal tariff reductions. These reform proposals have been important in agenda setting at various international conferences, culminating in the formation of the Group of 77 and the creation of the UN Conference on Trade and Development (UNCTAD). UNCTAD and the Group of 77 are embodiments of efforts by the developing states in negotiations with the developed states to improve the benefits from trade received by the developing states. Under the initial leadership of Prebisch, UNCTAD has tried to exert collective pressure for improvements in the trade regime, which ultimately led to the call for a New International Economic Order, the details of which are discussed in Chapter 3.

Various specific programs and measures for changes suggested by reformists are designed to help rectify the existing inequities of the trade regime as perceived in the developing countries and to increase their benefits from participation in trade. Since most of the suggested changes have largely been within the framework of the existing pattern of interactions, reformists have not necessarily disavowed the present trade regime in its entirety. As the notation for this perspective implies, the approach to the trade regime has been to attempt to reform the existing structures and norms rather than replace them. Reformist criticisms of free trade theory have raised important policy questions for the world trade regime by directly pinpointing some of the potentially adverse effects that may result from a trade regime primarily built on the concept of free trade.

Dependency-Neocolonial Views

The dependency-neocolonial view, unlike the reformist, displays much more concern over the workings of the world economic system and calls for greater action to rectify what is perceived to be a series of difficulties. Adherents of the view feel that the problems of the developing countries result from purposeful action rather than from historical accident. It is argued that historical occurrences helped to create the situation of dependency (Duvall 1978, p. 68; McGowan and Smith 1978, p. 181). Further, the industrialized countries have exploited the developing states both economically and politically (Alschuler 1976, p. 46; Barongo 1980, pp. 5, 19-20). The theory assumes that political ramifications result from the situation of economic weaknesses in the developing countries, which permit the industrialized nations to create, maintain, and perpetuate political influence or control.

The dual notation is being used for this school because there are subtle distinctions between the dependency view and that of the neocolonialists. Whereas dependency is a term generally used in Latin America, a continent long politically independent, neocolonialism is more prevalent in

Africa, Asia, and the Middle East, where most of the countries have had more recent colonial experiences. The dependency theories tend to place more emphasis on the proposition that the present Western domination has resulted from economic activities supplemented by political actions. Neocolonialists, on the other hand, regard the recent economic disadvantage of the developing countries to be more a result of direct imperial occupation of their territories. These differences in interpretations of the historical roles of economics and politics, while important, are more a matter of emphasis than basic disagreement. There is general consensus on the nature of present problems as well as the reasons for the continued existence of these difficulties; therefore, these two views can be treated as a composite theory. Also, in contradistinction to the reformist view, the dependency-neocolonial theorists have concentrated more on dyadic relationships between a dominant Western country and a set of controlled satellite states, rather than on the international regime.

It is not surprising that this perspective sees comparative advantage to be a form of economic exploitation by the rich countries. Even the classic textbook example of comparative advantage--the trade of British textiles for Portuguese wine--has been called into question. Baumgartner and Burns (1975) have argued that this trade permitted English merchants to eliminate the new Portuguese textile industry and to raise prices after the disappearance of the domestic competition. The eighteenth-century Portuguese economy was thus hurt, a process that was subsequently carried out in other territories as well. The world economic system is therefore seen, in an extension of this argument, as operating to maintain underdevelopment in the developing countries and to perpetuate the exploitive nature of the relationships between developed and developing countries, thereby hindering economic development (Alschuler 1976, p. 77; Dos Santos 1971; Mahler 1980, p. 1; McGowan and Smith 1978, p. 205; Sunkel 1969, pp. 135-36; Walleri 1978, pp. 607, 611). In fact, dependency theory has been described as a theory that is, in essence, "an explanation of the failure of the Third World countries to develop" (Stallings 1972, p. 5) (Emphasis in original).

Given the underlying belief in the presence of economic exploitation, these theorists argue that exporting traditional products at higher prices or in greater amounts will not solve the problems of underdevelopment. Reliance on markets in the developed countries will, in fact, result in some other state controlling the local economy of the developing state with concomitant political consequences. Even industrialization by the developing countries may not loosen dependency on the foreign markets. The developing countries will often remain reliant on markets for manufactured products in the developed states, as was the case for primary commodities (Michalet 1982, pp. 42-43). The capital goods and the technology for the new industries must come from the industrialized countries, which can then maintain political dominance through threats to withhold essential materials or inputs (Frank 1970; Mahler 1981, p. 469; Stallings 1972, p. 38; Sunkel 1969). Multinational corporations involved in the industrialization process can also be used to distort the local economies and drain the profits from these new industries (Lall 1975, p. 801; T. Smith 1979, p. 250; Sunkel 1969; Walleri 1978, p. 608).

The dependency-neocolonial theorists have also argued that the world trade regime has had adverse effects on income distribution and negative economic impacts in the developing states. The benefits of trade are seen to be uneven in the sense of favoring either certain elite groups or only certain sectors of the society. Also, the inequitable distribution of benefits at the international level will progressively lead to the poverty of the masses of the populations in the developing countries (Mahler 1980, p. 2; McGowan and Smith 1978, p. 184; Sunkel 1973, p. 146). Also, many of the export sectors of the developing economies are likely to be of an enclave nature. Since these enclaves are tied to the international market, they are seen to contribute relatively little to the local economy and to create geographic and sectoral maldistributions (Duvall 1978, p. 71).

Ultimately, this perspective views the present trade patterns, especially trade between developed and developing countries, as ones where the advantages are skewed on the side of the industrialized states, states unlikely or unwilling to surrender the present advantages. Dependency constitutes a whole syndrome going beyond economic distortions to include the social, political, and cultural realms as well (Caporaso 1978; Duvall 1978). Ultimately, the solution to these problems of inequities is seen not with greater integration into the world economic system but in greater self-reliance and self-sufficiency (Cardoso 1982, pp. 161-62).

Neo-Marxism

Neo-Marxist theorists dealing with world trade have both advantages and disadvantages by virtue of their subscribing to an already established and developed underlying world view. The prefix "neo" is attached to the theory since they are attempting to deal with a situation not originally perceived by Karl Marx in his writings, at least not in any great detail. The emphasis that neo-Marxists place on class conflict and capitalism tends to distinguish them from the dependency-neocolonial school:

> Great differences, however, exist between
> the two camps as to the means of ending
> neo-colonialism. While to the Marxists neo-
> colonialism is seen as an extension of
> class conflict to the world state sowing
> seeds of universal revolution, in the na-
> tionalist's view, class analysis has no
> relevance to the relationships of depen-
> dence. (Barongo 1980, pp. 47-48)

This view is economically deterministic and thus may ignore other relevant variables, and adherence to an economic deterministic perspective limits flexibility in analyzing or understanding particular activities. Actions of national governments are often seen to result from the operation of class factors rather than from activities pursuant to the national interests of a state, such as the neomercantilists argue exist or should exist. Neo-Marxists, on the other hand, can draw upon an extensive body of literature of Marxian theoretical writing on economic and political issues. They can also interrelate historical occurrences in the various domestic arenas rather easily with activity in the international system. As a result, the neo-Marxist perspective of world trade purports to be a totally systemic explanation of the world economic regime, including within it many exogenous variables to a much greater extent than the other composite perspectives presented.

According to neo-Marxist theorists, the international system thus reflects a global class division with the developing countries exploited by the bourgeois states of the West. The world trade regime allegedly serves as a mechanism for this exploitation and for keeping the developing countries in a position of receiving fewer benefits deriving from trade (Chase-Dunn 1975; Denoon 1979, p. 9; Galtung

1971; Gantzel 1973). While differences are noticeable among various neo-Marxist theorists regarding the question of exactly how and why the dominant capitalist classes control politics in individual countries and how they order the operation of the trade regime, a general consensus prevails that such controls do exist (cf. Krasner 1978, pp. 21-26; McGowan and Walker 1981, pp. 348-65). The neo-Marxists are also in complete accord as to the need for great changes in the world trade regime, as well as appropriate domestic action within developing states. In addition, cooperation with the socialist states ("the vanguard of the international proletariat"?) that will not exploit the developing countries is useful (Chase-Dunn 1983b, p. 272). Ultimately, revolutionary changes are needed in the class systems of the Western capitalist states.

The lack of economic development in the Third World is thus claimed to be a result of capitalist domination of the international economic system. True economic development would require radical measures whereby the developing countries take the hard choice of disassociating their domestic economies from the exploitive world capitalist system (Denoon 1979, p. 9; Gantzel 1973, pp. 208-09). The neo-Marxists do not necessarily advocate autarky, as trade with the socialist countries is seen as an exception to the rule of exploitation of developing countries by industrialized ones (Chase-Dunn 1983a, p. 45; Fagen 1978). Class factors play other roles in the limiting of economic progress in the developing countries. Increases in exports will perpetuate economic problems since the export sectors tend to favor exactly those class elements most disposed to capitalist interests in the industrialized states (Chase-Dunn 1983a, p. 26; Senghass 1975, p. 267; Senghass-Knoblock 1975, p. 283; Stallings 1982, p. 199). Import substitution policies will be likely to fail since the capitalist classes in the West will either prevent effective industrialization or channel it into areas where exploitation can continue, often through the multinational corporations that operate as instruments of the capitalist classes in the industrialized countries (Bornschier 1982, p. 60; Borrego 1983; Chase-Dunn 1982, p. 121; Martinelli 1982, p. 107; Senghass 1975, p. 268; Senghass-Knoblock 1975, pp. 283, 288). Even the socialist countries will have considerable difficulty in escaping from this situation of dominance since the world economy and trade regime are assumed to be dominated by capitalist states (Chase-Dunn 1983a).

The world class structure also contributes to distribution problems within the developing countries as well as
the developed ones. For the international exploitation to
work, there must be an indigenous class in the developing
countries that will profit by participation in trade, with
any existing benefits being concentrated in the hands of
this class. It will serve the Western capitalists and in
return is suitably rewarded as their paid intermediaries
(Arrighi 1970, pp. 222-23; Fagen 1978, pp. 204-05; Duvall
and Freeman 1981, p. 109; Hveem 1973, p. 322). Galtung
(1971, p. 85) has argued that if this class does not exist
in a given country, then the country cannot be structurally
integrated into the existing form of imperialism represented
by the present international economic and political regime.
Further, better terms of trade, while improving the international distribution of benefits, does not solve the internal distribution problems that prevail within individual
countries (p. 88).

In the final analysis, the neo-Marxian solution to
problems in the world economic system will require the replacement of the existing world trade system, or a large
portion of it, with a socialist world order (Chase-Dunn
1983a, p. 48; Gantzel 1973, p. 203). Replacement of the
local classes collaborating with capitalist interests in the
industrialized states would be a positive and helpful step
(Bodenheimer 1971), although it would not directly remove
the problems created by the presence of capitalism in the
industrialized states. Also, for the neo-Marxists an appropriate course of action might be to let conditions in the
developing country become so bad that internal revolutions
to create a socialist society may be the only available option (McGowan and Smith 1978, p. 184). This possibility
of revolutionary change separates the neo-Marxists from
the dependency-neocolonial theorists. Adherents of the
latter school have not noticeably favored permitting conditions to get worse; instead, they have favored measures for
improving conditions in the developing countries.

CONTRASTING THE PERSPECTIVES

All five perspectives postulate definite images of the
world economic order and provide views of the world trading system and the consequences of the existing patterns
of world trade. The free trade view is concerned virtually

only with trade. The other views, particularly the neo-Marxist and dependency-neocolonial ones, consider trade within the broader context of the global economy. In all five cases, however, trade tends to constitute an important part of the overall perspectives on the world economic order. All five perspectives also tend to provide definite views on the role that world trade should ideally play for individual countries.

The perspectives do have differing views on the current distribution of international and domestic benefits from trade. The classic liberal view, for example, assumes that all countries would gain from participation in trade, although the theory is silent on the exact nature of the division of those benefits and avoids the important question of equity. Neomercantilism developed under the assumption that benefits from participation in trade were not being distributed in an appropriate fashion. Adherents of this school, in effect, suggest that individual states should undertake policy actions to gain a greater share of the benefits resulting from participation in trade. This greater share should be attained in its own right, but a particular distribution of benefits should also be sought so that the distribution facilitates the implementation of domestic economic policies of whatever kind that are being pursued. Reformists are obviously very concerned about the distribution of benefits occurring in the present trade regime, and their criticisms have been grounded in questions of equity involving the existing arrangements.

The dependency-neocolonial and neo-Marxist perspectives have also clearly concentrated on questions related to the distribution of benefits from trade. Both views perceive that the developing countries in particular have received less than their fair share of the benefits of world trade. The perception of exploitation of the developing countries by the rich industrialized states is central to both perspectives. These schools also see the present pattern of trade as having negative consequences for domestic distribution within the developing countries in terms of both income and benefits derived from trade. The neo-Marxists, however, differ from the dependency-neocolonialists in their emphasis on the role that class plays. Whereas dependency-neocolonialist adherents tend to focus more on relationships between a major industrialized state and a group of developing countries, the neo-Marxists tend to place more emphasis on the structure of the international economy and political system.

The five perspectives have differing views on the role of trade in a country's economic growth and development, although it should be remembered that growth cannot necessarily be equated with development. The free trade theory assumes that economic growth will occur since all participating states will benefit from trade. The neomercantilists, on the other hand, expect appropriate trade policies to enhance growth in at least some countries. The assumption underlying the reformist view is that a fairer trade regime that improves upon the existing structure will further economic growth in the developing countries. Thus, they accept the idea that trade can help to generate additional economic growth. The dependency-neocolonialists view the role of trade more critically. They claim that only certain kinds of trade will favor economic growth, while other types will not. Not only the world trade regime needs to be changed but so also do the types of economic interactions and linkages between the developed and developing states. The neo-Marxists assume that changes in trade patterns by themselves will not lead to economic growth. They maintain that changes in the class structures in the developing and developed states are necessary and ultimately a socialist world order must replace the existing capitalist system. One difference between the neo-Marxist and dependency-neocolonialist perspectives is the extent to which economic development is perceived to be possible within the present global capitalist system (Caporaso 1981, p. 351).

It is possible that any relationship between trade and economic growth and development is unclear. While trade that is exploitive or that leads to negative domestic consequences, such as sectoral imbalances or maldistributions of income, may present difficulties, even more trade may be necessary for many countries so that they can reach a point where trade can be used constructively to aid domestic economic growth and development. A country with a growing economy might even actually attract more trade and investment, leading to greater dependence on the world trade regime (Ray and Webster 1978, p. 417). The additional trade and investment could ultimately provide greater freedom of action for many of the countries involved. Thus, those nations that are presently more dependent on trade, particularly the developing ones, may possibly be experiencing greater growth and may also, somewhat ironically, be closer to rectifying the problems that involvement in world trade may bring (Rothstein 1977, pp. 45-46).

Underlying differences in the perspectives also concern action called for in different arenas. The three key
areas where action might be specified are the world trade
regime, the developing countries, and the developed industrialized states. The contrasting emphases of the five perspectives are integral to many of their disagreements,
plans of action, and prescriptions for change or continu-
ance. In terms of these three areas of concern, the classic
liberal theory concentrates on the trade regime and suggests no changes. The neomercantilists are, in effect,
principally concerned with the industrialized states, since
the policies they often suggest have greatest relevance to
these states and can probably be implemented effectively
by only developed countries. Reformists attach greater importance to the world trade regime as well as to the situation of the developing countries. Their perceptions of the
problems that the developing countries are facing led to
their advocacy of structural and policy changes in the
world trade regime. The dependency-neocolonial theorists
parallel reformists in terms of specific areas of concern.
The neo-Marxists are the only group that specifies all three
arenas of action as being important. Unlike the dependency-
neocolonialists, the neo-Marxists are often less interested in
specific nations (Barongo 1980, p. 48) and, instead, focus
more on the broader trading system and patterns of interaction. They also ultimately see the need for radical
changes in the developed states and the developing countries and also in the structures of the world trade regime.
They seem to suggest that changes in the world trade regime would logically follow from the appropriate changes
in the developed and developing countries.

TRADE POLICY IMPLICATIONS

The five perspectives on the world economy have
had important impacts on the policies undertaken by individual countries or groups of states on issues relevant to
world trade. The free trade theory, which itself was a
response to earlier mercantile practices, has been the dominant image since World War II. The free trade idea has
also been important among policymakers in the United States
in particular (Calleo and Rowland 1973, p. 20; Gilpin 1971,
pp. 58-59; Mingst 1980; Monroe 1975, p. 1; Russet 1981-82;
Ruggie 1982, pp. 393-98). Although the United States has

not demonstrated total commitment to the free trade ideal in all cases, it is still one of the leading countries that has displayed a strong commitment.

Neomercantilism reflects dissatisfaction with the free trade concept. Protectionist practices in terms of particular commodities or industries or encompassing specific geographic areas have become increasingly prevalent, as will be discussed in the following chapters. Such trade protectionism for promoting national interests and domestic policies is acceptable, in principle, to neomercantilists. Protectionism in one state tends to lead to protectionism in others. Western European countries adopted some protectionist measures, especially against imports from Japan, partially as a reaction to Japanese protectionist measures (Denoon 1979, p. 11; Hollerman 1975, pp. 174-75). Protectionism in Japan and Western Europe has also led to suggestions that the United States abandon the commitment to free trade and adopt similar policies against foreign competitors (Calleo and Rowland 1973, p. 140; Cohen 1977).

The criticisms of reformists and dependency-neocolonialists have also been important for alternate policies advanced for the world trade regime. They have provided an intellectual basis for the calls for changes in the present international economic order (Denoon 1979, p. 10; Krasner 1981, p. 121). These demands, which will be discussed in detail in Chapter 3, have been an important policy issue for many developing states. This demand for change in the world economic system has been influenced by the two perspectives, and the critiques of the trade regime by their adherents helped to mobilize the developing states to form the Group of 77 and UNCTAD.

The neo-Marxist perspective has had perhaps the least impact on the policies of different countries to date, although the fact that this school shares criticisms of the trade regime with the reformist and the dependency-neocolonial groups is itself important. Arguments in favor of a socialist world order did gain an economic component, but neo-Marxists already accepted the need for such a world order on a variety of other grounds. This perspective, or portions of it, could have greater implications for the policies of different states in the future if new governments that accept the arguments of this school should come to power.

All five theoretical perspectives, and the interactions among them, have played still another important role in shaping the future of the world trade regime and the policies of the countries participating in the world trading system. They have collectively raised important normative questions about what the goals of international trade and the structure of the trade regime should be. Such normative questions are obviously implied in the calls for changes in the international order that will be discussed in Chapter 3 in particular, although they also appear in a variety of other forms in the remaining chapters of this volume as well. There will obviously be continuing disagreement over the important questions of who controls and who benefits in regard to world trade, as well as disagreements over policy preferences on how the regime structure should be altered. The raising of these issues, combined with the weakened hegemony of the United States in the world trade regime, has probably been most responsible for the dissension, conflict, and confusion about the role and value of trade. This dissension and confusion are typified by the disputes over the questions of what the structure of the world trade regime should be, why the worldwide economic recession of the 1970s with its associated problems appeared, and what roles different groups of countries should play in the world trading system and the world trade regime.

3 The Call for a New International Economic Order

The existing world trade regime was constructed after World War II without the active participation of the developing countries (the South) many of which were yet to be born, and it was designed primarily to serve the needs of the developed countries (the North). The call for a New International Economic Order (NIEO) has thus been an effort by the developing countries to implement changes in the main areas of North–South interaction that they consider necessary to make the international economic system maximally conducive to their development (Sauvant 1981, p. xxiv). International exchanges, especially world trade, are to trigger and then to maintain this development process.

The call for the NIEO represents the appearance of North–South economic relations at the forefront of international economics and politics. This demand for the establishment of the NIEO by the South, as well as the problems that have been raised for the developed states in preparing to deal with the concrete proposals related to the NIEO, now define the agendas of the numerous conferences and intergovernmental negotiating groups on international economic matters (Bhagwati 1977, p. 1). The substance of the NIEO proposal, therefore, reflects the evolution of the economic and political philosophy of the developing countries in the post–World War II era. In view of the stalemate in the North–South negotiations on the condition of the world economy, attention to the substance of the NIEO demands is necessary.

ORIGIN AND BACKGROUND

The adoption by the Sixth Special Session of the UN General Assembly of the "Declaration on the Establishment of a New International Economic Order" without a vote on May 1, 1974, marked the formalizing of the process of moving toward the demand for the NIEO. The United Nations has often been criticized for indulging in a high degree of idealism while failing to give due regard to world reality and practical matters. Such high-sounding idealism is reflected in the following opening statement of the declaration (UN General Assembly Resolution 3201-S-VI):

> We, the Members of the United Nations, . . . solemnly proclaim our united determination to work urgently for the establishment of a new international economic order based on equity, sovereign equality, interdependence, common interest and co-operation among all States, irrespective of their economic and social systems, which shall correct inequalities and redress existing injustices, make it possible to eliminate the widening gap between the developed and developing countries and ensure steadily accelerating economic and social development—in peace and justice for present and future generations.*

This declaration of intention was backed by an implementation plan, the Program of Action, also adopted on May 1, 1974, in an effort to translate idealism into practical measures of policy action. Seven months later, in December 1974, the developing countries in the South moved during the regular General Assembly session to pass the "Charter of Economic Rights and Duties of States." The charter was adopted by a majority of 120 to 6, with 12 abstentions. The passage of the charter, promoted by the Group of 77 and members of the Non-Aligned Nations Movement, found key industrialized countries in opposition or abstention. The United States and five other industrial

---

*The full text of the declaration and related NIEO documents can be found in UNITAR (1976).

countries (Belgium, Denmark, West Germany, Luxembourg, and the United Kingdom) voted against, with ten other industrialized countries (Australia, Canada, France, Ireland, Israel, Italy, Japan, the Netherlands, Norway, and Spain) abstaining (Vastine 1977, pp. 418–19). The passage of the charter thus marked a showdown between the voting power of the South in the UN General Assembly and the economic power of the North in the real world, with the latter overcome by the pressure of the former in the politics of the UN General Assembly.

Since the basic idea of the NIEO, at least as reflected in the preceding three documents, has been questioned by some in the developed countries, closer attention to the nature of the demands advanced by the South, as well as to the basis for some skepticism expressed through criticism of the NIEO, is necessary. The main point of criticism has been that the NIEO demand is one-sided in terms of the rights the developing countries claim and the duties the South seeks to impose upon the developed countries. Although some of the imbalance was corrected subsequently by the United Nations in the Seventh Special Session resolution on "Development and International Economic Co-operation" adopted on September 16, 1975, the basic difference of positions and perceptions between the South and the North still remained intact.

Seven noteworthy principles were laid down in the "Declaration on the Establishment of a New International Economic Order." First, it called for full and effective participation on an equal basis for all countries in the efforts to solve world economic problems in the common interest of all countries. Second, it stated that every country had the right to adopt the economic and social system it deemed most appropriate for development. Third, every state should have full and permanent sovereignty over its natural resources and economic activities. Fourth, it specified the need for regulation and supervision of transnational corporations. Fifth, it called for the creation of a fair relationship between the prices received by the developing countries for their exports and the prices they pay for the goods that they import. Sixth, the declaration called for the transfer of technology to developing countries and the promotion of indigenous technologies within them. Finally, there was a call for greater cooperation among the developing countries in economic, trade, financial, and technical areas (UNITAR 1976).

These principles were subsequently elaborated upon and incorporated into the "Charter of Economic Rights and Duties of States." The main thrust of the charter was contained in the following four basic demands put forward by the South in calling for the NIEO.

1. Every state has and shall freely exercise full permanent sovereignty, including possession, use and disposal, over its wealth, natural resources and economic activities.

2. Each state has the right to nationalize, expropriate or transfer ownership of foreign property in which case appropriate compensation should be paid by the state adopting such measures taking into account its relevant laws and regulations and all circumstances that the state considers pertinent. In any case where the question of compensation gives rise to controversy, it shall be settled under the domestic law of the nationalizing state and by its tribunals. . . .

3. It is the duty of states to contribute to the development of international trade of goods particularly by means of arrangements and by the conclusions of long term multilateral commodity agreements, where appropriate, and taking into account the interests of producers and consumers.

4. All states have the right to associate in organizations of primary commodity producers in order to develop their national economies to achieve stable financing for their development, and in pursuance of their aims assisting in the promotion of sustained growth of the world economy, in particular accelerating the development of developing countries. Correspondingly all states have the duty to respect the right of producing countries by refraining from applying economic and political measures that would limit it. (UNITAR 1976)

Obviously, the developing countries in the South have been advancing a demand for altering the standards of conduct and norms governing economic relations between the South and the North through these declarations and other NIEO documents. These and similar norms, if implemented, would result in the enhanced sovereignty of the developing countries. The advanced industrial countries have not accepted or even agreed to negotiate on these principles, which would alter the long-standing principles of international law regarding the rights and obligations of the states and their foreign investors and which would replace the market mechanisms with commodity agreements and/or commodity cartels in international commerce for raw materials. This attempt at "legislation by declaration" that the UN resolutions seem to represent, however, does not carry any legal or political binding authority except to the extent that it draws world public opinion to the cause of the developing countries and to the extent it lays out a foundation for altering international economic practices in the future (Blake and Walters 1983, p. 194).

SUBSTANTIVE ISSUES AND PROGRAMS

The elements and blueprints of the NIEO, as envisioned by the Group of 77 working through UNCTAD, consist of both short-term goals, embodying institutional arrangements through a complex of negotiations within and outside the UN system, to promote the economic and social progress of the developing countries, and long-term objectives for achieving the structural changes that it considers necessary to overcome the "defects and inequities" of the existing system. A number of the specific short-term issues related to creating an "economic security system" for the developing countries were an integrated program for commodities, improved compensatory financing facilities, and debt relief for developing countries. Examples of long-term objectives and policy issues included reducing the economic dependence of developing countries on the North, by means of expanding trade in manufactures, a strengthened technical base for the developing countries, and improvement in the marketing and distribution system for primary commodities; strengthening trade and economic cooperation among developing countries; and creating a more efficient global management of resources by such measures as changes in international trading rules, international monetary reform, and rational use of resources.*

---

*UNCTAD, "Trade and Development Issues in the Context of a NIEO," February 1976, as reprinted in Sauvant and Hasenpflung (1977, pp. 39-62).

The problems of raw materials and primary commodities are particularly important for the developing states
(as is noted in Chapter 6), as most of their export earnings come from primary commodities, and even some of the
manufactures involve limited processing of mineral resources
(see Chapters 4, 5, and 6). Improved earnings from commodity exports, therefore, would make a substantial contribution to the welfare of many developing countries.
The NIEO provisions on trade and development reflect the
perspective of the developing countries, often elaborated
in the reformist and dependency-neocolonial views, that the
liberal international economic system has been dominated
by industrialized states. The result has been the maldis-
tribution of global income and economic influence at the
expense of the developing countries. The resource trans-
fers demanded in the NIEO provide hope to the developing
countries that they will be able to eliminate what are seen
as the international sources of their economic impotence and
political weakness (Anell and Nygren 1980, pp. 120-21;
Blake and Walters 1983, p. 191). Even so, and perhaps
despite "occasional rhetorical excesses," the program em-
bodied in the NIEO documents basically accepts the idea
that trade and even foreign investment can contribute to
the growth of the developing countries through a more
equitable division of the benefits from such activities
(Fishlow 1978, p. 14).

In the trade arena, the NIEO program seeks various
forms of preferential treatment for the developing countries.
The program includes the ideas of price stabilization and
indexation for primary commodity exports. There have also
been desires for improving the prices received for manufactures, semimanufactures, and semiprocessed goods, including
special trade preferences for the exports of the developing
countries. Finally, a call has been included for better
domestic adjustment programs in the developed countries to
meet the transitional pains that would accompany the restructuring of the industrialized economies to facilitate the
increased importation of manufactures from the South.

Concern with the export of primary commodities
appears in a number of forms in the principles of the
NIEO. The desire for domestic control of natural resources
and the emphasis given to producer associations demonstrate
an important interest in such exports. There also been
an interest in expanding the markets for natural products

in relation to synthetics and promoting the processing of raw materials in the developing countries where they are produced.

More comprehensive and integrative approaches to the commodity problems specified in the NIEO have been considered in subsequent international forums. UNCTAD IV in Nairobi in 1976, for example, adopted an Integrated Program for Commodities and set up a timetable for the negotiation of the program. There were provisions for a Common Fund and International Commodity Agreements for a substantial number of materials of export interest to the developing countries. The Common Fund was established with a capitalization of $6 billion. Initially, $1 billion was to be contributed from member states with another $1 billion contributed later, and the remaining $4 billion was to be borrowed. The fund would finance buffer stocks and support other price stabilization measures. Subsequent negotiations in 1979 reduced the initial capital from $1 billion to $400 million (Brandt 1980, pp. 149–50; Vastine 1977, pp. 419–23). International commodity agreements involving cooperative arrangements between producers and consumers, however, have yet to be concluded in most cases, even though negotiation and dialogues have taken place at various international forums. The fact that the developed countries have not found it in their short-run interest to develop concerted implementation of the UNCTAD commodity policies has also been a major barrier (Gosovic 1972, p. 114).

As for food production and trade, the NIEO recommends that land in the developing countries that is unexploited or underexploited owing to lack of the necessary means be reclaimed and put into practical use. In the Program of Action the international community is called upon to undertake concrete and speedy measures to arrest desertification, salination, pest damage, and other phenomena afflicting various developing countries, particularly in Africa. Further, concrete measures are needed to increase food production and storage facilities in developing countries so as to prevent additional deterioration of natural resources and food supplies through pollution and contamination. The essential inputs for these measures need to come from the developed states and should be provided on favorable terms. Exports of food products from the developing countries should also be promoted through various arrangements, including the progressive elimination of protective and other barriers that constitute unfair competition. The Common Agricultural Policy of the EC and measures in other developed nations are an obvious focus of this last demand.

Regarding exports of manufactures, the General System of Preferences (GSP) has been a key component of the NIEO. The GSP concept first appeared at the UNCTAD II meeting in New Delhi in 1968 (Feld 1976, p. 239), but it has been included in various subsequent NIEO documents. The GSP basically argues for special treatment for certain products exported by the developing countries in the form of lower tariffs while leaving tariffs at higher levels for similar products exported by the developed countries. Manufactures and semiprocessed products are the items usually mentioned for inclusion in the GSP. In theory, these preferences in the industrialized states would make developing country exports more competitive with the export of the industrialized countries. In addition, no reciprocal privileges would be granted to the developed states in return for the special tariff considerations.

The GSP idea initially envisioned that all the developing countries would adopt a common system, but differing GSPs have actually been put into effect. For example, the United States has numerous potential exceptions to GSP provisions that exclude most Communist states, developing countries that have granted reverse preferences to other developed states, members of OPEC or other groups limiting the supply of vital resources or raising their prices to "unreasonable" levels, countries that have expropriated US property without fair compensation, and states that fail to cooperate in suppressing the movement of narcotics into the United States (Meyer 1978, pp. 117–18; Morrison 1976, pp. 27–28). The system adopted by the EC also includes similar limitations. Quotas for specific items were instituted, for instance, to protect the exports of the developing countries that have association agreements with the Common Market (Feld 1976, p. 240). The various schemes adopted also contain escape clauses to protect domestic industries that could be adversely affected by such imports from developing countries, a further reflection of the new protectionism to be discussed in Chapter 5.

There was initial opposition among the developed countries, including the United States, to the idea of the

GSP on a number of grounds. Since the GSP clearly con-
tradicted the free trade ideals, it has been argued that
one such deviation from the norm could easily lead to
others (Calleo and Rowland 1973, p. 234; Matthews 1977,
p. 83). Krasner (1979, pp. 526-27) has noted, however,
that past deviations from the principle of free trade frequently occurred after World War II and that they did not
directly undermine the general free trade orientation of the
regime. A related potential problem with the GSP is that,
in order for such tariff preferences to be effective, present
tariff levels on manufactures could not be reduced on the
ground that, as these tariffs approach zero, any positive
benefits from the GSP would be lost (Matthews 1977, p. 83).
Thus, institutionalization of the GSP idea might make it
more difficult for the developed countries to reduce the
tariffs on the trade among themselves. Another problem is
that the manufactures favored by a GSP scheme would in
many cases compete with declining domestic industries in
some of the developed countries. Escape clauses have been
designed to avoid domestic political problems that result
from factory closings and higher unemployment.

The NIEO has also included stipulations regarding
transportation and insurance provisions. The Program of
Action requested efforts be made to promote increasing and
equitable participation by the developing countries in world
shipping for the purpose of minimizing the cost of insurance and reinsurance for developing countries. It also
called for an early implementation of the code of conduct
for liner conferences adopted by UNCTAD. It also requested
that urgent measures be taken to offset the disadvantages
suffered by landlocked and island countries with regard to
transportation and transit costs (Anell and Nygren 1980,
pp. 143-45).

The NIEO demands thus address general trade questions as well as specific policy issues. The NIEO has included measures to ameliorate the terms of trade problems
of developing countries and to eliminate their chronic trade
deficits. The measures include improved access to markets
in the developed countries, through more specific schemes
such as GSP, expeditious formulation of the oft-mentioned
commodity agreements, and possible reimbursement by importing developed countries to exporting developing states
of receipts derived from customs duties, taxes, and other
protective measures applied to imports originating in the
developing countries. This new principle of remuneration

for developing producers and exporters was designed to generate additional income and provide an expanding resource base for economic development (Gosovic 1972, p. 31).

PERSPECTIVES ON THE NIEO

From a historic perspective, the call for a NIEO was inevitable as the number of newly emergent countries increased and the membership of the international system became more diverse and heterogenous. Because of the widening gap between the rich industrialized countries (the North) and the poor developing countries (the South) in terms of wealth and power, the idea for reforming the existing norms and institutions was unavoidable and natural from an evolutionary perspective of the world economy.

Although there have been divisions among the developing states, including recently industrialized countries that have gained from the existing operations of the trade regime (Krasner 1981, p. 137; Frey-Wouters 1980, p. 210), there has been a growing perception in the South that the existing trade regime based on GATT principles, nondiscrimination, and most favored nation treatment is largely irrelevant to the developmental tasks and needs of the developing countries. Moreover, GATT safeguard mechanisms, such as Article 19, which permits the imposition of emergency restrictions on imports and other nontariff barriers, are inherently discriminatory to developing countries attempting to export their products to the North. Although some developing countries have benefited from the GSP, most of the economically poor developing countries were largely excluded from the benefits. Most of these countries have special disadvantages: They need both finance and technical assistance to strengthen their commercial capacities in credit facilities, insurance, freight rates, or marketing, and they need assistance to help them to participate more effectively in international trade negotiations (Brandt 1980, p. 183).

The NIEO as an Institution

The call for the NIEO by the developing countries is understandable in light of these "perceived" and real inequities and the less than active and enthusiastic

participation by the developing states in the existing GATT
trading framework. GATT was founded in 1949, after all,
as a temporary and provisional arrangement for world
trade. The proposed International Trade Organization negotiated at the Havana Conference in 1948 did not materialize
because of the failure of the US Congress to ratify the
treaty. In recognition of their special development needs,
the newly independent developing countries acted in 1964
to create UNCTAD, which provided a forum for dialogue,
debate, and negotiation on matters pertaining to trade,
finance, and development of the South.

The fact that GATT did not and could not completely
serve the interest of many poor countries in the South in
their efforts to change the trading system seems to be generally valid. Although many developing countries have
joined GATT, they cannot exert sufficient influence to gain
trade concessions from the industrialized countries. Their
criticisms have included the fact that GATT is too preoccupied with the interests of industrialized countries and
that it has not been strict in efforts to limit protectionism
in the North. From the position of those advocating the
NIEO, GATT does not include all of Eastern Europe or
China, and large flows of world trade, including intradeveloping country trade, remain outside its scope (Brandt
1980, p. 184).

UNCTAD, from the perspective of those advocating
the NIEO, has become a principal forum for the important
debates and negotiations about changes in the world economic system. Unlike GATT, it has near universal membership. The developing countries, moreover, have raised
their major proposals for restructuring and reform at
UNCTAD; various commodity arrangements are being negotiated in UNCTAD; and the Secretariat in Geneva monitors
trade relations, particularly between North and South and
between South and South. UNCTAD has been the focus for
negotiations on many other issues, such as the transfer of
technology, that the developing countries consider to be
important. The GSP, as already noted, was negotiated
through UNCTAD and subsequently incorporated into the
statutes and practices of GATT.

In one sense, the two organizations tend to reflect
the differing viewpoints of the developed and the developing countries regarding trade and expectation of benefits
from their participation in a world trade regime. Whereas
the developed countries are more interested in efficiency in

the allocation and use of resources through world trade, the developing countries are more concerned with questions of redistribution and equity (Matthews 1977, p. 98; Krasner 1982, p. 188).

In the light of these facts, the call for the NIEO may provide a basis for establishing a new trade organization that accommodates the needs and activities of both GATT and UNCTAD. Whereas GATT is a limited body, covering an agreement on tariffs and trade, UNCTAD is a more encompassing body that provides a forum for dialogue and negotiation on wide-ranging topics pertaining to trade, finance, and development. Although the structure of a new world trade organization is difficult to specify, the possibility of a larger framework of organization that encompasses both GATT and UNCTAD and that serves world trade and development needs is not out of the question, as long as the trading regime that resulted would ensure fairer treatment of all nations and represent the common interests of all countries, both North and South. The historic relevance and role of NIEO rest upon the possibility of attaining this convergence of interests between North and South. A new world trade regime should, ideally, be more participatory, representative, and equitable in promoting the common interests for all.

The NIEO as an Ideology

There exist definite links between the theoretical analysis of a world trade regime, on the one hand, and the strategic options for reform advocated by the NIEO ideology, on the other. Five perspectives of "opinion clusters" on the NIEO are thus identifiable in terms of the ideologies of the establishment, social democrats, the third world movement, neomercantilists, and historical materialists (Cox 1979). Likewise, the five political economy perspectives on world trade enumerated in Chapter 2 are reflected in the NIEO ideology. Each of the five theoretical perspectives can be placed along the continuum of defending the existing international economic order that includes more or less a free trade regime prevailing under the GATT framework in the post-World War II era.

Free trade theorists are establishment-oriented and generally opposed to radical restructuring of the existing trade regime that NIEO entails. Neomercantilists are also basically opposed to the NIEO ideology and programs for reform, although their putative posture based on pragmatic considerations make them more flexible and willing to listen to the NIEO demands. So long as the national interest is promoted, they are more than prepared to negotiate with the NIEO advocates and to accommodate their demands on a case-by-case basis. Reformists are basically in support of the NIEO ideology, as are those subscribing to dependency-neocolonialist and neo-Marxist theorists of world trade.

On the question of assessing the value and expecting the probability of implementing the NIEO program, however, the three reform-oriented theories vary considerably. Whereas reformists will continue to entertain a desire for gradual change and reform in the existing world trade regime through the process of global negotiation and dialogue with the North, the dependency-neocolonialist and neo-Marxist theorists are not so sanguine about evolutionary change. Rather, they tend to be more radical and even revolutionary in their respective expectations of the possibility of structural change. Whereas those advocating a posture of gradual change consider the strategy of North-South negotiation through bargaining and compromise as viable, those taking a revolutionary position would consider such strategy as counterproductive and likely to fail. Neo-Marxism rejects and blames the capitalist world economy and advocates in its place a socialist world system that would allegedly promote international solidarity and mutual benefits rather than exploitation and domination of the weak by the strong (Fishlow 1978, p. 13).

THE POLITICS OF GLOBAL REFORM

The call for the NIEO is a product of the interplay of political forces exerted at a global level. The NIEO demands in the 1970s were the result of a political process engineered by the developing countries as an expression of collective action against the industrialized countries (Krasner 1981). The call for the NIEO as a demand for change in the international economic system was more a reformist-oriented action than a radical revolutionary act of transformation in the sense that the proponents of the NIEO advocated global dialogue and negotiation. Three political acts and styles characterize the strategic moves made by the proponents of the NIEO: organization of an international economic pressure group through the mobilization of the developing countries in the context of forming "trade unions of the poor countries against the rich countries"; the politicization of the development issue, by making development the highest policy goal of the poor developing countries; and group assertiveness of the developing countries, by promoting a militant posture of collective self-reliance and assertiveness through the Non-Aligned Nations Movement (Sauvant 1977, p. 6).

As the response by the North to the idea of conducting global negotiation proved to be predictably lukewarm (Frey-Wouters 1980, p. 267), the South has increased its own collective posture and endeavors, in rhetoric if not in deeds, such as occurred at the 1976 UNCTAD meeting in Nairobi. In addition, the South is exploring the promotion of regional cooperation and integration among the developing countries as an alternative to global negotiations. The 1981 study by the UN Institute for Training and Research (UNITAR) (cf. Nicol, Escheverria, and Peccei 1981) of regionalism and the NIEO is a case in point. Following the model of the European Economic Community, speaker after speaker at a 1981 conference suggested more "practical" alternatives to the "altruistic global approach" or the "piecemeal unilateral approach" to development. This approach, endorsed by UNITAR, the Club of Rome, and the Mexico City-based Center for the Study of Third World Development, which together sponsored the conference, was hailed by the conference participants as an appropriate response to the challenge of the NIEO at a time when economic recession in the industrialized countries and the failure of the global negotiation with the North were clearly evident (Nicol, Escheverria, and Peccei 1981).

Finally, the debates and disputes over the merit of the NIEO are not likely to disappear for the simple reason that they entail political conflict at the global level that is couched in economic terms. Depending on whether one agrees or disagrees with the basic philosophy of the NIEO, positions can be largely differentiated in a dichotomy of those in favor of the status quo and those in favor of change. The NIEO debate, in short, reflects the political conflict between the have nations and the have-not nations, between the rich countries and the poor countries, and between the satisfied and established nations and the dissatisfied and reformist nations. Since the NIEO will entail redistribution of wealth and reallocation of power and authority in the global system, the conflict between the two sides will not easily disappear, nor can it be wished away without a showdown in the arena of international relations.

PART II   Changing Commodity Structures

4 Trade in Manufactures I: The Industrialized Countries

IMPORTANCE OF MANUFACTURES

The importance of trade in manufactures has been recognized in the various ideas and theories presented in the previous chapter. The role that manufactured goods are seen to play is evident in the terms of trade arguments of the structuralists, and various import substitution policies are ultimately geared to trading in these products. A variety of neomercantilist practices in the developed countries have been implemented in response to the competition for world markets or as threats to domestic industries resulting from world exports. Such trade has indeed been of increasing importance in the international economy. The simple exchange of primary commodities for industrial products, while still occurring, is no longer the norm for international trade. Instead, an increasing proportion of world trade consists of the exchange of manufactured products between countries. The developed countries are the main contributors to trade in manufactures because most of this trade is among themselves rather than between them and the countries of the developing world (Calleo and Rowland 1973, pp. 122–23; Grotewold 1979, p. 34; Monroe 1975, p. 29; Wilkenson 1968, p. 14).

Table 4.1 indicates this pattern clearly. For example, the industrialized countries account for roughly three-quarters of the exports of manufactures of the non–Communist world, which, given the trading levels of the developed countries, is equivalent to more than half of the overall exports of both developed and developing countries. The slight decline in the percentage of manufactures from the developed countries in world trade between 1968 and

49

1978 may not necessarily represent a diminished role for such trade in the world economy. The decline of manufactured exports from the developed countries was compensated by the exports of the developing countries in part, and also represents the price increases for petroleum exports (presently reversing themselves).

TABLE 4.1
Importance of Manufactures Exports of Developed Free Market Economies

Measure	1968	1972	1976	1978
Exports of developed free market economies as percentage of total exports of free market economies	79.5	80.1	71.8	74.4
Exports of manufactures as percentage of total exports of developed free market economies	76.6	78.0	77.6	78.8
Exports of manufactures of developed economies as percentage of total exports of free market economies	60.9	62.5	55.6	58.6

SOURCE: Compiled by authors from Yearbook of International Trade Statistics, various years.

A number of factors are responsible for the enhanced role of manufactures in world trade, particularly among the industrialized countries. The formation of the European Common Market has led to greater intra-industry specialization among countries with a resulting expansion of trade in manufactures (Bracewell-Milnes 1976, p. 116; Meyer 1978, p. 180). The transnationalization of production processes by multinational corporations has also contributed to an increase in such trade (Frank 1975, pp. 12-13; Michalet 1982, pp. 39-44; Vaitsos 1980; Whitman 1981, pp. 11-12). Tariff reductions have particularly facilitated trade in manufactures among the industrial countries, since it has been technological progress in industrial areas that has permitted greater intra-industry specialization. Such expansion possibilities as a result of tariff reduction have not generally been present for trade in primary commodities or agricultural products (Makler, Martinelli, and Smelser 1982, pp. 10-11; Meyer 1978, p. 170).

The importance of these types of interactions among the developed states was evidenced by the Tokyo Round of tariff negotiations completed in 1979. The 1979 agreements generally lowered tariff barriers on trade in manufactured products and even reduced some of the nontariff barriers to such trade (Lipson 1982, p. 420). Other recent negotiations, moreover, have dealt principally with products traded among the industrialized nations and failed to enhance the price competitiveness of semiprocessed export goods common to many parts of the Third World (Anell and Nygren 1980, pp. 60-61; Monroe 1975, p. 55), reflecting perhaps a protectionist response of the industrialized nations to their declining share of the overall world market for manufactures.

TRENDS IN THE TRADE OF MANUFACTURES

Nations and Manufactures Data

Data for exports of manufactures by the free market economies for the decade from 1968 to 1978 provided a base for studying trends in the trade of manufactures. Data were collected for 34 categories of manufactured products for each of 14 individual industrialized nations and 2 other categories of countries. Various annual issues of the Yearbook of International Trade Statistics published by the United Nations served as the source from which the data were drawn. Data for two additional years, 1972 and 1976, were also included so as to determine the nature of shifts within the decade and any effects of the increase in oil prices that occurred. The analysis was limited to these ten years because of data availability. The necessary detailed information was only available starting in 1968, and 1978 was the last year for which such information was complete. Exports were used as the appropriate measure instead of imports or total trade, since the level of exports was determined to be a better indicator of international competitiveness. Imports partially reflect ability to buy, whereas exports reflect ability to sell particular products. Individual governments also have greater control over imports through various policy measures, particularly in an era when neomercantilist practices are becoming more common. Import data also may reflect the potential intrusion of foreign aid and the effects of export earnings (Coppock 1962, p. 18; Green and Lutz 1978, pp. 35-36).

The 14 industrialized countries studied were the United States, Canada, the United Kingdom, France, West Germany, Belgium/Luxembourg, the Netherlands, Italy, Sweden, Switzerland, Spain, Yugoslavia, Japan, and Australia/New Zealand. Belgium and Luxembourg constituted a joint entry because the two countries have had a complete customs union since 1921, and all trade data are listed under the dual entry in UN publications. Australia and New Zealand were also combined since it was not always possible to find or identify export levels for both. It was possible to determine their joint export totals since there was an entry for Oceania, Developed Economies, included in the source volumes. Australia and New Zealand are the only two countries that belonged to this category. While it would have been more useful to include the two countries separately, particularly since Australia is the larger economy by far, it was still considered useful to include the joint entry to provide geographic diversity. Yugoslavia and Spain were included as separate entries in part to ascertain trends among the larger of the less developed industrialized economies of southern Europe.

Two residual categories were included in addition to the 14 individual entries. First, the other countries classified as developed by the United Nations were combined in one group. The countries involved were Iceland, Ireland, Norway, Denmark, Finland, Austria, Portugal, Greece, Israel, and South Africa. While almost all of these countries are important traders in some manufactured commodities, they are very minor traders in others. Only the top 40 exporters were listed for the various manufactures categories that were used, thus detailed data were often lacking for these smaller countries. Their absolute and relative contributions as a group were important, and the aggregate levels could be determined since the levels for the 14 individual entries were known and there were totals for all the developed free market economies. The other residual category was that of the developing free market economies. The inclusion of this group of states provided a total for all trade in manufactures. Since trade data for the centrally planned economies (except Yugoslavia) were not available, none of the Communist states were included, even though these countries export some types of manufactures.

The 34 categories of products consisted of export levels at the two-digit or three-digit levels of the Standard International Trade Classification (SITC) format used by the United Nations. Four of the ten one-digit categories were included in total as well as parts of three others. Data were collected at the three-digit level for some products since a few two-digit groups included both manufactures and primary commodities. SITC 5 (with nine two-digit groupings) consists of chemical products, including various compounds, medicines, and manufactured fertilizers. SITC 6 (also with nine two-digit categories) classified manufactures according to basic material inputs, such as rubber, wood, or type of metal. These manufactures are collectively termed "basic manufactures" in the present study since many of them serve as inputs into other manufacturing processes, even though some are end-use products. SITC 7 (three two-digit categories until 1980) included machinery and transport equipment, and SITC 8 (with seven two-digit categories until 1980) consisted of miscellaneous manufactures, principally end-use consumer goods with no dominant material component. The final groups of manufactures drawn from the other major SITC groups were categories 013, 032, 04, and 431 (processed foods), SITC 11 (beverages, mainly alcoholic), and SITC 122 (tobacco manufactures).* There still remained small levels of manufactured products not included in these groups since two- and three-digit level categories almost always had subdivisions composed of products not otherwise specified. These categories may have contained small amounts of manufactured goods. These missing data, however, were minimal, since such categories contained no identifiable product groups that were major items in world trade. Also, SITC groups 5, 6, 7, and 8 composed the bulk of world trade in manufactures.

---

*The complete list of the classifications at the relevant two- or three-digit level is given in Appendix A with a brief description of the manufactured products involved.

Of the various types of manufactures, certain categories of products were much more important than others
(see Table 4.2). Processed food products, beverages, and
tobacco were relatively small components of the overall
trade. Chemicals and miscellaneous manufactures had
much larger shares. Basic manufactures were even more
important to world trade, though such products were declining relative to other categories. The three component
parts of SITC 7 are displayed separately, given their great
importance to total trade in manufactures. The products
in these three two-digit classifications accounted for roughly one-third of all trade in manufactures. This importance no doubt was one reason for the reclassification,
effective in 1980, of SITC 7 products into ten categories at
the two-digit level.

The various categories of manufactures have shown
different growth patterns throughout the decade. Overall,
trade in manufactures has increased about fivefold in dollar value. Food products, beverages, and basic manufactures have lagged behind that rate of increase, while
chemicals, miscellaneous manufactures, electric machinery,
and transport equipment have been growing in value at
rates greater than the average. The general trend appears
to be a move toward more complex products and less emphasis on simpler manufactures and semiprocessed raw materials. Trade in manufactures may be replicating the increasing economic complexity of the world in general.

Country Patterns

For the 14 countries for which data were collected,
exports of manufactures comprised a very important portion
of their total trade (see Table 4.3). Manufactures usually
accounted for a minimum of 70 percent of total exports in
the years selected, and the share often reached 90 percent
or better. The countries most reliant on manufactures were
those, such as Switzerland, that lack significant raw materials bases. The countries falling below these percentages were the ones exporting raw materials. The very
noticeable major shift in the manufactures percentage for
Australia/New Zealand in 1972 reflected the rapid development of various mineral deposits in Australia. Even the
countries exporting some raw materials, however, remained
large exporters of manufactured goods in absolute terms.

TABLE 4.2

Importance of Manufactures in World Trade of Free Market Economies by General Type

Category	1968	1972	1976	1978
Total exports (millions $US)	212,376	372,644	895,274	1,175,472
Exports of manufactures (millions $US)	138,448	249,416	538,945	758,805
Manufactures share of total exports (%)	65.2	66.9	60.2	64.6
Type of manufacture (millions $US)				
Food products (SITC 013, 032, 04, 431)[a]	2,060	3,135	6,036	8,426
Beverages (SITC 11)	1,676	3,013	4,924	7,437
Tobacco (SITC 122)	527	842	1,674	2,502
Chemicals (SITC 5)	15,622	27,010	64,188	88,901
Basic manufactures (SITC 6)	44,291	72,555	148,973	208,272
Nonelectric machinery (SITC 71)[b]	24,670	44,785	97,367	124,240
Electric machinery (SITC 72)[c]	11,077	22,327	52,243	86,778
Transport equipment (SITC 73)[d]	22,302	44,170	97,658	132,741
Miscellaneous manufactures (SITC 8)	16,222	31,580	65,883	99,058

[a] 013 and 032 were eliminated as separate categories at the three-digit level in 1980.

[b] Equals SITC codes 71, 72, 73, and 74 in 1980.

[c] Equals SITC codes 75, 76, and 77 in 1980.

[d] Equals SITC codes 78 and 79 in 1980.

NOTE: Figures may not sum due to rounding.

SOURCE: Yearbook of International Trade Statistics, various years.

TABLE 4.3
Importance of Manufactures as Exports for Selected Countries

| | Manufactures as Percentage of Exports | | | |
	1968	1972	1976	1978
Developed countries	76.6	78.0	77.6	78.8
Developing countries	20.7	22.2	16.6	23.3
United States	71.1	71.2	69.8	68.9
Canada	61.4	59.6	58.0	58.4
United Kingdom	90.8	88.4	86.0	83.8
France	77.9	77.7	79.6	81.8
West Germany	90.5	90.6	89.9	89.4
Belgium/Luxembourg	83.7	83.5	83.4	79.8
Netherlands	62.5	67.5	58.5	58.6
Italy	83.8	86.5	86.3	87.2
Sweden	74.2	78.3	80.5	83.7
Switzerland	92.7	93.8	93.0	95.0
Spain	55.8	71.3	74.8	78.2
Yugoslavia	71.8	75.8	85.3	81.3
Australia/New Zealand	77.8	25.8	24.9	27.9
Japan	95.6	95.7	96.7	97.1
Other developed countries	55.6	60.7	62.5	69.3

SOURCE: Compiled by authors from Yearbook of International Trade Statistics, various years.

The importance of a number of the industrial nations as exporters of manufactures has shown considerable variation in the 1968–78 decade (see Table 4.4). The North American countries have evidenced a rather steady decline. In 1968, the United States was the leading exporter of manufactures, but, by 1978, it was in second place, with Japan a close third. There was a brief competitive resurgence in 1976, but the recovery was brief. Canada showed a steady decline for the ten years and did not share in the brief US resurgence. As an exporter of manufactures it ranked sixth in 1968 and had fallen to ninth in 1978.

In Western Europe the United Kingdom lost a significant portion of its share of the world market. There was an improvement from 1976 to 1978, indicating that the post-

TABLE 4.4
Shares in Exports of Manufactures

Country	1968	Percentages			Change 1968–78
		1972	1976	1978	
United States	17.6	14.0	14.7	12.8	-4.8
Canada	5.6	4.9	4.1	3.5	-2.1
United Kingdom	10.1	8.6	7.4	7.9	-2.2
France	7.1	8.1	8.2	8.3	1.2
West Germany	16.2	16.8	17.0	16.7	0.5
Belgium/Luxembourg	4.9	5.4	5.1	4.7	-0.2
Netherlands	3.8	4.5	4.3	3.9	0.1
Italy	6.2	6.5	5.9	6.4	0.2
Sweden	2.6	2.8	2.7	2.4	-0.2
Switzerland	2.7	2.6	2.6	2.9	0.2
Spain	0.6	1.1	1.2	1.4	0.8
Yugoslavia	0.7	0.7	0.7	0.6	-0.1
Australia/New Zealand	0.7	0.8	0.7	0.6	-0.1
Japan	9.0	11.0	12.0	12.5	3.5
Other developed nations[a]	5.7	5.6	5.6	6.1	0.4
Developing nations	6.5	6.6	7.8	9.3	2.8

[a] Austria, Denmark, Norway, Ireland, Portugal, Iceland, Greece, Finland, Israel, and South Africa.

SOURCE: Compiled by authors from Yearbook of International Trade Statistics, various years.

World War II decline may finally have stopped. Also, entry into the Common Market may finally have begun to yield
benefits, although one early study found that the United
Kingdom actually lost export markets as a result (Fetherston,
Moore, and Rhodes 1979), a conclusion supported by the
trend from 1968 to 1976. Of the other EC members, France
showed consistent gains, the bulk of which came in the
early part of the period. France's export trade has been
more diversified than that of the United Kingdom (Meyer
1978, pp. 35-36), and this diversity might have aided that
country's ability to at least maintain its overall share of
the world market. West Germany's gains over the period
were relatively small. After a peak in 1976, it is possible
that a long period of steady increases in terms of world
market shares had stopped and a time of stability or even
decline may be approaching. Belgium/Luxembourg, the
Netherlands, and Italy had only minor changes over the
period as a whole. The trends would indicate that the
first two are facing future declining shares. Italy's performance has been rather volatile.

Among other European countries, Sweden may also be
experiencing the possibility of a declining percentage of
the world market, while Switzerland may be on a competitive upswing. Yugoslavia has been rather constant in its
performance. The other developed nations and Spain have
upward trends, with Spain showing a remarkable increase
in ten years by more than doubling its world share and
demonstrating consistent improvement throughout the decade.
This performance also explains the increasing importance of
manufactures in the Spanish export mix apparent in Table
4.3.

In the Pacific Basin the two Commonwealth dominions
lost some ground, although their performance was rather
constant. The region also contained the world's major
gainer of manufacturing markets—Japan. The Japanese
gain for the decade was almost three times as large as
that of any other country. The trend is also an upward
one, not showing signs of stabilization, as in the case of
West Germany. This rapid advance of Japanese competitiveness has been one of the factors responsible for increasing
neomercantilist sentiment in the United States and the long-
standing reluctance of the European countries to open their
markets to Japanese competition.

RELATIONSHIPS AMONG THE
INDUSTRIALIZED NATIONS

The preceding overview demonstrates the overall importance of trade in manufactures and its pivotal role for
the industrialized countries. Losses of foreign markets and
increased competition domestically from imports have concerned most of the developed nations at some time. Pressures for protectionist measures have occurred widely, particularly in times of worldwide economic slowdown, such as
that which occurred in the aftermath of the jump in oil
prices, although the causes of those difficulties were much
more diverse than a simple increase in prices for energy.
As a result, relationships among the industrialized nations
in their export performances, particularly possible connections between the losers and gainers, is an important question. For example, the revival of the United Kingdom noted
above suggests that membership in the European Communities could have had a positive impact, and if such is indeed the case, it would be reflected in associations with
the trade of other members of the EC.

Measures

The basic measure used was the change in shares of
the 14 individual nations and the two residual categories
for various types of manufactures. Correlations between
the changes in share for these 16 cases were derived for
the 34 categories of manufactures. These categories were
the two-digit SITC groupings, except for the four three-
digit levels that were used. Use of the various categories
provided an opportunity to better detect relationships among
the various states, as well as possible associations of
losses on one side with gains on the other, or mutual gains
and losses, reflecting shared characteristics among countries. The changes for these categories for the 16 cases
were correlated for the periods 1968–72, 1972–76, 1976–78,
and 1968–78. The changes over the decade provided an
overview of relationships, while the shorter time periods
uncovered changing relationships for different pairs of
countries over time.

The changes in shares of world exports for the various countries were used in four forms in the correlational
analysis. First, the raw percentage change figures were

used. Second, a shift or shift-share measure was used.
Third, a weight reflecting their volume of trade in the 34
categories was applied to the raw change figures. Finally,
the shift figures were similarly weighted. The weighting
procedure was necessary since the various products had
highly variable shares of the world market. Obviously,
SITCs 71, 72, and 73 were much more important to world
trade than SITC 11 or 122. In order to facilitate comparisons of correlation coefficients, the weight used was the
percentage of world trade in manufactures accounted for by
a given two- or three-digit SITC category at the end of the
time period in question multiplied by 34. Thus, the n for
the weighted and unweighted correlation analyses was kept
constant.

The percentage net shift referred to is a measure
that avoids overemphasizing small starting bases or under-
emphasizing large initial ones. For example, in one of the
smaller SITC categories, a small change in absolute levels
for one nation would lead to exaggerated percentage changes
in the form of market share. Similarly, large absolute
changes in the export of transport equipment would be less
noticeable in the form of percentage changes. The net
shift is the difference between a country's actual change
in trade over a given time period and the expected change
that would have occurred if the country's exports held
their share of the market. The positive or negative change
in the share of the world market for the country required
dividing the change for each country by the sum of the
positive changes if that country experienced a positive
shift or the corresponding sum of negative changes if it
experienced a loss. Since the losses and gains summed to
zero, the divisor was the same except for sign. The following formula summarizes the calculations:

$$NS_i = \frac{\Delta T_i(t,\ t-1)}{\sum_{n=p}^{} \Delta T_i(t,\ t-1)} (100)$$

where NS_i = net shift for the ith country,

$$\Delta \underline{T}_{i(\underline{t}, \; \underline{t} \; - \; 1)} \quad = \quad \text{the change in share for the } \underline{i}\text{th}$$

nation with a change of the same sign from period $\underline{t} - 1$ to period $\underline{t}$, and

$\underline{p}$ = countries with changes of the same sign.

If only one country lost shares in a given manufactures category in a given time period, its net shift would be 100 percent.

Given its means of derivation, the use of the shift measure provided an additional advantage for the correlation analyses in that it standardized changes across the various categories of manufactures and across time. The percentage losses or gains reflected different magnitudes, but this standardization, combined with weighting, provided a truer picture of changing patterns of exports and the positions of various countries relative to one another. One disadvantage of the net shift measure is that, as used, it tended to overemphasize the magnitude of changes among the individual countries. The two residual categories contained nations that both lost and gained in most, if not all, of the 34 SITC groupings, but since they were combined, the total losses and total gains were both understated and the denominator was much smaller than would be the case with a larger group of countries. Thus, a net shift measure is sensitive to the number of cases included.* Still, the shift measures in conjunction with the straight changes in shares should discover important relationships that existed for this time period.

Results

For each time period, only the correlation coefficients that were significant at least at the .05 level (two-

---

*More detailed discussions of the net shift measure can be found in Ashby (1964), Green and Lutz (1978, pp. 151–56), Huff and Sherr (1967), and Sternitzke (1979). For debates on its value, see Houston (1967), Richardson (1971), Ricks, Czinkota, and DeJesus (1980), Ashby (1968), and Sternitzke (1980).

tailed test, since the direction of the association was not prespecified) are included in the tables and discussion. Each of the significant correlations that were found is listed twice in the relevant tables under the headings for each country of the pair so linked, except for the two residual groups. The changes in shares for the ten-year period were considered first. The most obvious result was that links varied greatly, depending on which measure was used (see Table 4.5). Given this situation, the following discussion primarily focuses on the weighted measures since they better reflect overall effects of various country–pair relationships.

For Canada and the United States most of the significant coefficients were found with the simple unweighted change in share measure. Since these levels of association generally disappeared with the other measures, it was obviously the smaller manufactures categories that explained the links. The overall decline in the US export position in this decade is most clearly negatively linked to the improvements in the French and Japanese positions. Canada also suffered from the Japanese gains and from German gains for the period. Somewhat surprisingly, there was no link, either positive or negative, between the two North American industrialized countries when the volume of the export categories was taken into account, notwithstanding their close economic ties and the similarity of their performances. Productivity differences, variable prices for inputs into the production process, and different rates of technological change led to different export patterns for Canada and the United States in the past (Stryker 1968, pp. 170–71). The persistence of such differences would explain the lack of association from 1968 to 1978.

For the European countries, a number of connections appeared. France, Belgium/Luxembourg, and the Netherlands had positive associations with each other, even when weighting or net shift impacts were included, indicating that they often lost or gained in the same categories. Often two of these three nations also had similar associations with various other countries. Italy and Spain had a positive association in terms of export performance and similar relationships with other countries, including a number of negative links with the other countries of the EC. Thus, they both would appear to have been responding to similar occurrences in the world economic system, even though the total Spanish export performance showed more consistent improvement in the decade.

TABLE 4.5

Significant Correlations for Country Pairs, 1968–78

Country Pairs	Change in Share		Net Shift	
	Unweighted	Weighted	Unweighted	Weighted
United States/				
Canada	$-.74^c$	--	--	--
United Kingdom	$-.43^a$	--	--	--
France	$-.49^b$	$-.55^c$	--	$-.57^c$
Belgium/Luxembourg	$-.37^a$	$-.45^b$	--	--
Netherlands	$-.58^c$	--	--	--
Sweden	$-.55^c$	--	--	--
Yugoslavia	--	--	--	$-.36^a$
Australia/New Zealand	$.36^a$	--	--	--
Japan	--	$-.61^c$	$-.39^a$	$-.54^b$
Canada/				
United States	$-.74^c$	--	--	--
United Kingdom	$.47^b$	--	--	--
West Germany	--	$-.47^b$	--	$-.45^b$
Netherlands	$.45^b$	--	--	--
Sweden	$.47^b$	--	--	--
Australia/New Zealand	$.49^b$	--	--	--
Japan	--	$-.43^b$	--	$-.41^a$
United Kingdom/				
United States	$-.43^a$	--	--	--
Canada	$.47^b$	--	--	--
Netherlands	--	--	--	$.38^a$
Italy	--	--	--	$.36^a$
Sweden	--	--	--	$.36^a$
Yugoslavia	--	--	--	$-.36^a$
Other developed nations	--	--	--	$-.44^b$
Japan	--	$-.58^c$	$-.37^a$	$-.53^b$
France/				
United States	$-.48^b$	$-.55^b$	--	$-.57^c$
West Germany	--	--	$.38^a$	--
Belgium/Luxembourg	$.42^a$	$.44^b$	--	--
Netherlands	$.36^a$	$.36^a$	--	--
Spain	$-.37^a$	--	$-.36^a$	$-.37^a$
Japan	--	$.39^a$	--	$.36^a$
Developing countries	$-.50^b$	$-.39^a$	--	--

(continued)

| | Measure | | | |
| | Change in Share | | Net Shift | |
Country Pairs	Unweighted	Weighted	Unweighted	Weighted
West Germany/				
Canada	--	-.47[b]	--	-.35[a]
France	--	--	.38[a]	--
Developing countries	-.47[b]	-.35[a]	--	-.35[a]
Belgium/Luxembourg/				
United States	-.37[a]	-.45[b]	--	--
France	.42[a]	.44[b]	--	--
Italy	--	-.36[a]	--	-.39[a]
Sweden	.37[a]	.36[a]	--	--
Spain	--	-.46[b]	--	-.39[a]
Yugoslavia	.44[b]	--	.34[a]	--
Developing countries	-.34[a]	--	--	--
Netherlands/				
United States	-.58[c]	--	--	--
Canada	.45[b]	--	--	--
United Kingdom	--	.41[a]	--	.38[a]
France	.36[a]	.36[a]	--	--
Sweden	.52[b]	--	--	--
Australia/New Zealand	.39[a]	.36[a]	--	.36[a]
Developing countries	--	-.41[b]	--	-.41[a]
Italy/				
Belgium/Luxembourg	--	-.36[a]	--	-.39[a]
Spain	--	.34[a]	--	.46[b]
Developing countries	--	.34[a]	--	--
Sweden/				
United States	-.55[c]	--	--	--
Canada	.47[c]	--	--	--
United Kingdom	--	--	--	.36[a]
Belgium/Luxembourg	.36[a]	.36[a]	--	--
Netherlands	.52[b]	--	--	--
Spain	--	-.34[a]	--	--
Australia/New Zealand	.43[a]	--	--	--
Japan	--	--	--	-.36[a]
Developing countries	-.34[a]	--	--	--
Switzerland/				
Spain	--	--	--	.36[a]

Country Pairs	Measure			
	Change in Share		Net Shift	
	Unweighted	Weighted	Unweighted	Weighted
Spain/				
France	$-.37^a$	--	$-.36^a$	$-.37^a$
Belgium/Luxembourg	--	$-.46^b$	--	$-.39^a$
Italy	--	--	--	$.46^b$
Sweden	--	$-.34^a$	--	--
Switzerland	--	--	--	$.36^a$
Yugoslavia/				
United States	--	--	--	$-.36^a$
United Kingdom	--	--	--	$-.36^a$
Belgium/Luxembourg	$.44^b$	--	$.34^a$	--
Other developed nations	--	$.34^a$	--	--
Developing countries	--	$-.49^b$	--	$-.38^a$
Australia/New Zealand/				
United States	$-.36^a$	--	--	--
Canada	$.50^b$	--	--	--
Netherlands	$-.39^a$	$.41^a$	--	$.36^a$
Sweden	$.43^a$	--	--	--
Japan/				
United States	--	$-.61^c$	$-.39^a$	$-.53^b$
Canada	--	$-.44^b$	--	$-.41^a$
United Kingdom	--	$-.58^b$	$-.37^a$	$-.53^b$
France	--	$.39^a$	--	$.36^a$
Sweden	--	--	--	$-.36^a$
Other developed nations	$.45^b$	--	--	--
Developing countries	$-.68^c$	$-.43^a$	$-.44^a$	$-.35^a$

[a] Significant at α = .05.

[b] Significant at α = .01.

[c] Significant at α = .001.

-- Not a significant correlation.

SOURCE: Compiled by authors.

Japan, as the prime gainer in terms of exports, naturally had predominantly negative associations with other countries. The Japanese changes were inversely correlated with the United States, the United Kingdom, and Canada and with the developing countries. Since the first three nations suffered declines for the period, the results indicate that Japanese gains were at their expense. Japanese competitiveness has also increasingly been in those fields with more technological sophistication (Lutz and Green 1983), a fact that would explain the gains at the expense of the other industrialized nations. Since the developing countries as a group were also net gainers for the decade, some former Japanese markets were apparently being transferred to them. Past studies of Japanese trade have noted the tendency of Japanese firms to abandon product lines that had become standardized and that had low technology inputs to developing countries (Hollerman 1975, pp. 196–98; Yoshino 1975, pp. 261–68). This trend was apparently continuing between 1968 and 1978.

Two other noteworthy observations are discernible in Table 4.5. Switzerland and West Germany had only limited associations with the other industrialized countries, a particularly surprising finding for West Germany, one of the founding members of the Common Market. Another pattern, particularly apparent with the unweighted share change, was the relationship among countries such as Sweden, Australia/New Zealand, Canada, the United States, and the Netherlands. These countries had numerous positive associations, with the exception of the United States, which had negative associations with many of them. These associations apparently reflected exports of manufactured products with more basic raw materials inputs, since many of the smaller volume two-digit and three-digit categories had important raw materials bases. Previous studies have found distinctive patterns for export manufactures based on raw materials inputs and their corresponding performance in the world market for Canada (Wilkenson 1968, p. 43) and Sweden (Carlsson and Ohlsson 1976, p. 173). Thus, it is not surprising that these nations were linked when the measure in the simple unweighted form was used. Exporters relying on raw materials inputs appear to have gained or to have lost together, although this pattern was generally submerged within the context of overall trade, since it does not survive in the weighted measures. The importance of the raw materials categories for Canada,

Sweden, and the Netherlands was somewhat unexpected, given that these countries have had either high or increasing reliance on exports with research-intensive inputs. Canada, in fact, ranked second only to the United States in terms of research and development (Balassa 1977, p. 333). US resource-intensive industries have been found to suffer a comparative disadvantage in international markets (Harkness and Kyle 1975, p. 161; Mitchell 1970), a finding supported by the negative correlations of the United States with the other nations in this group.

There were fewer significant correlations for the period from 1968 to 1972, and some of the relationships were different (see Table 4.6). Both the United States and the United Kingdom had a series of negative correlations with the various original members of the Common Market, indicating that these two countries were losing market shares to these countries. The United Kingdom had its largest negative relationship with France, and the United States had highly negative ties with Japan on three of the measures. The coefficients were not only significant but they explained approximately 45 percent of the variance in the changes for both countries.

Among the European countries the association of France, Belgium/Luxembourg, and the Netherlands was not present in this period. There were in fact some signs of negative associations between the Netherlands and Belgium/ Luxembourg. The Netherlands had a number of other surprising links--negative ties with West Germany and positive ones with Japan, hardly results expected for an EC country. Spain and Italy still had a connection in this period, although it was less pronounced than for the whole decade. The negative link between Spain and Yugoslavia would indicate competition for markets between these two countries in various manufactures categories.

Yugoslavia had some of the strongest associations of any individual nation for this period. The positive association with Australia/New Zealand accounted for approximately half of the variation for the two countries. Both had positive associations with the other developed countries group and noticeably negative ones with the developing countries. Taken together, these relationships may indicate multiple actor competition for specific markets. Since Spain and the developing countries group had the biggest overall gains in exports of manufactures in this period, while the other countries group was static, the negative

TABLE 4.6
Significant Correlations for Country Pairs, 1968–72

Country Pairs	Change in Share		Net Shift	
	Unweighted	Weighted	Unweighted	Weighted
United States/				
United Kingdom	--	.34[a]	--	--
France	--	-.37[a]	--	--
Belgium/Luxembourg	--	-.44[b]	--	--
Netherlands	--	-.50[b]	--	--
Other developed nations	--	.51[b]	--	--
Japan	--	-.69[c]	-.66[c]	-.66[c]
Developing countries	-.80[c]	--	--	--
Canada/				
France	-.37[a]	--	--	--
United Kingdom/				
United States	--	.34[a]	--	--
France	-.41[a]	-.63[c]	--	--
Italy	-.60[c]	-.41[a]	-.36[a]	--
Other developed nations	--	.37[a]	--	--
Australia/New Zealand	--	--	--	.35[a]
Japan	--	-.40[a]	--	--
France/				
United States	--	-.37[a]	--	--
Canada	-.36[a]	--	--	--
United Kingdom	-.41[a]	-.63[c]	--	--
Italy	.42[a]	--	--	--
Sweden	--	.37[a]	--	--
Other developed nations	--	.38[a]	--	--
Developing countries	--	--	-.35[a]	--
West Germany/				
Netherlands	--	-.36[a]	--	--
Developing countries	-.57[c]	--	--	--
Belgium/Luxembourg/				
United States	--	-.44[b]	--	--
Netherlands	--	--	-.40[a]	--
Italy	--	--	--	-.42[b]
Yugoslavia	-.44[b]	-.44[b]	-.49[b]	-.39[a]
Netherlands/				
United States	--	-.50[b]	--	--
West Germany	--	-.36[a]	--	--
Belgium/Luxembourg	--	--	-.40[a]	--
Yugoslavia	-.46[b]	--	-.40[a]	--
Other developed nations	--	-.43[b]	--	-.40[a]
Japan	--	.41[a]	--	--

Country Pairs	Measure			
	Change in Share		Net Shift	
	Unweighted	Weighted	Unweighted	Weighted
Italy/				
United Kingdom	$-.59^c$	$-.41^a$	$-.36^a$	--
France	$.42^b$	--	--	--
Belgium/Luxembourg	--	--	--	$-.42^a$
Spain	$.37^a$	$.37^a$	--	$.35^a$
Other developed nations	--	--	--	$-.35^a$
Australia/New Zealand	$-.36^a$	--	$-.34^a$	--
Sweden/				
France	--	$.37^a$	--	--
Switzerland/				
Australia/New Zealand	--	--	--	$.36^a$
Developing countries	--	--	--	$-.34^a$
Spain/				
Italy	$.37^a$	$.37^a$	--	$.34^a$
Yugoslavia	$-.34^a$	$-.50^b$	$-.34^a$	$-.51^b$
Japan	$-.48^b$	--	$-.34^a$	$-.38^a$
Yugoslavia/				
Belgium/Luxembourg	$-.44^b$	$-.43^b$	$-.48^b$	$-.39^a$
Netherlands	$.46^b$	--	$.40^a$	--
Spain	$-.34^a$	$-.50^b$	$-.34^a$	$-.51^b$
Other developed nations	--	$.41^b$	--	$.46^b$
Australia/New Zealand	--	$.69^c$	--	$.76^c$
Developing countries	--	$-.50^b$	$-.34^a$	$-.51^b$
Australia/New Zealand/				
United Kingdom	--	--	--	$.35^a$
Italy	$-.36^a$	--	$-.34^a$	--
Switzerland	--	--	--	$.36^a$
Spain	--	--	--	$-.38^a$
Yugoslavia	--	$.69^c$	--	$.76^c$
Other developed nations	--	--	--	$.35^a$
Developing countries	--	$-.49^b$	--	$-.73^c$
Japan/				
United States	--	$-.69^c$	$-.66^c$	$-.66^c$
United Kingdom	--	$-.40^a$	--	--
Netherlands	--	$.41^a$	--	--
Spain	$-.48^b$	--	$-.34^a$	--
Other developed nations	--	$-.56^c$	--	--

[a] Significant at α = .05.
[b] Significant at α = .01.
[c] Significant at α = .001.
-- Not a significant correlation.

SOURCE: Compiled by authors.

TABLE 4.7

Significant Correlations for Country Pairs, 1972-76

Country Pairs	Change in Share		Net Shift	
	Unweighted	Weighted	Unweighted	Weighted
United States/				
United Kingdom	--	--	--	-.48[b]
Other developed nations	-.43[a]	-.45[a]	--	--
Canada/				
United Kingdom	--	--	.40[a]	--
Other developed nations	--	-.38[a]	--	-.41[a]
Australia/New Zealand	--	.43[b]	--	.38[a]
Japan	--	-.38[a]	--	-.41[a]
United Kingdom/				
United States	--	--	--	-.48[b]
Canada	--	--	.40[a]	--
France	--	--	--	-.46[b]
West Germany	--	--	--	.45[b]
Italy	--	--	--	-.39[a]
Australia/New Zealand	--	.37[a]	--	--
Japan	--	-.53[b]	-.36[a]	-.50[b]
France/				
United Kingdom	--	--	--	-.46[b]
West Germany	--	--	--	-.44[b]
Belgium/Luxembourg	.50[b]	.43[b]	--	--
Netherlands	.50[b]	--	--	--
Italy	--	--	--	.45[b]
Sweden	-.46[b]	--	--	--
Developing countries	-.67[3]	--	--	--
West Germany/				
United Kingdom	--	--	--	.45[b]
France	--	--	--	-.44[b]
Yugoslavia	-.36[a]	--	--	--
Other developed nations	--	-.36[a]	--	-.37[a]
Japan	--	--	--	-.37[a]
Belgium/Luxembourg/				
France	.50[b]	.43[b]	--	--
Netherlands	.54[b]	--	--	--
Sweden	.50[b]	--	--	--
Switzerland	--	--	--	-.35[a]
Australia/New Zealand	--	--	--	-.35[a]
Developing countries	-.54[b]	--	--	--
Netherlands/				
France	.50[b]	--	--	--
Belgium/Luxembourg	.54[b]	--	--	--
Sweden	.82[c]	--	.36[a]	--
Spain	.35[a]	--	--	--

Country Pairs	Measure			
	Change in Share		Net Shift	
	Unweighted	Weighted	Unweighted	Weighted
Australia/New Zealand	.54[b]	--	--	--
Japan	--	-.52[b]	--	-.59[c]
Italy/				
United Kingdom	--	--	--	-.39[a]
France	--	--	--	.45[b]
Yugoslavia	--	--	--	.35[a]
Developing countries	--	-.55[c]	--	-.55[c]
Sweden/				
United Kingdom	--	-.34[a]	--	--
France	.46[b]	--	--	--
Belgium/Luxembourg	.50[b]	--	.36[a]	--
Netherlands	.83[c]	--	--	--
Australia/New Zealand	-.79[c]	--	-.46[b]	--
Switzerland/				
Belgium/Luxembourg	--	--	--	-.35[a]
Spain/				
Netherlands	.35[a]	--	--	--
Japan	.62[c]	--	.40[a]	--
Developing countries	-.57[c]	-.47[b]	-.43[a]	-.54[c]
Yugoslavia/				
West Germany	-.36[a]	--	--	--
Italy	--	--	--	.35[a]
Other developed nations	-.42[a]	--	--	--
Australia/New Zealand/				
United Kingdom	--	.37[a]	--	--
Canada	--	.43[b]	--	.38[a]
Belgium/Luxembourg	--	--	--	-.35[a]
Netherlands	.54[c]	--	--	--
Sweden	.75[c]	--	--	--
Other developed nations	-.37[a]	-.49[b]	--	--
Japan	--	-.43[a]	--	--
Developing countries	-.56[c]	--	--	--
Japan/				
United Kingdom	--	-.53[b]	-.36[a]	-.50[b]
Canada	--	-.38[a]	--	-.41[a]
West Germany	--	--	--	-.37[a]
Netherlands	--	-.52[b]	--	-.59[c]
Spain	.62[c]	--	.40[a]	--
Developing countries	-.51[b]	-.41[a]	-.36[a]	-.42[a]

[a] Significant at α = .05.
[b] Significant at α = .01.
[c] Significant at α = .001.
-- Not a significant correlation.

SOURCE: Compiled by authors.

associations represented the successes of the former and the failures of the latter to gain new markets.

In the four years from 1972 to 1976, the United States no longer had negative associations with changes for either Japan or the nations of the EC (see Table 4.7). Of course, the United States improved its total export performance in this period, so negative associations were less likely. Changes in Canadian exports were again negatively associated with the ongoing Japanese increases. The United Kingdom also had a negative association with Japan's changes, as well as negative links with changes occurring with French and Italian exports of manufactures. While the United Kingdom suffered a relative decline in manufactures exports for this period, France showed a slight gain and Italy a slight decline. Obviously, the effects of these two countries on British exports were different and somewhat complex. British export changes were negatively associated with the improved US performance as well. At the same time, West Germany's slight overall gain was positively linked with the United Kingdom's continued decline. Again, a complex pattern existed. The United Kingdom's changes in various manufactures followed other nations' changes in some cases and were inversely related for other countries. France's and West Germany's slight gains apparently were partly at each other's expense.

Among other relationships for this period was the reversal of the significant positive link between the Netherlands and Japan to a significantly negative one. Similarly, the link between Spain and the developing countries demonstrated a reversal. Obviously, at least some of these changed links reflected short-term factors in the world economy. The raw materials-based producers also appeared as a group in this period, represented by Sweden, the Netherlands, Australia/New Zealand, and Canada. Export changes among these countries resulted in the positive correlations that appeared for them in many cases for the first two unweighted measures. For this group, the overall world setting seemed to determine the connections rather than competition among the countries for relative market shares, as the associations were positive.

For the shorter period from 1976 to 1978, some different patterns emerged. US exports were again in a period of relative decline, and this situation was reflected in negative associations with Japan and for the first time

West Germany (see Table 4.8). The United Kingdom no longer had negative ties with various members of the Common Market. West Germany, as well as Switzerland, again had few links, although the negative association of West Germany with the United States was not unimportant. Various other members of the EC had mixed patterns, indicating that market share changes came partially at each other's expense. Spain and Yugoslavia now had a positive association in contradistinction to the whole decade and earlier periods. Japan had the usual set of negative relationships with a differing set of countries, with Belgium/Luxembourg in this period being the European country with which there was a positive link.

There were again numerous associations between countries more reliant on raw materials inputs. Some relationships were negative and others positive. The significant coefficients were no longer restricted to the straight change measure but included the other three measures as well. Apparently, these export markets were in a state of some flux in this period. Many of the significant associations for the United Kingdom appear to have been related to this group of countries, as there were positive links with the Commonwealth while its links with the other countries in the group tended to follow the pattern of the Dominions.

SUMMARY

The preceding discussion and analyses indicate that the developed countries interact with each other in a number of significant and often complex ways. The correlational analyses found some unexpected patterns in many cases. The major trading countries did not interact as directly as is often assumed. Changes in export shares of the United States, the United Kingdom, France, West Germany, or Japan were not linked either in the decade or in the shorter periods of time with any great frequency. Patterns were either nonexistent or inconsistent over time. Germany in particular had few significant relationships. Japan usually had high negative correlations, as might be expected for a country with rapidly expanding shares of the world market. These negative correlations, however, varied for the shorter periods in terms of the countries

TABLE 4.8
Significant Correlations for Country Pairs, 1976–78

Country Pairs	Change in Share		Net Shift	
	Unweighted	Weighted	Unweighted	Weighted
United States/				
Canada	-.66[c]	--	--	--
United Kingdom	-.62[c]	--	--	--
France	-.37[a]	--	--	--
West Germany	-.50[b]	-.49[a]	-.36[a]	-.48[b]
Sweden	.58[c]	--	--	--
Yugoslavia	--	--	--	-.34[a]
Other developed nations	--	-.34[a]	-.36[a]	--
Japan	--	--	--	-.51[b]
Developing countries	.39[a]	--	--	--
Canada/				
United States	-.66[c]	--	--	--
United Kingdom	.79[c]	--	--	--
France	.40[a]	--	--	--
West Germany	--	--	--	-.42[a]
Sweden	-.66[c]	--	--	--
Japan	--	--	--	-.36[a]
Developing countries	-.61[b]	--	--	--
United Kingdom/				
United States	-.62[c]	--	--	--
Canada	.79[c]	--	--	--
France	.49[b]	--	--	--
Sweden	-.56[c]	--	--	--
Australia/New Zealand	-.71[c]	--	-.44[b]	--
France/				
United States	-.37[a]	--	--	--
Canada	.40[a]	--	--	--
United Kingdom	.49[b]	--	--	--
West Germany	.41[a]	--	--	--
Belgium/Luxembourg	--	-.45[b]	--	-.42[a]
Sweden	--	.47[b]	--	.53[b]
Other developing nations	--	.34[a]	--	--
Japan	--	--	--	-.36[a]
Developing countries	-.54[b]	-.41[a]	--	-.48[b]
West Germany/				
United States	-.50[b]	-.49[b]	-.36[a]	-.48[b]
Canada	--	--	--	-.42[a]
France	.41[a]	--	--	--
Netherlands	--	--	--	.41[a]
Developing countries	-.56[c]	--	--	--
Belgium/Luxembourg/				
France	--	-.46[a]	--	-.42[a]
Italy	-.47[b]	--	-.45[b]	--
Yugoslavia	--	--	.41[a]	.35[a]
Other developed nations	--	-.51[b]	--	-.39[a]
Japan	--	.51[b]	--	.43[a]

	Measure			
	Change in Share		Net Shift	
Country Pairs	Unweighted	Weighted	Unweighted	Weighted
Netherlands/				
West Germany	--	--	--	.41[a]
Yugoslavia	--	--	-.43[a]	--
Italy/				
Belgium/Luxembourg	-.47[a]	--	-.45[b]	--
Sweden	--	--	-.47[b]	--
Sweden/				
United States	.59[c]	--	--	--
Canada	-.66[c]	--	--	--
United Kingdom	-.56[c]	--	--	--
France	--	.47[a]	--	.53[b]
Italy	--	--	-.47[b]	--
Switzerland	--	.49[b]	--	.52[b]
Other developed nations	--	.36[a]	--	--
Japan	--	-.56[c]	-.35[a]	-.63[c]
Developing countries	.37[a]	--	--	-.44[b]
Switzerland/				
Sweden	--	.49[b]	--	.52[b]
Developing countries	--	--	--	-.42[a]
Spain/				
Yugoslavia	.53[b]	.41[a]	.36[a]	--
Other developed nations	.36[a]	.41[a]	.35[a]	.41[a]
Yugoslavia/				
United States	--	--	--	-.34[a]
Belgium/Luxembourg	--	--	.41[a]	.35[a]
Netherlands	--	--	-.42[a]	--
Spain	.53[b]	.41[a]	.36[a]	--
Australia/New Zealand	--	--	--	.41[a]
Developing countries	-.43[b]	--	--	--
Australia/New Zealand/				
Canada	.45[b]	--	--	--
United Kingdom	.51[b]	--	--	--
Yugoslavia	--	--	--	.42[a]
Developing countries	-.40[a]	--	--	--
Japan/				
United States	--	--	--	-.51[b]
Canada	--	--	--	-.36[a]
France	--	--	--	-.36[a]
Belgium/Luxembourg	--	.51[b]	--	.43[a]
Sweden	--	-.56[b]	-.35[a]	-.63[c]

[a] Significant at α = .05.
[b] Significant at α = .01.
[c] Significant at α = .001.
-- Not a significant correlation.

SOURCE: Compiled by authors.

that were negatively linked with Japan. Thus, neomercantilist approaches implemented to counter competition from any single country would be unlikely to be effective across the total export mix, as one country is unlikely to be the culprit, although they might be more relevant for a particular product line. The Common Market restrictions on Japanese imports may be a possible exception to this generality, given their presence since the 1950s, but these restrictions have at best obviously only slowed the expansion of Japanese exports of manufactures.

The analyses of the various shorter periods, perhaps especially the 1976–78 period, clearly demonstrate the impact of probable short-term factors. There were reversals in signs from previous periods with the coefficients retaining their levels of significance. Thus, policies undertaken in response to these occurrences in one period could be nonproductive in that short-term phenomena are at work. In any event, since the underlying causal factors are likely to change, many such policies are predestined to be ineffective (although they might appear to be great successes at the time).

While the formation of the Common Market has had an obvious impact on trade in industrial products, especially for intra-EC trade, there are at least some signs that it has been a mixed blessing for the countries concerned. Some of the nations have begun to suffer declines in shares of the market, and there are some indications that these losses have been to fellow members. The expansion of the European Communities could exacerbate this potential problem. Spain (a likely member in the near future) and Italy had some of the more consistent relationships among the country pairs, but they had fluctuating ties with other EC states and particularly with the other developed nations category, a group including other EC members and many associate members.

Raw materials inputs rather consistently had a role to play in the relationships among the industrialized countries most reliant on such inputs. These ties, however, like many others, also demonstrated inconsistent patterns. At times these countries tended to rise or fall as a group, and in other time periods there were mixed patterns among them, indicating either competitive effects or differential world demand for various products. Some raw materials inputs could have remained important in a period while others declined in impact. Notwithstanding the complexity, such inputs do appear to continue to be a relevant consideration for trade patterns.

Overall, the trade in manufactures by the developed countries is a multifaceted phenomenon. Its importance is undoubted, but its complexity would seem to preclude easy approaches to the resulting (perceived) difficulties. Neomercantilist policies may simply turn out to treat symptoms rather than causes of export difficulties or domestic problems. The results of a free trade solution would be hard to measure, and advantages or disadvantages accruing to those nations opting for such policies would be unclear. Various other theoretical views of the international trade regime only touch on the trade among the industrialized countries, but the complexity of this trade may well caution against other simple solutions to the difficulties in the world trade regime.

5 Trade in Manufactures II: The Newly Industrializing Countries

World trade takes place primarily among the developed free market economy countries, and, as noted in Chapter 4, trade in manufactures constitutes the largest proportion of world trade. These figures suggest that trade among the developing countries (that is, intradeveloping country trade) is relatively small as a proportion of total world trade (5 to 7 percent in the 1970s) and that primary commodities, not manufactured products, are the principal export items of the developing countries to the world market, especially to the developed countries. The discussion of trade in primary commodities and agricultural products will be left to Chapters 6 and 7, respectively. The present chapter will examine the trade in manufactures between the developed countries and developing countries, especially the small number of those countries known as the "newly industrializing countries" (NICs).

MANUFACTURES EXPORTS FROM THE DEVELOPING COUNTRIES

Exports of manufactures by the developing countries, although still a small proportion of the world total, have steadily increased in recent years, thus constituting an important portion of the world trade in manufactures. Between 1955 and 1974, for instance, the output of manufactures in the developing countries as a whole grew at an annual rate of about 7 percent as compared with a rate of about 5 percent in the developed free market economy countries. Between 1970 and 1976, manufactures exports from the developing countries increased almost twice as fast as

did the growth of production and four times as fast as
the growth of production in the developed countries (UNCTAD
1977, p. 3).

The exports of manufactures by the developing countries accounted for a slightly larger proportion of the
total world exports of the free market economies with 6.0
percent at the end of 1978, compared to 4.3 percent of the
total in 1968 (see Table 5.1). These gains were far short
of the target of about 25 percent of the world manufactured
exports set for the year 2000 by the Nonaligned Nations
Conference in the Lima Declaration and the Plan of Action
in 1975, but the trendline for the decade was definitely
upward (UNIDO 1975). During the 1968-78 period, manufactures generally increased in importance in the export
mix of the developing countries, ranging from 20.7 percent
in 1968 to 23.3 percent in 1978. The decline to 16.6 percent in 1976 was largely due to the increase in the price
of oil that raised the proportion of primary commodities in
the export mix of the developing countries, a trend reversed by 1978. These exports of manufactures by developing countries continued to grow throughout the decade in
spite of the recession in the developed countries that followed the energy crisis of the mid-1970s.

TABLE 5.1
Importance of Manufactures Exports of Developing Free Market
Economies

| | Year | | | |
Indicator	1968	1972	1976	1978
Exports of developing free market economies as percentage of total exports of free market economies	20.5	19.9	28.2	25.6
Exports of manufactures as percent- age of total exports of developing free market economies	20.7	22.2	16.6	23.3
Exports of manufactures of developing economies as per- centage of total exports of free market economies	4.3	4.4	4.6	6.0

SOURCE: Compiled by authors from Yearbook of International Trade Statistics, various years.

Just as relationships existed between the performance of the developed countries in terms of export shares, interactions between the developing countries and the industrialized nations have been present. The developing countries' share of total world exports of manufactures increased between 1968 and 1978 from 6.5 to 9.3 percent (see Table 4.4), an increase that reflected the increasing importance of these countries as traders in manufactures. This increase, obviously, could only have come at the expense of the developed countries. Ideas about comparative advantage and the product life cycle theory, as well as efforts at regime reform, import substitution, and the creation of free trade areas to stimulate exports of manufactures, all might partly explain this increase.

Table 5.2 contains the significant correlations between the export shares of the developing countries as a group and the export shares of the various developed countries that were derived in the analyses in Chapter 4. The recapitulation shows that for the entire decade West Germany, the Netherlands, Yugoslavia, and Japan had the most consistent weighted correlations, all of which were negative associations, with the performance of the developing countries. All of these countries except Yugoslavia increased their total shares of the world market slightly in the decade; thus, the gains by the developing countries were selective in some product areas and corresponded to losses by these countries. As mentioned in the case of Japan in the previous chapter, the developing countries may have been taking over the production and export of products that had become standardized and were at the end of the life cycle where labor costs or locational advantages would be particularly relevant. In some cases the Japanese government and some industrial firms have encouraged such relocations (Hadley 1981, pp. 309–12).

There were only a few significant correlations for the 1968–72 period, with the negative associations of Yugoslavia and Australia/New Zealand with the developing countries most prominent. While these two countries and the developing countries all gained small market shares in the four years, it was apparently partially at each other's expense in different product areas. The more substantial overall gains by the developing countries from 1972 to 1976 were negatively associated with the performance of many developed nations. The largest associations were with Italy, Spain, and Japan, all of which also gained

TABLE 5.2

Significant Correlations Between Developing Countries and Developed Countries

Year and Developed Country	Change in Share		Net Shift	
	Unweighted	Weighted	Unweighted	Weighted
1968–78				
France	$-.50^b$	$-.39^a$	$-.45^b$	--
West Germany	$-.47^b$	$-.35^a$	$-.38^a$	$-.35^a$
Belgium/Luxembourg	$-.34^a$	--	--	--
Netherlands	--	$-.41^a$	--	$-.41^a$
Italy	--	$-.35^a$	--	--
Sweden	$-.34^a$	--	--	--
Yugoslavia	--	$-.49^b$	--	$-.37^a$
Japan	$-.68^c$	$-.43^a$	$-.44^a$	$-.35^a$
Other developed nations	--	$-.36^a$	--	--
1968–72				
United States	$-.80^c$	--	--	--
France	--	--	$-.35^a$	--
West Germany	$-.56^c$	--	--	--
Switzerland	--	--	--	$-.34^a$
Yugoslavia	--	$-.50^b$	--	$-.66^c$
Australia/New Zealand	--	$-.49^b$	--	$-.73^c$
1972–76				
France	$-.67^c$	--	$-.62^c$	--
Belgium/Luxembourg	$-.54^c$	--	--	--
Netherlands	$-.70^c$	--	--	--
Italy	--	$-.55^c$	--	$-.55^c$
Sweden	$-.79^c$	--	$-.46^b$	--
Spain	$-.57^c$	$-.47^b$	$-.43^a$	$-.54^c$
Australia/New Zealand	$-.56^c$	--	--	--
Japan	$-.51^b$	$-.41^a$	$-.36^a$	$-.42^a$
1976–78				
United States	$.39^a$	--	--	--
Canada	$-.61^c$	--	--	--
France	$-.54^c$	$-.41^a$	--	$-.48^b$
West Germany	$-.56^c$	--	--	--
Sweden	$.37^a$	--	--	$-.44^a$
Switzerland	--	--	--	$-.42^a$
Yugoslavia	$-.43^a$	--	--	--
Australia/New Zealand	$-.40^a$	--	--	--

[a] Significant at α = .05.
[b] Significant at α = .01.
[c] Significant at α = .001.
-- Not a significant correlation.

SOURCE: Compiled by authors.

81

export shares in this period. Again, the developing countries were obviously gaining shares in areas where these countries were less competitive and remaining stable in product areas where these three nations were improving their export performance. From 1968 to 1978, there were few significant associations on the weighted measures. France was the only country with consistently negative weighted association, indicating another possible transfer of production in some manufactures areas.

In general, the export performance of the developing countries for the decade was more sensitive to the European countries and Japan than the North American nations, notwithstanding the fact that the developing countries were consistent gainers and Canada and the United States suffered rather consistent declines. France, with a relatively small world share of manufactures exports, was the European country that most regularly interacted with the developing countries. The relationship with Japan was also quite important and probably did reflect the transfer of some manufacturing production to the developing states. There was no particularly clear identification with raw materials exporters apparent in the unweighted associations, although in some periods there were links between the developing countries and some of the developed nations that exported manufactures more reliant on raw materials inputs. The only two positive correlations in Table 5.2, those with the United States and Sweden for the simple change in share measure from 1976 to 1978, might fall into this category.

THE NICS: A PROFILE

The NICs are distinguishable from other countries, both developing and developed, in the type of economic policies pursued and in the kinds of adjustment problems arising from the successful implementation of the policies of economic growth (Balassa 1981; OECD 1979b; Saunders 1981). According to a 1979 OECD report, "What distinguishes the NICs from most of the non-oil developing countries is the emphasis they place on outward-looking growth policies as a means of promoting rapid industrialization." The successful implementation of this developmental strategy has often led to what has been called "a steady, and in some cases dramatic, enlargement of export market shares and of the domestic market" (OECD 1979b, p. 47). The NICs' fourfold characteristics, according to this report, were outward-looking growth policies, rapid economic growth through industrialization, enlargement and expansion of trade, and heavy reliance on foreign capital and technology (pp. 45-47).

A 1979 study by the Washington-based Overseas Development Council noted similar characteristics of the more advanced developing countries. They generally satisfied a set of four conditions. They attained relatively advanced levels of development, based on relatively rapid and uninterrupted rates of economic growth; they possessed relatively large, sophisticated, and diverse industrial sectors; they had major economic impacts on the industrial countries through their international transactions, resulting primarily from their penetration of world market for manufactures; and they implemented effective development strategies, a major element of which was a shift toward outward-looking growth policies (Mathieson 1979, pp. 5-6).

The change in developmental strategy and policies of the NICs came about in the 1960s due to two views that were widely shared by some policymakers in the developing countries at the time (Morrison 1976, p. x). First, there was a dissatisfaction with the results of import substitution, which had failed to stimulate and accelerate the process of economic growth for most of the developing countries; and, second, there was a realization of the inadequacy of most primary exports as bases of long-run economic growth for many developing countries. Those developing countries that subsequently became NICs, therefore, experimented with new economic policies, including a trade policy of expanding manufactured exports. Such measures were seen as having a favorable impact on economic growth. This approach and expectation, in retrospect, proved to be valid as the world economy was receptive to the NICs' expansion at least during the 1970s. Manufactured exports as such, of course, will not automatically improve the income distribution and employment situation. But, with proper government policy directives and adjustments to domestic and external circumstances, some of these NICs have succeeded in attaining the desired goals of rapid economic growth and transformation of their economic structure through industrialization.

The concept and acronym of the NICs was made popular by the 1979 OECD report, which selected some ten countries from what was described as the "dynamic continuum" of developing economies (Saunders 1981, p. 2). Four of these countries--Greece, Spain, Portugal, and Yugoslavia-- are in southern Europe. Since these countries are considered developed by the United Nations and included in the aggregate trade figures for the developed economies, as noted in the previous chapter, the discussion will focus on the other states: Brazil and Mexico in Latin America and Hong Kong, Taiwan, South Korea, and Singapore in East Asia. These countries are, in effect, leaders in the Third World in terms of levels of economic development and industrialization.

The emergence of the NICs has obviously been conditioned by the circumstances of specific time and place. The current generation of the NICs, at the outset of the 1980s, are heterogeneous and diverse in terms of size, culture, and resource endowment. Depending on the resource base of the economy, two types and varieties of the NICs may be broadly differentiated--the resource-rich NICs and the resource-poor NICs. Whereas the Asian NICs are generally resource poor, the Latin American NICs are generally resource rich. Of course, all the NICs are blessed by abundant human resources and have the advantage for the industrialization process of relatively cheap labor.

While the physical resources or raw materials for manufacturing industries are in short supply for most of the Asian NICs, the Latin American states enjoy a relative abundance of raw materials. Mexico in particular has the advantage of the recently revealed large deposits of oil and natural gas, although the decline in the price of oil in 1982 and 1983 posed a serious threat to the financial viability of Mexico's economy. In 1983, the Mexican government took a series of economic measures that included, among others, a prohibition of the transfer of Mexican currency out of the country. The Mexican peso floated against the US dollar at a ratio of 150 to 1 in April 1983, and Mexico's external debts totaled some $80 billion. Also, while these six NICs are considered free market economy countries, the variation in size among them is enormous. Whereas Brazil and Mexico have large domestic markets, South Korea and Taiwan fall between the large and small domestic market economies. Hong Kong and Singapore have trade-oriented offshore economies, with limited domestic markets.

This brief overview of the NICs during the late 1970s suggests that drawing a simplistic cause and effect association between the NIC status, on the one hand, and cultural traits, on the other, must be avoided. If there is any lesson to be drawn from study of the current generation of the NICs, it seems that many developing countries may aspire to bring about industrialization as long as their economies are efficiently managed with clear policy goals and directives, and as long as an appropriate level of determination and skill to carry out these goals is present (Hofheinz and Calder 1982; Kahn 1979).

To the extent that the NICs provide a model of "export-led growth" and developmental strategy that may be followed by other countries, some states in the developing world have been mentioned either as actual or potential NICs and near-NICs. These states include Malaysia, India, Thailand, and the Philippines in Asia, Algeria, Egypt, and Nigeria in Africa, and Argentina, Chile, and Colombia in Latin America. The present discussion will concentrate on the non-European NICs identified by the OECD report--the four Asian NICs of Hong Kong, South Korea, Singapore, and Taiwan and the two Latin American states of Brazil and Mexico.

EXPORT COMPOSITION AND PARTNERS OF THE NICS

The increase in exports of manufactures by the NICs and the developing countries in general has been more concentrated in some product areas than in others. The most important manufactures categories for the developing states as a group, both in terms of total absolute volumes of exports and as percentages of total world exports, are shown in Table 5.3. From the table, it is clear that the most important SITC groups for the developing states in terms of both volume and shares of the world market were clothing, textiles, travel goods, footwear, other or nonferrous metal manufactures, and miscellaneous manufactures (eleventh in terms of the developing countries' share of the world market). The other SITC categories in Table 5.3 represent either large shares of smaller volume SITC groups or small shares of categories accounting for relatively large trade volumes. The three components of SITC 7, for example, are present in the first part of the table because of the sheer size of total world exports included in these groups. These volumes, of course, are important for the developing states, but the lower percentages indicate that they are product areas where the industrialized countries still dominate.

Those product categories in which the developing countries have fared relatively well have been ones that would

TABLE 5.3
Major Exports of Manufactures of the Developing Countries

SITC Category	1968 Total Exports (000)	Percentage of World Exports	1978 Total Exports (000)	Percentage of World Exports
Share of developing countries of all manufactures exports		6.5		9.3
Ten SITC categories with largest developing country volumes in 1978				
84 Clothing	739,764	20.4	9,667,981	41.6
72 Electric machinery	249,296	2.3	8,317,058	9.6
65 Textiles	1,455,727	16.0	7,350,656	19.3
68 Other metals	2,845,044	32.0	6,256,128	25.4
89 Miscellaneous manufactures	566,339	9.7	4,595,671	15.8
73 Transport equipment	166,558	0.7	4,181,879	3.2
71 Nonelectric machinery	244,446	1.0	3,471,181	2.8
66 Cement and construction materials	459,613	9.5	3,172,275	10.6
67 Iron and steel	259,815	2.7	2,669,289	5.2
69 Metal manufactures NES	163,940	3.8	2,378,798	8.5
Ten SITC categories with largest developing country shares in 1978				
83 Travel goods	32,294	14.1	1,013,473	51.9
84 Clothing	739,764	20.4	9,667,981	41.6
63 Processed wood products	202,764	17.2	2,058,916	32.1
85 Footwear	118,299	9.9	2,167,367	29.2
61 Leather manufactures	172,672	19.3	1,164,241	26.5
68 Other metals	2,845,044	32.0	6,256,128	25.4
032 Canned fish	61,354	13.3	479,118	25.2
013 Canned meat	180,508	24.7	449,147	24.7
65 Textiles	1,455,727	16.0	7,350,656	19.3
431 Processed vegetable and animal oils	30,633	17.3	148,730	17.1

SOURCE: Compiled by authors.

86

have been expected. Many of the manufactures in question were ones with relatively simple, standardized inputs or ones based on important raw materials inputs, as in the case of nonferrous metal products. These products were also ones that the product life cycle concept and shifting comparative advantage would have suggested as being areas in which the developing states would first begin to export to world markets. Many of these exports, such as textiles, clothing, and footwear, however, have been facing increasing protectionist measures in various developed nations. Thus, the concentration of exports of manufactures in these types of product lines has created conditions that may limit the eventual size and share of the world market in a number of cases. Even so, with the exception of the nonferrous metal products, the SITC groups that appear in both parts of Table 5.3 are ones in which the developing countries have held or increased their shares of the world market.

The NICs' exports are also generally highly concentrated and focused in terms of specific partner countries. During the 1970s, the United States, for instance, was consistently an important trade partner for a number of NICs including Brazil, Mexico, Hong Kong, South Korea, and Singapore. In addition, the pattern of NICs and market nation relationship was generally stable over time, although there were some exceptions. In the 1970s, for instance, Argentina's trade with the United States as share of the former's total exports decreased dramatically, from 42.79 percent in 1970 to 7.29 percent in 1979, reflecting the changing nature of US–Argentina diplomatic relations during the 1970s. Likewise, South Korea's trade with the United States declined from 46.76 percent in 1970 to 29.1 percent in 1979, reflecting South Korea's diversification in the pattern of trade relations, particularly toward Japan (Morrison 1976, p. 17). Singapore and Hong Kong also were exporting more to Japan at the end of the 1970s.

The role of the NICs in world trade has also changed over time in terms of their exports to the specific developed market economy country as a percentage of the latter's total imports. Generally speaking, the market share of the individual NICs in the partner country's total imports is stable over time. Any change has been very slow and small in magnitude. During the 1970s, more NICs gained than lost in the share of their partner countries' markets. Argentina and Chile, however, were dramatic examples of NICs losing their market share with a partner country. The Argentine share of the US and Italian mar-

kets decreased from 1.91 percent and 1.81 percent in 1970 to
0.26 percent and 0.79 percent in 1979, respectively. Likewise,
Chile's market share in the United States declined from 0.45
percent in 1970 to 0.19 percent in 1979.

Other NICs were moderately successful in increasing
their market shares in the partner countries. Some notable
examples include Chile with Brazil, Mexico with Spain and
Israel, and South Korea with the United States, Japan,
Hong Kong, and Thailand. South Korea's market share in
the United States, for instance, increased from 0.98 percent
in 1970 to 2.02 percent in 1979, while its share with Japan
increased from 1.24 percent in 1970 to 3.03 percent in 1979.
The fact that more NICs gained than lost in their market
shares with specific partner countries in the 1970s indicated that their export performance in the 1970s was generally good, at least as reflected in trade with specific
developed market economy countries.

THE NIC PHENOMENON: DEPENDENCY OR DIFFUSION?

Of the several theoretical explanations that may be
advanced regarding the origin of the NIC phenomenon, two
stand out as the most promising--the diffusion theory and
the dependency theory. Whereas the diffusion theory seeks
an explanation for the NIC success in the indigenous capabilities of the country involved and the policies pursued
by its government in response to the external environment,
the dependency theory gives more emphasis to the structure
of the world capitalist system by treating the NICs as an
integral part of transnational business links.

The diffusion theory assumes that by enlarging the
export market shares, the NICs were able to attract foreign
investment that facilitated, among other things, the introduction of advanced technology for manufacturing processes
(Anell and Nygren 1980, p. 73; Morton and Tulloch 1977, p.
213; OECD 1979b, p. 47). The dynamics of the capitalist
business expansion abroad provided the stage at which the
NICs could prosper. The NICs merely responded to the opportunity made available to them internationally through
the opening up of the world market as a result of the increased demand for the manufactured products. The NICs'
process of adaptation to the changing environment of the
world economy included taking advantage of factors of production made available to them internationally in areas
where they were formerly deficient. Due to the need to

recycle petrodollars, the international lending agencies and private banks have been more than willing to make available investment capital to the NICs since the mid-1970s. The multinational enterprises, moreover, have been helpful to the NICs in supplying the necessary technology and the inputs of production, except for labor, which has been provided by the NICs themselves.

The product life cycle theory (discussed in Chapter 2) constitutes a variation of the diffusion hypothesis. The last stage of standardization with the concomitant economies of scale available in production is the establishment of manufacturing facilities in the developing countries for export to the industrialized states and the rest of the world. Taiwan is just one example of such a process. Early exports of manufactures were low in technology inputs and not competitive in the domestic markets of developed states. As industrialization developed, Taiwanese industries moved into new product lines, and later exports of manufactures became competitive with the products of the developed states, both worldwide and in their domestic markets (Roe and Shane 1979, pp. 176-77). It is possible, in fact, that the developing countries might be able to identify products approaching the "mature phase" of the product life cycle and formulate plans to take advantage of the resultant opportunities (Hirsch 1972, p. 50). The possible shifting of industrial production in some product areas from industrial locations in Japan to the developing states that was noted above would fit the concept of the product life cycle and the diffusion theory quite well.

The export-led growth of the NICs, according to dependency theory, reflects the process of worldwide capital accumulation. While the rise of the NICs occurred for a number of potential reasons, it can be seen as part of the ongoing dynamics of the world capitalist system rather than a process specific to individual countries (Frank 1982, p. 22; Caporaso 1981, p. 273). The structural theory of imperialism developed by Galtung (1971) is another example of a dependency theory that views the development of the NICs within the context of the world capitalist system. Industrialization in these countries resulted from the transnational links that integrated the developing states into the world capitalist system as part of a feudal interaction structure wherein the weaker states are dominated and exploited by the stronger.

While adherents of the dependency view accept the fact that some manufacturing production is relocated to the NICs, and the socialist countries of East Europe, to lower production costs, they have noted that this relocation process also leaves the technologically sophisticated manufacturing processes in the developed countries (Frank 1982, p. 22; Galtung 1973, p. 59; Luke 1983, pp. 999-1000; Martinelli 1982, pp. 99-101). The transfer of industrial facilities to the developing countries is also far from trouble-free since it generates protectionist pressures in traditional manufacturing sectors in the developed states and has generated financial and trade imbalances that have affected the overall trade regime and its corresponding financial system (Frank 1982, p. 22; Rothstein 1977, p. 242). There is also disagreement among dependency theorists and with neo-Marxists over the advantages of such "dependent development (that is, development which relies extensively on the global capitalist system)," with some arguing that there are consequent adverse effects on the distribution of the gains from such industrialization within the developing countries (Caporaso 1981, p. 351).

Access to markets in developed economies is also deemed essential for the continued expansion of the NICs' trade and exporting of manufactured products. In this sense the economic welfare of the NICs is closely tied with the economic health of the developed market economy countries. Since the NICs are highly vulnerable to shifts and fluctuations in the economies of the developed countries, they are increasingly interdependent and integrated into the world economic system. This vulnerability is shown by the integration of the respective NICs with the developed countries in trading blocs.

THE POLITICAL CONSEQUENCES OF THE EMERGENCE OF THE NICS

What have been the implications of the emergence of the newly industrializing countries in the world trade system and politics? What impact did their emergence have on the structure of the global and regional trade systems? The NIC phenomenon must be placed in its proper historical and comparative perspective. The consequences of the NIC phenomenon have been severely felt by the developed market economy countries, most of which have adopted neomercantile policy measures. Further elaboration and scrutiny of these developments will aid in providing a rational policy solution beneficial to both parties of trade disputes, that is, the developed market economy countries and the NICs.

Neomercantilism in the Developed States

    The increase in the manufactured exports by the NICs has led to the adoption of various protectionist measures by the developed market economy countries, intended primarily to discourage rapid and expansionist export drives by the NICs. Many developed countries have succumbed to mounting domestic pressures generated by labor and business interest groups in the ailing industries that have been adversely affected by the increased competition from abroad. These voices of protectionism have been vociferous and the politicians have often been sympathetic, in the name of defending the market and employment of the workers who otherwise would lose their jobs. Domestic programs of trade adjustment, in the form of monetary payments and compensations to the affected industries and regions, have been implemented as one means of responding to the challenge from abroad. But these adjustment measures have not generally been adequate or effective thus far (Baldwin 1981; Frey-Wouters 1980, p. 270).
    In spite of the official adherence to an open trading system, evidenced by the conclusion of the Tokyo Rounds of the Multilateral Trade Negotiations under the GATT framework in 1979, many developed countries have instituted a variety of restrictive measures on imports from the developing countries in general and the NICs in particular. These protective measures include, among others, new import quotas and OMAs (Orderly Marketing Arrangements), price floors on imports (especially for steel and agricultural products), new VERs (Voluntary Export Restraints), countervailing duties, administrative obstacles to imports, and subsidies to domestic industries to sustain levels of production in excess of those justified by demand (Gosovic 1972, p. 8; Keesing 1979, p. 15; Morrison 1976, p. 25). These calls for protectionism were made not only to control the market shares on a regional or worldwide basis but also to extend controls to a wide array of manufactured products. Under a VER, for instance, quantitative restrictions in imports from the developing countries and NICs

were imposed upon individual supplier countries urging them to cut back their exports to a particular market where they were considered "disruptive" (Murray and Walter 1978, p. 40). These measures have been imposed on the NICs under the explicit threat of quantitative or other import restrictions in the case of failure to act. Such bilateral restrictions on trade were in fact on the increase throughout the 1970s (Page 1981, p. 26).

In the 1970s neomercantilism was a response by the developed market economy countries to the challenge posed by expanded manufactures exports by the NICs, a challenge that necessitated the structural adjustment of their economies. Three characteristics of such protectionism were noticeable, each of which entailed an appropriate policy response to alleviate the temporary economic hardships and disruptions—long-term structural adjustment in specific industries, nontraditional forms of import restrictions, and government interventions in the market (OECD 1979b).

The erection of trade barriers in the 1970s reflected less and less an attempt to correct an overall imbalance in current trade and more and more a response to long-term structural difficulties in specific industries that were associated with the changing international division of labor for manufactures production. For instance, the growth of manufactures exports by the NICs was the major cause of protective measures in textiles and clothing, footwear, household electrical appliances, and television sets, while the shift in trade flows in the OECD area was influential for protective measures in the steel, shipbuilding, and automotive industries where the NICs were not as yet fully competitive as other OECD countries (Frey-Wouters 1980, p. 115; OECD 1979b, p. 102). Moreover, the new protectionism made less use of the conventional techniques of unilateral imposition of quotas and customs duties and gave preference to other forms of discriminatory actions, such as bilateral or multilaterally negotiated trade restrictions. Coercion and barriers such as cumbersome administrative regulations specific to certain products were also employed even if the nontariff barriers provision of the Tokyo Round adopted in 1979 prohibited such discriminatory practices. Finally, governments adopted various policy measures that were not directly linked with trade itself, but intended to protect domestic industries indirectly from foreign competition. These practices included government intervention in the market with employment subsidies, tax exemptions, state holdings in firms, and the like (Morrison 1976, p. 25; Malmgren 1981, p. 433, Page 1981, pp. 36-37).

The case of textiles may be cited to illustrate the point of this new protectionism. New restrictions on the export of textiles and clothing severely curtailed the prospect of the developing countries' trade expansion into the markets of the developed countries. For the years 1978 through 1982, under the new protectionist guise, the EC countries have imposed quotas on textiles and clothing imports that not only limit growth but actually reduce the level of imports. The quotas for 1978 were set well below their actual 1976 trade levels in several major product categories for the three leading NIC suppliers of Taiwan, Hong Kong, and South Korea. The possibility of expanding their exports was thus severely restricted by quotas that grew only slowly from the past trade levels, usually by between 0.5 and 4 percent a year, as compared with the previous norm of 6 percent per year. The new agreements also established low "trigger levels" for further quotas that would limit the scope for diversification of exports into new products. These new rules were expected to result in a growth rate of less than 6 percent for clothing and textiles imports by many of the developed countries from the developing countries (Balassa 1978, pp. 414-15). As a result of these restrictive measures, capital investments in these industries were either being canceled or cut back, not only in the NICs but also in the developing countries in general (Keesing 1979, pp. 60-61).

Under the guise of the VERs, new trade restrictions were also imposed by the developed countries on the NICs' export of electronic components, television and radio sets, calculators, steel, motor vehicles, motorcycles, and ball bearings, most of which were accepted in the face of threats of unilateral measures (Keesing 1979, pp. 60-61). Under the OMAs, pressure tactics and coercion were also applied to the NICs' exports of manufactured products and commodities, such as the US negotiations with Taiwan and South Korea in 1977 to restrict the export of footwear.

Authoritarian Politics

The impact of the NIC phenomenon upon the domestic political process and structure of the NICs has generally been toward strengthening the position of the central gov-

ernment and authoritarian political tendencies. Although
the NICs are more heterogeneous than homogeneous, most of
them have strong central governments that are controlled
by dominant elites and that are more or less nondemocratic
and authoritarian. Thus, the three Far Eastern NICs of
South Korea, Singapore, and Taiwan are controlled by authoritarian political leaders, while British Hong Kong is
administered as a type of colony. The two Latin American
NICs of Brazil and Mexico are also dominated by strong
leaders, Brazil by a military oligarchy and Mexico by a
single, generally noncompetitive party. South Korea is a
civilianized military regime that has been turning the country into a bureaucratic authoritarian state.

Although both old and new industrial countries must
operate under the system of the capitalistic principles of
competition and comparative advantage, the NICs as industrial newcomers have not generally been welcomed. The
ruling elites in the NICs have tended to use the presence
of severe competition abroad as a threat to the survival
and viability of the state and society itself. The sense of
crisis thus engendered by the governing elite in the NICs
has aroused public concern and consciousness, which, in
turn, is exploited politically to enhance the regime's claim
for legitimacy of rule.

The NIC phenomenon thus has domestic impact and
fallout upon the process of political development in each
NIC. The external environment in the world economy tends
to affect the domestic political trends in the NICs in terms
of type of government and ruling coalition (Borrego 1983;
Collier 1979; O'Donnell 1973). It has also been suggested
that transnational corporations favor authoritarian polities
since such regimes supply stability and are easier to influence (Martinelli 1982, p. 89). The dynamics of the
politics of industrialization have been operative in the
NICs much as in the developed market economy states. In
fact, the effect may be more exaggerated in the NICs because of their late entry into the race for industrialization.
Gerschenkron's (1962) notion of late industrialization and
development has some application to the NICs in this respect.

Because of the dynamics of competition in the world
marketplace and changes in technology, each NIC as a recent competitor has faced a new game, with the rules altered by protectionism. The entry cost for the NICs seeking
to join the world trade regime as manufactures exporters

has been generally much higher than it was for the old established industrial nations. There have been more complex economic and political requirements for late industrializers, which faced greater competition, than was the case for the countries able to industrialize earlier. Paying these costs required greater collective mobilization of energies, which, in turn, required greater central coordination of efforts. The societies that had previously developed strong central institutions prior to industrialization would naturally have found these institutions useful when they attempted to catch up with the earlier industrializers (Gerschenkron 1962; Gourevitch 1978; Luke 1983).

TOWARD INTEGRATION AND ACCOMMODATION

The NICs are the recent entrants into the world of industrialization, and as such they are the new actors and competitors in the arena of world trade. They have attained limited success in exploiting favorable circumstances through such policy measures as adopting an outward-looking growth policy and pursuing an aggressive trade policy of manufactures export. In these endeavors the NICs skillfully utilized the comparative advantage in wages and productivity in certain industrial sectors. In this sense the NICs are the newest members of the industrialized world, and they share the experience of all the earlier industrializers, such as West Germany, Japan, and Italy. Whereas West Germany successfully reentered the world trade system in the 1950s, Japan and Italy did so in the course of the 1960s. The fact that the NICs succeeded in their export drives in the late 1960s and in the 1970s, therefore, should not be taken as an exception to the historic pattern.

Although the current economic difficulties of the advanced industrial countries have little to do with the NICs, the fact that many developed market economy countries blame NIC competition as the source of their problems must be taken seriously. To be sure, the phenomenon of economic recession and stagflation in the economies of most industrialized developed countries was caused more directly by the energy-related economic disturbances and less by NIC export expansion in manufactured products into the domestic markets of developed countries. The current problem of surplus capacity in the old industrialized countries, it can be argued, is due to the policy failure on the part of these countries to bring about structural adjustments in their national economies. Balassa (1981, pp. 422-28) has argued that the unemployment in the industrial countries was not caused by imports from the developing world, but reflected the growth of indigenous technologies within the industrialized states themselves. Obviously, the developing countries of the NICs that are rapidly industrializing as a result of their successful economic policies should not be criticized for their success, nor should they be forced to pay for the policy failures of some of the old industrialized countries.

From the standpoint of utilizing the world economic resources efficiently and attaining a higher degree of international division of labor, both developed countries and NICs should be better integrated into the global economic system. The trade relationship between the developed countries and the NICs, in short, should be viewed not as a zero-sum game but as a positive-sum game. The contribution of the NICs to the world economic development through trade expansion should be duly recognized and their legitimate demands and status respected. From the perspective of maintaining the proper balance between the two parties to trade conflicts, the solution to the problem of the rise of neomercantilism and the emergence of the NICs can be found in the accommodation of mutual interests of the two concerned parties. The posture of an accommodation of interests between the developed countries and the NICs, in short, may suggest a formula for the success and an appropriate strategy for the management of the current difficulties of world economic recession and stagflation.

6　　Trade in
　　　Primary Commodities

　　　　Although trade in manufactures has come to represent the largest component of world trade, a wide variety
and significant quantity of primary commodities or raw
materials continue to be traded in the world market.   Many
countries principally participate in the world trade regime
as exporters of raw materials that in turn are used by
importing countries either directly as consumer goods or as
inputs into manufacturing processes.   The uneven geographic
distribution globally of some basic resources has encouraged trade between producing and consuming countries.
While there is flexibility in terms of which mineral products
are to be exploited and which agricultural and forestry
resources utilized, there are natural limitations in terms
of potential sources of supply and thus exporting countries.
Given the overall importance of trade in primary commodities, the policy issues connected with this trade that
have arisen are relevant not only for the countries participating in such trade but for the world trade regime as
well.

THE ROLE OF COMMODITIES IN WORLD TRADE

　　　　Since manufactures have come to play a larger role
in international trade, primary commodities have become
less prominent as a proportion of world trade, even when
increasing in absolute terms.   A victim of the increasing
complexity of products present in the world, commodity
trade has given way to manufactures that in turn require
more and more manufactured inputs and lower relative
levels of commodity inputs (McCullock 1978, p. 235).   It is

safe to predict that commodities will play a relatively smaller role in the foreseeable future and that the world trade regime is unlikely to return to the situation where trade was principally conducted on the basis of exchanging raw materials or semiprocessed commodities for manufactured goods. For example, in the 1970s the United Nations projected total world demand for manufactures to grow at two to three times the rate of growth for primary products (Morrison 1976, p. 7).

The relative decline of trade in most primary commodities, including some food products to be discussed in greater detail in Chapter 7, is shown in Table 6.1. Almost without exception, individual primary commodities represent a smaller proportion of trade in 1978 than in 1968. Petroleum exports are an obvious exception, but even here there was a decline between 1976 and 1978. Fibers such as jute, cotton, and wool showed particularly sharp declines, amounting to less than half of their 1968 index levels in 1978. Iron ore also displayed a similar pattern. The performance of the basic manufactures in the SITC 6 group, compared to SITC 7 products, likewise reflected the declining role of commodities in trade. Thus, with the major exception of crude petroleum, commodities have been declining in relative importance, whether as unfinished products or in semiprocessed forms.

The shrinking role of primary commodities in world trade has varying and differential implications for different countries. Whereas some developed countries, such as Japan, Germany, and Switzerland, are involved in commodity trade almost exclusively as importers, others export manufactured products and raw materials. The group of commodity-exporting developed nations includes the United States, Canada, Australia, Sweden, Spain, Finland, and the Soviet Union. The impact of natural resources on the export performances of the developed countries in at least some product categories was noted in Chapter 4; they have an interest in trade in commodities as exporters as well as importers. Ultimately, however, for all of these developed countries (with the possible exceptions of Australia and New Zealand), their overall export positions in world trade and their levels of economic development will remain buttressed by trade in manufactures.

The countries more directly affected by trade in raw materials and changes in the trade regime affecting these products are the developing countries (Frey-Wouters 1980,

TABLE 6.1
Indices of Shares in World Exports

	1968	1972	1976	1978
Primary Commodities				
Coffee	11.8	9.2	9.9	10.0
Cocoa	4.0	2.7	2.8	4.7
Tea and mate	3.0	1.8	1.1	1.4
Sugar and honey	8.6	9.4	8.8	6.7
Meat	15.1	16.8	11.0	11.7
Fish	7.8	8.7	7.1	8.6
Wheat	11.8	9.7	10.0	7.8
Rice	4.4	2.7	2.3	2.3
Maize	6.8	6.0	8.2	6.6
Other grains	3.3	3.4	3.8	2.8
Flour, meal, and cereal preparations	3.7	3.1	2.9	3.0
Tobacco	5.0	3.9	2.9	3.0
Rubber (including synthetic)	7.8	5.1	5.1	5.2
Wood (rough and shaped)	13.9	12.7	10.4	10.7
Jute	.8	.5	.2	.1
Cotton	9.6	7.1	4.7	4.3
Wool	8.9	5.9	4.1	3.0
Iron ores	8.4	6.2	5.6	4.1
Nonferrous ores	9.7	8.4	6.3	6.3
Iron scrap	2.3	1.7	1.8	1.6
Nonferrous scrap	2.7	1.5	1.5	1.4
Crude petroleum[a]	55.4	69.9	149.5	123.4
Petroleum products[a]	24.0	22.6	35.9	30.5
Manufactures				
Basic manufactures (SITC 6)	208.5	194.7	166.4	177.2
Other manufactures (SITC 7)	273.4	298.6	276.3	292.4

[a] Indices based on total free world imports due to lack of complete export data.

Index = commodity volume/total exports of free market economies x 100.

SOURCE: Yearbook of International Trade Statistics, various years.

p. 235). Many of these countries, not surprisingly, rely on primary commodities for their major exports. The percentage of trade of the free market developing countries devoted to manufactures, while generally on the increase, was relatively small, as indicated in Table 5.1. Since most of the trade in manufactured products from developing countries has been accounted for by a small group, principally the NICs, the reliance on commodities by the remaining developing countries is even greater.

Commodity trade is also important for many developing countries because their commodity exports are not diversified into many different product categories (Mikdashi 1976, p. 172; Morton and Tulloch 1977, p. 90). Many countries export principally one product or a group of related products. Some examples of such export concentrations are copper and copper products in Zambia and Chile; petroleum in Saudi Arabia, Kuwait, and the United Arab Emirates; groundnuts and associated products in Gambia and Senegal; cacao in Ghana; meat products and hides from Somalia; and bauxite and alumina in Jamaica. Changes in world demand or prices for particular materials consequently will have significant impacts on the economies of some developing countries. Unlike developed countries whose exports of manufactures and diversified export mixes have provided them with a cushion, commodity-exporting developing countries have been more critically affected by global commodity trade. This sensitivity to the position of commodities in world trade led the UNCTAD conferences to focus on the issues of terms of trade and price stability for commodity exports (Vastine 1977).

COMMODITY PRICES AND PROPOSED SOLUTIONS

Terms of Trade for Primary Commodities

The concern over declining terms of trade for raw materials was one issue underlying the call for reforms in the world trade regime. Supporters of the NIEO have argued that the same volumes of commodity exports have been buying progressively less and less of the manufactures of the industrialized countries, and that such declines have been particularly difficult for the developing countries whose export structure is generally undiversified. Dos Santos (1971, p. 230) further argued that it is monopoly

conditions in the world market that lower the prices for
raw materials and raise the prices of industrial products.
The declines in the relative prices of commodities also
tend to lead to many political strains and pressures
(Kuznets 1964, p. 70).

In fact, however, it has not been clear that commodities have generally had declining terms of trade, even
when petroleum is excluded from consideration (Anell and
Nygren 1980, pp. 134–35; McCullock 1978, p. 236; Mutti and
Richardson 1979, p. 61; Uri 1976, p. 99). Part of the
difficulty in determining long-term trends in the case of
exports of commodities by the developing countries (and
the developed ones as well) lies in the choice of the base
year. Compared to the Korean War years, for example,
when prices for most commodities were high, there has
indeed been a decline. Compared to other periods, however, there has been greater variability in changes in the
terms of trade.

Data on the terms of trade for 25 developing states,
mostly larger ones, from different areas of the world, as
well as the industrialized countries and some of the centrally planned economies, were available. The data covered the period from 1970 to 1978, with 1975 serving as
the base index year (see Table 6.2). The developing
countries for which data were available included exporters
of a variety of commodities. Exporters relying on petroleum shipments, however, were excluded since petroleum
prices for this period have usually been seen as an exception to the declining terms of trade argument. The data
for the industrialized states and the centrally planned
economies in Europe provided an opportunity for a comparison of trends in this period. It is possible that the
comparisons would totally reflect long-term trends for the
developing countries given year-to-year fluctuations in the
prices of particular commodities. For example, in 1979,
Jamaica gained greatly from increased royalty payments
and prices for bauxite and alumina exports that would
clearly be reflected in improved terms of trade for that
country if more recent data were available. In the case of
the developed countries, the trends can be considered more
meaningful since there are a wide variety of products involved, and changes in any one product price would have
been offset by changes in the prices for other products.
In spite of these difficulties, the figures in Table 6.2 provide a useful indication of overall trends in the 1970s.

TABLE 6.2
Terms of Trade for Developing and Developed Countries

Developing Country	Terms of Trade		Developed Country	Terms of Trade	
	1970	1978		1970	1978
	(1975 = 100)			(1975 = 100)	
Bolivia	74	99[a]	Australia	89	87
Brazil	117	116	Austria	100	97
Cyprus	113	100	Belgium/Luxembourg	105	97
El Salvador	119	198[b]	Canada	92	93
Egypt	165	113	Denmark	107	101
Fiji	75	88	Finland	94	91
Hong Kong	100	103	France	105	101
India	151	119	Greece	119	98
Jamaica	121	97	Iceland	106	120
Kenya	141	132	Ireland	101	104
Korea, South	146	128	Israel	118	121
Malawi	123	104	Italy	126	102
Mexico	83	111	Japan	139	113
Morocco	74	94	Netherlands	110	100
Pakistan	117	124	New Zealand	118	113
Panama	118	94	Norway	93	95
Philippines	135	89	Portugal	135	116[b]
Sri Lanka	184	173	South Africa	108	81
Syria	94	120	Spain	134	100
Thailand	114	88	Sweden	98	93
Trinidad and			Switzerland	97	108
Tobago	75	99	United Kingdom	119	107
Tunisia	65	97	United States	122	95
Uganda	178	203	West Germany	101	101
Zambia	232	99	Yugoslavia	106	104
Zimbabwe	105	81			
			Bulgaria	104	87
			Czechoslovakia	110	88
			East Germany	115	100
			Hungary	120	98
			Poland	98	100
			Soviet Union	94	113

[a] 1976.
[b] 1977.

SOURCE: Yearbook of International Trade Statistics, 1979, pp. 1142–45; 1980, pp. 1191–93.

No clear pattern for the terms of trade for the developing or developed countries is reflected in Table 6.2. Compared to 1970, for example, 11 of the developing countries had better terms of trade in 1978, 13 had worse terms of trade, and 1 (Brazil) remained relatively the same. Among the developed countries of the West, 5 improved, 2 changed by a point or less on the index, and 18 had declining terms of trade. Only two of the centrally planned European economies improved in the eight years, and four experienced declines. Between 1975 and 1978, 13 developing countries showed improvement, 4 had virtually no change, and 8 experienced declines. Among the developed countries, ten had gains, ten had declines, and five showed little change. For the centrally planned economies, three had declines, two were relatively stable, and only the Soviet Union had improved terms of trade. Thus, over the period as a whole, the group of developing countries included in the table fared better than the developed Western countries or the centrally planned economies in terms of general trends. Although these findings are tentative, since the developing countries included in the table are not a random sample, the results provide some insight for one period of time.

A number of institutional reforms and measures have been proposed to counter the perceived inequity in world trade in the prices received for primary commodities. These measures are designed to improve the returns to the developing countries exporting raw materials. Among the proposals are those stressed by NIEO proponents, including schemes indexing the prices received for commodities with the prices of manufactures, stabilization of the international prices of commodities, and cooperation among the commodity exporters.

Indexation of Raw Materials Prices

As noted in Chapter 3, one proposal for securing better prices for commodity exports has been to peg the prices of important commodities to the prices of a market basket of manufactured goods exported by the developing countries (Brandt 1980). The indexation idea has been put forward by members of the reformist school as one means of correcting existing imbalances in the world trade regime that work to the disadvantage of the developing states.

For dependency-neocolonialist and neo-Marxist theorists, how-ever, the terms of the trade problem is more a symptom of underlying problems than a key issue in its own right. Even with higher prices the developing countries would still be tied into the world trade regime in a subservient position and suffer the negative consequences of such an association. The idea of indexing commodity prices ob-viously runs counter to free trade theory, and to the extent that free trade ideas exist in developed nations there will be opposition to the indexation concept.

A number of problems are extant in the idea of in-dexation, some of which have been raised by developed countries. First, the choice of a base year presents some difficulties since some commodities (and exporters) would be favored over others in any particular year. Even run-ning averages over a number of years might present prob-lems. Second, a number of industrialized countries that export commodities would no doubt gain from higher prices since it would be difficult to effectively exclude some ex-porters from the gains. While some developed states might be willing to pay higher prices for exports from the de-veloping countries, they might oppose a situation where other developed countries gained noticeably. A third dif-ficulty, and an argument used by some industrialized states, is that indexation, however arrived at, would penalize developed countries on the basis of their imports of raw materials rather than on the basis of their contribu-tions to higher world prices for manufactures (Morton and Tulloch 1977, p. 298). A fourth problem, also argued by some developed states, is that since commodities are a basic input for manufactures, the pegging process would start a round of price increases that would be destabiliz-ing for the world economy (Frey-Wouters 1980, p. 243). Fifth, there is a possibility that gains would not be equally distributed among the developing countries, and some could even be net losers in such an indexation pro-cess (Anell and Nygren 1980, p. 135; Uri 1976, p. 98). A final potential problem is that such an indexation scheme could encourage substitutions of some materials for the in-dexed commodities. Such substitutions could be to the ultimate detriment of some developing exporters, as the higher prices received would be for a smaller volume of exports.

Notwithstanding the potential difficulties associated with indexing the prices of commodities with manufactures,

the basic idea does reflect a desire to improve the returns the developing countries would receive from trade.
It also demonstrates the complexity of problems faced by
commodity exporters in their attempts to improve the gains
from participation in the world trade regime. While improving such gains for developing states may be worthwhile
and even necessary for the long-term stability of the regime, solutions such as indexation are likely to be difficult to achieve because of disagreements between exporting
and importing states, regardless of their development status, and even possible disagreements among the exporters
or among the importers. While indexation theoretically
could be a solution to many of the problems of the developing states, its implementation in the near future is
unlikely from a practical standpoint.

Price Stabilization

Another policy issue important to exporters of commodities is that of stable prices. Price stability has advantages for facilitating economic planning by governments
and formulating effective budgets. Fluctuating prices
make it difficult for governments to implement long-term
projects and plan investments since a significant portion
of revenues may be based in one form or the other upon
the export sector (Morrison 1976, p. 6). While it has been
argued that price fluctuations do not impede development
in the long run and that there is no indication that stable
prices have led to increased growth (Anell and Nygren
1980, p. 141; Mutti and Richardson 1979, p. 69), it does
seem clear that instability does create uncertainty. Table
6.2 clearly shows that the developing countries did suffer
from much greater fluctuations in their terms of trade on
the average than either the developed nations or the centrally planned economies. Such price fluctuations also have
the disadvantage for the exporting countries of permitting
buyers to play different commodity producers off against
each other (Frey-Wouters 1980, p. 235).
One reason why price stability may not have contributed to growth in the past is that fluctuations may
have indicated rapid improvement in prices. In the 1950s,
after the end of the Korean War, prices for commodity exports were actually more stable than those for manufactures.
This fact, however, reflected a situation in which prices

for manufactures were increasing; thus, they were more "unstable" (Coppock 1962, p. 35). The increases in petroleum prices in the 1970s also reflected great price instability, although the higher prices could hardly be considered a handicap to the economic growth of the OPEC nations.

Stable prices for exports often are of interest to all countries, regardless of development status. Many developed countries prefer stable prices for raw materials to facilitate their domestic economic planning and to aid local industries in terms of planning production and avoiding major rises in the prices of inputs that could contribute to domestic inflation. But, as is often the case in the area of commodities, stable prices are more a concern for the developing countries. The industrialized states have a mix of exports, and while unstable prices can hurt particular industries, the national economy as a whole is less affected. Developing countries are more vulnerable as a general rule. Since such variations could contribute to political difficulties for the governments of many developing nations, price stability has both economic and political benefits.

The price variations for raw materials occur for a variety of reasons, many of which limit the potential for stabilizing prices in the world market. Agricultural products, for example, are affected by weather and crop yields in a given year. Diseases have also dramatically affected the output in particular countries, such as coffee in Brazil and cacao in Ghana. In the case of minerals, new discoveries may lead to lower prices. Finally, for all primary commodities, an economic downturn in the industrialized countries will generally lead to lower demand and price drops. The generalized recession in the West in the late 1970s had exactly this type of impact on prices for raw materials. Even when the prices paid for the commodities remained the same, difficulties still remained because total revenues from the commodities declined because of lower volumes of exports.

Thus, solutions to problems of price instability or revenue instability are not any easier to achieve than those related to the problems of terms of trade. Stabilizing prices at too high a level, for instance, may encourage new exporters, leading to further competition. If the chosen price is too low, there may be an undersupply of commodities. The question of allocation of market shares among exporters will also appear if prices are stabilized, and there will be difficulties if there are new entrants into the market. Negotiations dealing with these problems will be difficult since the countries involved will have different goals and interests, goals and interests that do not always correspond to their positions in the market as exporters or importers.

Past efforts to achieve price stabilization in the past have had some positive effects. Action has been taken by countries with strategic stockpiles to sell portions of these reserves when prices have been high and to replenish them when prices decline. The end result of this type of unilateral measure has been more stability in the world price and greater domestic economic stability in some countries. The Common Market has created a stabilization fund for some commodities, particularly agricultural materials and timber, exported by the developing EC associate members. Exporters themselves have on occasion established stockpiles or withheld surpluses in efforts to stabilize world prices, usually with only limited success. The ultimate extension of this type of multilateral effort has been the formation of commodity export groups, such as OPEC, which will be discussed below.

Agreements between producers and consumers have also been used in efforts to stabilize prices by, in effect, fixing purchasing power. For example, the sugar quota as operated in the United States provided some guarantees in terms of prices since countries had access and fixed market shares. France provided price supports for products from most of its former colonies with guarantees on volumes of the commodities as well. The EC agreed to continue this practice in the first association agreement reached with the African associates in 1963 in the first Yaoundé Convention (Zartman 1971, pp. 29-30), later replaced with a stabilization fund for some commodities in the Lomé Convention of 1975. The developing countries themselves have at times made barter agreements for exchanging specified volumes of raw materials (cf. Karunatilake 1969). While potentially uneconomic from a free trade point of view, since the producer with the comparative advantage is not necessarily the supplier, a barter agreement does aid the partner countries by disposing of commodities for needed or useful imports. Even if world prices for the commodities are high, usually scarce foreign currency reserves are preserved for other purchases. Such barter agreements, if

undertaken on a massive scale, could be potentially counterproductive if production were diverted from more efficient
sectors to facilitate the barter.

AGREEMENTS AMONG COMMODITY PRODUCERS

The successes of OPEC in both negotiating better
royalty and ownership agreements with the multinational
oil companies and in raising prices on the world market
for petroleum emphasized the potential for agreements
among exporters of at least nearly essential and not overly
abundant commodities. These producer associations, or
cartels (a more pejorative term), are seen as one means of
reversing the perceived negative price movements for raw
materials in the world market. The five political economy
perspectives discussed in Chapter 2 have varying views of
such producer associations. They do run counter to free
trade theory, and consuming nations periodically have encouraged OPEC members to adhere to free trade principles.
Neomercantilists can, of course, accept such associations if
they work. As noted in Chapter 3, the reformists in particular have seen producer associations as one means of
correcting inequities in the world trade regime, and their
views have been reflected in the efforts to form such
groups. For dependency-neocolonialist adherents and neo-
Marxists such associations are an important form of countervailing economic and political influence vis-à-vis the industrialized states. For the neo-Marxists such associations
could be a mixed blessing. If the higher prices gained
aid the local capitalist classes (as they might argue), the
associations could be counterproductive in the short run in
terms of class advantages in the developing countries.

The Success and Failure of OPEC: A Case Study

The major price increases for petroleum instituted
by OPEC were a major international economic fact of life
in the 1970s and early 1980s. The impact of the cooperation among the oil exporters can clearly be seen in Table
6.1 in the role that crude petroleum played in international trade. The index for crude petroleum exports increased tremendously, reflecting the price increases rather
than volume increases. The initial success of this or-

ganization can be attributed to the conjunction of a number of factors related to the international market for oil--the resources of the member states, the key moderating position of Saudi Arabia, and even some fortuitous circumstances.

OPEC's gain of higher prices resulted from its ability to meet three significant criteria for a group of commodity-exporting states. First, the exporters had to account for a significant portion of the world market for the commodity, including control of both actual and potential sources of supply. Second, relative price in elasticity among consumers had to exist, that is, higher prices would not lead to a proportional drop in consumption. Third, agreement and continued cooperation among the exporters had to be possible (Fishlow 1978, p. 33; Woods 1979, pp. 220-21). The ability of OPEC to meet these conditions for a period of time was the basis of its initial success, and its subsequent failure to continue to completely meet these criteria helps explain its recent difficulties.

OPEC's ability to raise prices was not an overnight phenomenon. The organization was in existence for two decades before it achieved this goal. In addition, a very specific political event created the impetus for joint action by the Arab exporters during a period when the three basic criteria were met. Control of sources was relatively assured, particularly since the chief non-Arab exporters, Iran and Venezuela, were in a position to gain more from joining price increases than from undercutting them. Venezuela, due to the relatively higher extraction costs for its petroleum, could generally only be a follower in terms of price increases. Iran was in need of greater revenues to meet internal development tasks. At the same time, the consuming industrialized nations were in a situation of relative price insensitivity that assured the exporters at least some gains from any higher prices that were established. The joint action initiated by the Arab countries in response to the Arab-Israeli war also provided the necessary spark for agreement and effective collective action. While such an arrangement might have eventually occurred with higher prices and returns as the primary concern, the political tensions in the Middle East hastened agreement, particularly once the actions taken for political and economic reasons proved to be successful.

An additional factor important in OPEC's ability to maintain cooperation and coordination of international prices for as long as it did was the presence of one

country able to play the role of a stabilizer in the organization. Saudi Arabia, due to its great reserves of
petroleum and its ability to postpone revenues to some extent, was able to play this role. OPEC's price increases
required in part the ability to create an "artificial" short-
age on the world market, more or less on demand. Ultimately, such a situation required an effective threat to
cutback production. Saudi Arabia, and Kuwait and the
United Arab Emirates to lesser extents, was in a position
to cut back production significantly without jeopardizing
domestic development plans or economic activities. The
Saudi economy was actually unable to absorb directly all
the revenues generated by the higher oil prices, so cut-
backs did not necessarily constitute a major sacrifice.
Similarly, Saudi Arabia could effectively threaten to increase production in conjunction with lower prices, thereby
gaining market shares from other exporters. Saudi Arabia
was in a position of being able to play the role of a
regime preserver within OPEC. Regimes normally require a
nation or nations to make sacrifices in the short term, and
Saudi Arabia was ideally situated to play this role. The
leadership of the country was also perceived to be willing
to take the appropriate actions. As a result, OPEC proved
to be very successful in the 1970s.

Events within OPEC, more noticeable in the late 1970s
and in the 1980s but present at all times since the formation of the organization, have demonstrated the difficulties
of maintaining the essential three conditions for a successful producer association. Agreement among the member
nations, and even among the Arab members, has always
been difficult to achieve (Mikdashi 1974). Without Saudi
Arabia serving as a regime maintainer, dissension might
have weakened the organization even earlier. Control
over supplies also decreased. As a consequence of higher
prices, new energy resources were exploited, as, for example, the North Sea oil and gas fields. The Mexican government's decision to reveal the extent of its domestic
reserves at the time of high prices was also in the nature
of opening up a "new" resource. Marginal oil fields in
many areas were more exploited. Similarly, substitute
energy forms were sought, a situation foreseen even before
the quadrupling of oil prices (Mikdashi 1974, pp. 29-30;
Monroe 1975, p. 68; Uri 1976, p. 15). Thus, effective
control over a variety of actual and potential production
was weakened. Finally, the necessary price in elasticity

was only short term to some degree, as consumers limited
demand by conservation efforts, changing technology reduced energy inputs, and shifts to other types of energy
sources occurred.

Overall, OPEC was obviously successful as an organization of commodity exporters. Although its achievements were related to a number of special circumstances,
the member nations were better off as a result of their
collective endeavors. Because of concerted actions they
received higher prices for their exports. OPEC was also
important in collectively establishing higher royalty payments, in bringing about the location of refineries in exporting states, in regaining control over unexplored concession areas, and in bringing about increasing levels of
state ownership and control of indigenous natural resources.
The OPEC experience has demonstrated the feasibility of
some developing countries using producer associations as a
mechanism to effectively change the division of benefits in
international trade to the advantage of developing countries. The oil-exporting states, with their natural resources, foreign currency reserves, and foreign investments,
have emerged to become very important actors, not only in
the world trade regime but also in the wider international
economic system as well.

Other Associations of Commodity Exporters

The initial successes of OPEC stimulated other efforts
at forming organizations of exporters for a variety of commodities, including copper, iron ore, tin, bauxite, other
minerals, and agricultural products. The accomplishments
of these organizations have been more limited, partly because they have been unable to match the circumstances
that favored OPEC. Even so, they have provided some
benefits for the commodity-exporting countries.

The Intergovernmental Council of Copper Exporting
Countries (CIPEC) was one such organization that drew its
inspiration from OPEC. It has not proven particularly
effective, however, in improving returns for the member
states of Peru, Chile, Zaire, and Zambia. There has been
an oversupply of copper on the world market, making the
achievement of higher prices difficult. Also, alternative
materials to replace copper have been readily available
(Moran 1974, pp. 46-48). Copper production exists in a

number of countries, including developed ones, and known reserves are located in yet other states, so that CIPEC members did not effectively control the market (Mikdashi 1976, pp. 83-84) and controlled a more limited portion of the potential sources of production. Prices have also proven difficult to establish since the different countries have had different production costs (Mikdashi 1976, p. 87; G. Smith 1979, p. 188). Agreements on production controls and market shares also proved difficult to achieve (Moran 1974, pp. 230-31). Even the successes of the individual countries in achieving either ownership of control of foreign mining firms were more related to the fact that there was already a large amount of fixed investment in the mining and processing facilities that could in effect be held hostage by the governments of the exporting countries (cf. Moran 1974; Sklar 1975, pp. 34-61).

In the case of bauxite exports, Jamaica has been a key actor. The formation of a bauxite-exporters group, including Australia, was effective in generating higher prices for bauxite and alumina. Jamaica led the way in raising taxes and royalty payments, an action that was successful in part because the major processing facilities were already in place and constituted a major fixed investment for the aluminum companies (Mikdashi 1976, p. 113; Vastine 1977, p. 415; Woods 1979, p. 212). Thus, as with copper, the success in generating additional income for the exporter was due to relative power in bargaining negotiations with the corporations exploiting the natural resource rather than power in negotiating better prices in the international marketplace, although the gains were facilitated by the existence of the organizations in at least some measure. The presence of a developed nation such as Australia in the group, however, demonstrates that cooperation among exporters of different development levels is possible and can increase returns.

Another organization, the International Tin Agreement (ITA), first started in 1956, has also been successful in terms of providing stable prices through the years for a commodity export. The ITA is not solely a producer organization since it includes both producers and consumers. The United States was a late-joining consuming nation, staying aloof for 20 years (G. Smith 1979, p. 184). The agreement provides for a stockpile with both price floors and price ceilings, thus providing potential advantages for both producing and consuming countries. Tin prices over the years have in fact been much more stable than prices for other nonferrous base metals, reflecting the successful operation of the stockpile (Mikdashi 1976, pp. 128–29). The ITA has worked reasonably well for a number of reasons. It includes both producers and consumers. Since all the principal exporters are included, quotas can be assigned relatively easily. Finally, no potential new deposits are known (Mikdashi 1976, pp. 128–29), although greatly higher prices might stimulate new exploration. The presence of alternative substitute materials has also emphasized price stability as opposed to higher returns, facilitating producer–consumer agreement. In the past when prices for tin have gone up, its use has declined (G. Smith 1979, p. 187), a factor that has favored price stability within the ITA. Finally, world demand is not high relative to present production potential; therefore, incentives for new exploration or production are limited.

Producer associations have been formed for such various agricultural commodities as bananas, coffee, and natural rubber, but the success of these groups has been relatively limited (cf. Vastine 1977, pp. 413–14). Agricultural producer associations are inherently more difficult to coordinate. Since harvests can vary from year to year, quotas are generally harder to fix and maintain than is the case for mineral products. Bumper crops in one country and poor harvests in another could easily upset quota arrangements. Higher prices for agricultural products at a point in time may also encourage other countries that are not members of the association to become exporters. Higher prices might also lead to substitutions of products, such as one tropical fruit replaced by another or rice by wheat. Agricultural protectionism in developed countries by limiting the world market has also hindered the benefits available to many prospective producer associations.

PROSPECTS FOR EXPORTERS OF RAW MATERIALS

The potential for generating higher prices for commodities within the mechanisms of the present world trade regime appears to be limited. It is true that improvements in the terms of trade can be achieved in some instances. Countries with control over large deposits of particular resources and facing few competitors, such as

Morocco in the case of phosphates, have advantageous bargaining positions. But even Morocco's gains face a limit
due to the exports of manufactured fertilizers from other
states. In fact, world increases in the price of phosphates
have been related to higher prices for petroleum, the
source material for most manufactured fertilizers (Morton
and Tulloch 1977, p. 95). In the future, therefore, exporters of any commodity that is favored by circumstances
of increased demand may derive additional trade benefits,
particularly since cooperative activities of the exporters in
some areas have demonstrated the potential for greater gains.

Continuing efforts at price stabilization, however,
are likely to provide some help to commodity exporters.
Evidence of positive examples, at least to some extent, is
found in such measures as stockpile reductions and build-
ups, EC support for the prices of some commodities exported
by the Common Market associate members, the US sugar
quota, and the ITA. Additional arrangements similar to
these are also possible in the future. However, progress
in the direction of price stabilization is more likely when
there are a limited number of producers, and perhaps consumers, given the dynamics and difficulties of bargaining
within large groups. Negotiations are likely to be much
easier in smaller groups, and the fixing of quotas would
be less contentious. For commodities produced and exported by many states, on the other hand, agreements on
stabilization will be more problematic, and many of the
uncertainties facing countries exporting at least some raw
materials are likely to continue in the foreseeable future,
particularly for developing countries that cannot rely on a
diversity of commodity exports or exports of some manufactures.

7 World Food Trade and Policy Issues

Historically, commerce tends to begin with nonessentials, such as luxuries, surplus raw materials, and manufactured goods. However, as international relations became more frequent and stable, commerce has gradually extended itself to include more essential products, such as food and energy materials. Because of the essential nature of food as a commodity, nations have been rather reluctant to promote food trade internationally. Instead, a policy of food self-sufficiency, although difficult to attain for many countries, has been pursued by governments throughout the world. Moreover, for domestic political reasons to be explained subsequently, agricultural protectionism rather than trade liberalism has prevailed in the world trade regime in agricultural and food commodities. No major state in the third quarter of the twentieth century has in fact allowed trade to integrate its agricultural sector with the world economy (Meyer 1978, p. 170).

As the prospect for stable external supplies of food products improved, countries began to see that they could afford to depend on foreign sources of food. In fact, as some proponents of liberal free trade argue, there is no inherent reason why food and agricultural trade should be treated differently from trade in manufactured products. Nonetheless, most of the developed and developing countries in the world, including the United States, that enjoy overall comparative advantages in food production have generally adhered to agricultural protectionism in certain commodities.

PATTERNS OF AGRICULTURAL PRODUCTION
AND TRADE

The world food situation in the 1970s, other than during the 1972-73 food crisis, has generally been favorable--a rather surprising and unexpected development that resulted from the world food supply keeping pace with global food demand (Johnson 1982). The primary reason for the favorable world food situation in the 1970s, in spite of the noticeable price instability and fluctuation in availability of food commodities, may be attributed to two surprises--the sharp decline in birth rates in many low-income countries and the rapid growth of grain imports by the centrally planned economies, facilitating production in other countries (Johnson 1982, p. 33). Agricultural prices rose 46 percent, for instance, between 1972 and 1974. The higher export prices of farm products naturally produced a net gain for the economy of food-exporting countries, although it also led to the income losses to consumers in many countries (Ford Foundation 1982, pp. 14-15).

As Table 7.1 shows, world exports of agricultural and food products expanded in value by almost sixfold between 1966 and 1981, although trade only doubled in terms of volume. Food trade was more vigorous among the developed market economy countries than among the developing countries or between the developed and developing countries. In fact, developing market economy countries had only a slight increase in the value of food trade, whereas the centrally planned economies did not register growth at all during the same time period.

Table 7.2 shows the market share in the world exports of agricultural products in terms of value and percentage of the total. A trend is clearly visible in that the developed market economy countries have increased their world market share from 60.5 percent in 1976 to 65.9 percent in 1981, while the developing market economy countries and the centrally planned economies have declined, decreasing, respectively, from 32.0 percent in 1976 to 28.4 percent in 1981 and from 7.4 percent to 5.7 percent. As agricultural prices have risen in world markets, a strong shift of income has taken place from the poor (consumer) to the rich (producer), not only within food-producing but also within food-consuming and -importing countries (Ford Foundation 1982, pp. 14-15).

TABLE 7.1

Increase in World Food Trade (Excluding Fish): Indices of Export Volume and Value

	Volume				Value			
	1966	1971	1976	1981	1966	1971	1976	1981
World	85	106	134	177	83	111	273	493
Developed market economies	85	109	149	211	81	115	299	568
Developing market economies	94	102	119	138	84	105	254	428
Centrally planned economies	94	100	88	90	86	105	186	250
All developed economies	85	108	141	196	81	114	283	528
All developing economies	97	102	117	135	87	105	251	417

Index: 1969-71 = 100.

SOURCE: FAO (1977, p. 36; 1982, p. 36).

In terms of the world regions, Western Europe and North America are the leading food-exporting regions. Western Europe increased its market share from 32.4 percent in 1976 to 35.6 percent in 1981, while North America had a slight gain from 21.1 percent in 1976 to 22.9 percent in 1981. The dramatic increase in Western Europe's market share was primarily due to the expansion of the EC and its Common Agricultural Policy (CAP), to be examined in more detail below. In terms of individual countries, the leading agricultural and food-exporting countries, measured by the values in agricultural and food commodities exported in 1981, included the United States, France, the Netherlands, and West Germany. Apart from the EC countries, Brazil, Australia, Canada, and Argentina were also important as food-producing countries, Thailand and Malaysia have been traditional food surplus countries in Asia, and China and India appeared as large exporters since they are among the most populous countries in the world.

TABLE 7.2

Share in World Exports of Agricultural Products by Major Regions and
Selected Countries

	Value ($ million)		Percentage	
	1976	1981	1976	1981
World	132,921	230,847	100.0	100.0
Developed market economies	80,450	152,218	60.5	65.9
North America	28,047	52,883	21.2	22.9
West Europe	43,029	82,080	32.4	35.6
Oceania	7,140	23,043	5.3	5.6
Other	2,233	4,281	1.7	1.8
Developing market economies	42,575	65,477	32.0	28.4
Africa	7,751	8,596	5.8	3.7
Latin America	19,986	31,464	15.0	13.6
Near East	3,914	5,470	3.0	2.4
Far East	10,663	19,428	8.0	8.4
Other	259	517	0.2	0.2
Centrally planned economies	9,895	13,181	7.4	5.7
Asia	2,805	3,520	2.1	1.5
Europe and Soviet Union	7,090	9,661	5.3	4.2
All developed countries	87,541	161,840	65.9	70.1
All developing countries	45,380	68,997	34.1	29.9
Selected countries				
United States	26,690	45,052	20.1	19.5
France	8,942	17,862	6.7	7.7
Netherlands	9,328	15,888	7.0	6.9
West Germany	4,797	10,587	3.6	4.6
Brazil	6,243	9,771	4.7	4.2
Australia	5,341	9,399	4.0	4.1
United Kingdom	3,481	8,175	2.6	3.5
Canada	4,358	7,831	3.3	3.4
Argentina	2,846	6,321	2.1	2.7
Belgium/Luxembourg	3,384	6,291	2.5	2.7
Italy	3,005	5,838	2.3	2.5
Denmark	2,910	5,071	2.2	2.2
Cuba	4,358	4,735	3.3	2.1
Thailand	1,977	3,969	1.5	1.7
Spain	1,975	3,486	1.4	1.5
Malaysia	2,002	3,479	1.5	1.5
China	2,470	3,110	1.9	1.3
India	1,728	2,742	1.3	1.2

SOURCE: FAO (1982, pp. 42-44).

As world demand for food grew steadily in the 1970s, it was the industrialized countries that were the principal beneficiaries of the trade expansion in agricultural goods. The developed countries dominated the world food market as both suppliers and consumers, while the developing countries, particularly as consumers, relied on the difference between the world supply and the demand of the developed states (Morton and Tulloch 1977, p. 132; Thompson 1981, p. 202). In spite of the protectionist practices and obstacles in agricultural trade, the world trade has expanded so that the effect of the "Green Revolution" that increased agricultural yields in developing countries has had minimal or inconsequential impacts in lowering the overall volume of agricultural trade. A consideration of some production and trade figures on specific commodities illustrates these points.

World production of grains, both food and feed, has expanded greatly in the recent decades, increasing from 845 million metric tons in 1960 to 1,503 million metric tons in 1981 (see Table 7.3). Trade in agricultural products also increased steadily, increasing from only 8.6 percent of the total production in 1960 to 9.2 percent in 1971 and 14.2 percent of the world total production of grains and cereals. The stock of grains for utilization and consumption purposes, however, declined somewhat from 23.8 percent in 1960 to 15.6 percent in 1971 and 14.6 percent in 1981. This decline suggests that a food security system is a matter of serious concern for policymakers in both food-producing and food-consuming countries. One important reason for the decline in grain stocks is that the United States and Canada have no longer been willing to maintain large reserves as they did in the 1950s and 1960s. As a result, stability of supply, and price, has declined (Hopkins and Puchala 1978, pp. 13, 23). The annual demand for world grain has also fluctuated over time. The annual rate of growth in total world grain trade was larger, on balance, in the 1970s than it was in the 1960s. It averaged 10.4 percent in the 1970s as compared with 3.7 percent in the 1960s, registering highs of 25.8 percent in 1979 and 24.5 percent in 1972 and lows of -6.5 percent in 1974 and 0.1 percent in 1971 (World Food Institute 1982, p. 8).

A disproportionate amount of world exports of grain is carried out by a handful of countries, including the United States, Canada, EC members, Brazil, Australia, and Argentina. For example, as shown in Table 7.4, the US shares of exports of agricultural products are very impressive.

TABLE 7.3
World Production and Trade of All Grains for Selected Years

	1960	1966	1971	1976	1981
Production (million metric tons)	845	1004	1193	1360	1503
Utilization (million metric tons)	831	978	1175	1307	1469
Trade (million metric tons)	73	104	110	156	214
Trade as percentage of production	8.6	10.4	9.2	11.5	14.2
Stocks (million metric tons)	198	170	183	193	214
Stocks as percentage of utilization	23.8	17.4	15.6	14.9	14.6

NOTE: Grains include wheat, rice, and coarse grains.
Trade year covers July to June of the subsequent year.

SOURCE: World Food Institute (1982, p. 6).

TABLE 7.4
US Shares of World Trade in Grains and Soybeans for Selected Years

	1961	1971	1976	1981
	(percent of world total)			
Wheat	46.7	31.9	40.9	49.0
Coarse grains	65.4	50.2	61.3	59.5
Rice	13.8	20.5	21.6	23.1
Soybeans	87.5	94.3	79.0	85.1
Soybean meal	98.4	89.9	68.4	34.2
Soybean oil	72.9	95.1	71.6	25.4

NOTE: Trade year covers July to June of the subsequent year.

SOURCE: World Food Institute (1982, p. 22).

In the case of wheat, the US share was relatively steady, with 46.7 percent in 1961, 31.9 percent in 1971, 40.9 percent in 1976, and 49.0 percent in 1981. The US share for soybeans in global trade was overwhelming, accounting for 87.5 percent of the total in 1961, 94.3 percent in 1971, 79.0 percent in 1976, and 85.1 percent in 1981. The US share in other grains, while substantial, composed a smaller portion of the world totals. These figures demonstrate why the United States has been a key actor in the world grain trade through the years.

Due to a worldwide economic recession, the global export demand for agricultural products in 1981-83 did not increase as fast as in the 1970s. In fact, the unit value of agricultural exports declined in 1981 and 1982, thus contributing to the overall relative decline in the value of world food exports. This decline was especially noteworthy since the food export volume actually registered increases in 1982 and 1983. As a result, total food trade is expected to grow more slowly in the 1980s than in the 1970s. Even though the world food situation has improved since the mid-1970s, food and agricultural trade in the 1980s will still experience difficult problems of adjustment as a consequence of the varied agricultural policies and practices in the world trade regime associated with trade in food and agricultural products.

POLICY ISSUES AND PROBLEMS
IN WORLD FOOD TRADE

As noted in Chapter 1, the liberal world trade regime established by GATT generally served well in expanding and sustaining the rapid growth in world trade in the post-World War II era. This remarkable achievement was more successful in increasing the exports of manufactured products by the advanced industrialized countries and the NICs, as already seen in Chapters 4 and 5. The benefits of GATT for trade in agricultural products and other primary commodities, with the important exception of petroleum and related energy sources, have not been as significant. The primary reason for this situation is the basically value-added nature of the merchandise traded by the industrial countries as compared with the agricultural and primary commodities exported by the developing countries. Agricultural trade may also have lagged behind trade in manufactures because of an international Engels law. Within countries as income levels increase, the percentage of income allocated to food purchases declines, and such a trend may also be operative in the international sphere as well (Fishlow 1978, p. 22).

Another important source of lessened influence of GATT principles on agricultural trade is the fact that domestic political and economic considerations usually prevail in national agricultural policies leading to such practices as heavy government price supports and export subsidies for agricultural products. Thus, agricultural trade relations between the EC and the United States and between Japan and the United States have led to some of the trade disputes that have brought havoc to the operation of the GATT system. Some of the resulting policy issues in food and agricultural trade may be examined from both long-term and short-term perspectives.

The long-term policy issues of world food trade include an efficient use of world food resources through the establishment of appropriate procedures for balancing global agricultural production and utilization, and an appropriate strategy for encouraging agricultural development in developing countries, while enabling them to finance agricultural imports to meet the basic nutritional needs of their populations. More specific long-term policy concerns involve such issues as promoting free trade in agriculture, overcoming agricultural trade protectionism and trade wars, and maintaining a food security system. More immediate short-term policy issues in world food trade, on the other hand, pertain to the need to cope with political economy questions, such as an increasing use of long-term grain agreements between food-exporting and food-importing countries and the use of food trade as a diplomatic tool, including embargoes and trade subsidies.

Agriculture and Free Trade

The agricultural sector has, to a large extent, remained on the fringe of the liberalization process, encouraged under the GATT principle, in the world trade regime. The GATT rules were often related to matters of import restrictions and export subsidies in the case of agricultural products. Waivers from GATT rules were even obtained by some countries, while others adopted new forms of protection (OECD 1972, p. 68).

The agricultural sector, therefore, has been experiencing severe problems of adjustment in most of the developed countries. Farmers have generally received price supports and protection from the government as the population engaged in agriculture dwindled and farm incomes declined relative to industrial wages (Monroe 1975, p. 82). Farmers almost everywhere in advanced industrial countries have been well organized politically; consequently, they have had political influence out of proportion to their declining numbers, and their interests are often represented disproportionately in legislatures. In contemporary Japan, for example, the ruling conservative Liberal Democratic Party has been in power since 1955, primarily with the support of the rural constituencies that under the Japanese form of legislative apportionment are greatly overrepresented in the Diet relative to their population (Fukui 1975, pp. 156–57). It is even said that a vote in some Japanese rural districts is worth five times a vote in some urban districts.

Both grain-producing countries and food-importing countries could benefit more from policy measures of liberal trade, such as reduction of restrictions on the international exchange and movement of agricultural products (Nau 1978, p. 232; Johnson 1978). However, at times of uncertain grain supplies, as in the 1970s, other policy objectives and considerations worked to moderate the efforts toward less restrictive food trade. Several countries have maintained domestic food prices well above world levels in an effort to increase domestic food production and discourage excessive consumption. Japan and most of the Western European countries are cases in point (Barr 1981, p. 1093). Other countries, however, set domestic food prices below world levels so as to insulate the economy from fluctuations in the world supply and demand of agricultural products, thereby encouraging food consumption and discouraging production. The Soviet Union and most of the centrally planned economies are examples of countries using this latter approach (Paarlberg 1978, pp. 93–95).

The conventional approach to trade liberalization under the GATT rules, in short, has not worked well in the agricultural sector. Many advanced industrialized countries are in the habit of making agricultural policy without regard to its international ramifications and consequences, although awareness of the international sector is increasing. The GATT ministerial meeting did set up an agriculture committee to launch a study of the effect of domestic agricultural policies on international trade, but progress has been rather slow and intangible. The 1982 GATT ministerial meeting in Geneva, for instance, had a clash of views among the agricultural and trade representatives from the member countries, particularly among representatives of the United States and the EC.

Even if free trade is acknowledged to be advantageous, various efforts to reduce trade barriers have been less successful in agriculture than in nonagricultural products. Major agricultural trade restrictions and practices include the EC's high internal prices for grain, the Japanese and European quotas and other restrictions on US exports of livestock products, and US imposition of quotas and other restrictions on imports of meat, dairy products, and sugar (JEI 1982). Through the mechanism of the CAP, the EC maintains variable import levies and taxes that are used to keep EC prices above world levels, thus preventing agricultural sales by the United States and others to the European market (Josling and Pearson 1981; Meyer 1978, pp. 168–69). The CAP has been sufficiently effective, for example, in raising the level of agricultural self–sufficiency within the EC from 91 percent in 1958 to 96 percent in 1968 (Monroe 1975, p. 45). It also enabled France to move from a position of being a net importer to being among the top three exporters of food in the space of 15 years (Rehfeldt 1980, p. 177). Japanese protectionism, in addition to forcing Japanese consumers to pay higher prices, also has had negative effects on food exports from the United States and some Southeast Asian countries (Monroe 1975, p. 48). These and other practices reinforce the trend toward agricultural protectionism that are manifest in frequent mutual threats to use export subsidies, price supports, and other incentives to expand domestic agricultural production, thus leading to larger market shares in world food trade (Josling and Pearson 1981, p. 36).

While the EC pressed for restrictions on imports of US corn and soybean products by encouraging increased use of domestic EC grains, Japan has resisted pressure to open up its market to US agricultural sales, especially in beef and oranges and other citrus products that are restricted through import quotas (Castle and Hemmi 1982). There is always a danger that these protectionist practices could get out of hand, and perhaps even lead to a trade war. Trade disputes are especially acrimonious during a sluggish world economy and declining world trade, as was the case in the early 1980s. A recent example of an agricultural trade war in the making was the 1982 conflict over wheat trade between the United States and the EC involving trade with third countries. The US flour sale to Egypt in 1982-83, for instance, was interpreted by the EC as coming at its expense, while the US loss of wheat sales in China to EC was not taken kindly by the United States. As a result of these trade conflicts and disputes, world food prices will likely be raised in the long run, if not in the short term. The needy in the poor developing countries will suffer the most from the higher food prices that may accompany trade conflicts.

World Food Security

Because of the world food crisis in 1972-73 and the subsequent World Food Conference of 1975, global public consciousness and policy measures for maintaining world food security have been greatly enhanced (Hopkins and Puchala 1978, p. 8). Price hikes in food and fertilizer in 1974, whereby the world price of wheat and rice roughly increased three times and that of fertilizer four times over those in 1972, most hurt the economically poor developing countries that depend on food imports for sustaining the basic diets and nutritional requirements of the population (Nicholson and Esseks 1978, p. 104). In 1976, however, the dramatic fall in prices for food grains and fertilizer injected an additional element of uncertainty and instability in world food prices (World Bank 1982, p. 55). Thus, while there is no consensus about the long-run food and agricultural situation in the world regarding adequacy of supply, there is agreement that there will be short-term fluctuations in grain production and consequently in grain prices (Cochrane 1979, p. 145).

Because of the unstable environment in world grain market, the governments in a number of food-importing countries, notably those in Western Europe and the centrally planned economies, took protective measures to insulate domestic markets from the effect of world food prices. These protective measures, as well as large grain purchases by the Soviet Union, kept food prices higher in the remainder of the 1970s, mainly hurting developing countries that were not protected and still dependent on imported food sold in the world market. The immediate concern for policymakers was, therefore, to prevent the repeat of the world food crisis and its aftereffects. These experiences in the 1970s gave a valuable lesson and an incentive to adopt a rational food security system.

Food security is particularly important to many developing countries. The poorest states often lack sufficient food to feed their populations and must rely on food imports to meet local demand. Unless such imports are in the form of grants, scarce foreign exchange must be used. In times of world shortages the higher world prices, often combined with declines in the levels of food aid, make importing the necessary food difficult and quite expensive (Barr 1981, p. 1094; Fishlow 1978, p. 59; Nicholson and Esseks 1978, pp. 103-04). In addition, rising worldwide food prices often trigger export constraints in developed countries, further exacerbating the supply problems of the poor countries (Barr 1981, p. 1095; Fishlow 1978, p. 58). Even nonemergency food aid, such as PL 480 food from the United States, may present unforeseen problems for poorer developing countries.

Such aid is more readily available in times of food surpluses, serving as a means of disposing of domestic overproduction on the part of food-producing countries. When dispensed in times of lower world food prices, food aid tends to discourage agricultural expansion in the food-importing countries (Destler 1978, p. 44; Paddock and Paddock 1976, pp. 175-77; Thompson 1981, p. 197). Thus, while food shortages are a matter of policy concern not only for the developing but developed countries as well, the issue of food security will have more immediate impacts on the economically poor and food-importing developing countries. As was the case for primary commodities in general, the low level of economic resources of these countries makes it more difficult for them to deal effectively with shortages and price fluctuations.

Some of the measures adopted to enhance world food security at the national and international levels have included a greater emphasis on food production, a more careful monitoring of food stocks and reserves, and a more efficient operation of the world grain markets through a better responsiveness to price changes in the market. A number of intergovernmental agreements have also been reached in an effort to improve world food security. These included an international emergency food reserve of 500,000 tons, established in 1976, and increased to 588,000 tons in 1981; the signing of a Food Aid Convention raising the minimum annual contribution of food aid from 4.2 to 7.6 million tons in 1980; and the Food Facility of the International Monetary Fund (IMF) established in 1981 as an extension of the IMF Compensatory Fund Facility to provide financial assistance to offset fluctuations in food import bills either because of shortfalls in domestic production or higher world food prices (World Bank 1982, p. 55).

Given the difficulties involved with world food security, it is clear that both food-importing and -exporting countries have an important stake in maintaining food reserves to offset fluctuations in world crop production. Without adequate reserves, agricultural trade will become increasingly subject to artificial trade restrictions, such as increased use of long-term grain agreements, and use of food trade as a diplomatic tool (World Food Institute 1982, p. 37).

Although much of the global grain reserves in the 1960s and 1970s were in effect held in the United States and Canada, there is no reason why a food reserve system cannot be worked out elsewhere on a global or regional basis. The 1976 World Food Conference in Rome established the World Food Council and the global food reserve system. Members of the Association of Southeast Asian Nations (ASEAN) agreed in 1979 to establish and maintain a rice reserve system of their own (Balaam 1981, pp. 136-37). Among unresolved world food policy issues are the size of reserves needed, where reserves should be stored, methods of sharing costs for the storage of reserve grain, prices or other conditions under which global stocks will be accumulated and released, and the impact on US grain prices, grain producers, and livestock feeders from storing global grain reserves in the United States (World Food Institute 1982, p. 37).

Use of Long-Term Grain Agreements

Since the United States negotiated its first five-year grain agreements with the Soviet Union in 1976, the practice of long-term agreements has multiplied and proliferated, thereby injecting a new factor in the world food trading system. The 1976 US-USSR agreement provided for 6 to 8 million metric tons of US grain to be sold annually to the

Soviet Union and for additional sales at about this level, subject to prior US approval. As a result, greater stability and predictability were added to Soviet grain purchases of US agricultural products. Subsequently, the United States signed a similar agreement with the People's Republic of China and one with Mexico on a more short-term and limited scale. Stimulated by the US practice, other grain-exporting countries, including Canada, Brazil, and Argentina, also entered into long-term grain agreements with the Soviet Union, China, and other developing countries (World Food Institute 1982, p. 36). By 1980, nearly 30 percent of wheat and coarse grains trade was moving under terms of bilateral and multilateral agreements that insulated these movements from market fluctuations (Barr 1981, p. 1093).

The plea for concluding effective international commodity agreements has included advocating better North-South cooperation in world trade and the call for the NIEO, which considers commodity agreements to be a means of stabilizing the world prices of commodities at remunerative levels (Brandt 1980, p. 158). From the standpoint of food-exporting countries, however, consideration of both the short-term and long-term benefits--and costs--of opting for the signing of long-term supply agreements as opposed to relying on the market for a determination of commodity prices must be carefully weighed. Also to be considered are the relative payoffs, positive and negative, of concluding long-term agreements to both food-exporting and -importing countries, as well as to the world trade regime in general. Obviously, usually the payoffs for negotiating bilateral commodity agreements are greater than those for negotiating multilateral commodity agreements from the standpoint of promoting a trading country's national interest and of the possible use of food trade as a diplomatic tool.

Food Trade as a Diplomatic Tool

Although economically undesirable, grain embargoes have been used by food-exporting countries for foreign policy purposes. The partial US embargo on grain sales to the Soviet Union in 1980 and 1981, the US embargo on exports to Iran in 1980, and Western European restrictions on trade with Argentina during the Falklands (or Malvinas) War in 1982 are some recent illustrations of the use of food trade as a diplomatic tool. Other exporting countries, like

Brazil, Argentina, Canada, Australia, and Thailand, have also halted sales of agricultural commodities due to limited supplies. Since their supplies individually were much smaller, there was little or no market impact.

One reason why the Soviet Union signed long-term agreements with the United States and other food-exporting countries was to protect itself from possible future embargoes and also to diversify its sources of food supply. The side effects of embargoes include distorted market signals to both exporting and importing countries. Embargoes also often provide an incentive for an increased domestic food production by importing countries. Food embargoes are ineffective unless other exporting countries are cooperating. Such cooperation is often difficult to attain, and even when it is achieved the substitutability of one foodstuff for another often weakens the impact of the embargo.

THE COSTS OF PROTECTIONISM

Agricultural protectionism poses as a flash point in the trade relations between the United States, on the one hand, and the EC and Japan, on the other. As the leading industrialized trading nations, the United States, the EC, and Japan favor free trade in principle and practice it when they are not competitive. But protectionism if also often invoked when they are competitive, as in textiles, steel, and automobiles, as well as in selected agricultural commodities. For sugar, for example, the United States has a high level of protection, as do the EC and Japan. In dairy products, the United States has quotas that limit imports to less than 2 percent of the total consumption in terms of milk equivalent. In beef, US legislation limits imports to less than 10 percent of consumption. The United States has been pressing Japan to liberalize its agricultural trade, especially by removing quotas on beef and oranges and other citrus products, while criticizing the EC for its increasingly protectionist practices in agricultural trade. Unlike Japan, the EC protects its agriculture from imports not only of food but of feed grains as well. Agricultural protectionism is thus a matter of degree, not kind, in Japan, the United States, and Europe.

Protectionism is the support provided by domestic consumers in the form of higher prices than those that would prevail in the absence of import duties and restric-

tions. Thus defined, the price for agricultural protectionism may be estimated. According to one study covering
1978-80, Japan had the highest agricultural support program in terms of cost to consumers and taxpayers, some
$15.6 billion to consumers and $5.9 billion in budget support from the Japanese Treasury. This cost amounted to
approximately a 140 percent surcharge over what it would
have cost the country to procure food on the world market.
In the EC, the equivalent figures were $28.9 billion for
consumers and $14.0 billion in budget support, a surcharge
amounting to 67 percent above the world prices. In the
United States, the comparable figures were $5.6 billion to
consumers and $3.6 billion in budget support, a surcharge
15 percent above world prices (JEI, 1982).

If the cost of agricultural subsidy programs is
taken into account, the price for agricultural protectionism is much higher than what the surcharges of food
prices indicate. The same study estimated that the EC,
through its common agricultural policies, spent well over
$30 billion in 1978-80, while Japan spent about $25 billion
and the United States some $20 to $30 billion to pay the
farmers in the same time period (JEI 1982). These amounts
are staggering expenditures for agricultural protectionism.
Although less defensible on an economic ground, the fact
remains that for political reasons all governments in industrial democracies have come to protect their farmers
with agricultural subsidy programs.

World food trade issues are difficult to settle on
strictly economic grounds. From a political economy perspective, a consideration of both political and economic
factors is necessary in any policy analysis. The linkage
between domestic and international policy concerns must
be given complete attention in the analysis of the issues
surrounding food trade. This linkage may become even
more important in the future since it has been suggested
that there will be a "significant shift toward protectionism"
to insulate food-importing countries from the vagaries and
fluctuations of the international market (Barr 1981, p. 1093).
Thus, notwithstanding the costs of protectionism enumerated
above, food trade will continue to be limited by national
policy decisions derived primarily from domestic concerns
in many countries of the world.

PART III   Regional Patterns and Trends

8   The United States and the Western Hemisphere

Of the four centers of major trading systems, the United States is the world's largest single trading nation. It is also the largest single national market given its population size and high per capita GNP (gross national product) level. The United States was also the chief architect of the liberal trade regime established after World War II. Although the primacy of the United States, both as a hegemon and as the world's leading trader, has waned in recent years, its present and past positions are reflected in the structure of its trading system and in the types of problems and patterns that are present in that system. After detailing the method used to establish membership in various trading systems, the US system will be described, including broad comparisons with other groups of countries. Then the specific problems, prospects, and responses of the states in the system will be evaluated. The fact that the United States was, and remains, a key factor has had a direct impact on the pattern of relationships among the members of the system.

DERIVATION OF THE TRADING SYSTEMS

The first step in describing various trading systems and in ascertaining continuity and change over time was to identify those countries included in each system for specific time periods. The periods chosen were 1961 to 1971 and 1971 to 1976. These two periods were selected for a number of reasons. Before 1961, reliable trade figures were available for a decreasing number of countries and territories. Other useful descriptive statistics were

even more difficult to come by for earlier periods. After
1976, data were also not complete. While the aggregate
trade figures used in earlier chapters for various commodity
groups were available after 1976 and data for major traders
were usually complete, data for many individual countries
were missing. Use of the time periods in question permitted the inclusion of most of the states and territories
of the world with reasonable certainty of accuracy. Even
so, a few countries were omitted from the 1971-76 period
due to the lack of data availability. Both time periods
were long enough to provide sufficient years to ensure that
trade ties between a country and the major trading nations
were consistent and indicative of lasting links as opposed
to a temporary phenomenon.

     Trade data were collected for all territories for
which information was available for 1961, 1971, and 1976,
as well as the intervening years from various issues of
the United Nations Yearbook of International Trade Statistics and various issues of Direction of Trade Annuals of
the International Monetary Fund. Trade data were reported
for all territories that reported trade separately, including independent countries, colonial areas, overseas departments of some of the European countries, and integrated
customs areas. For inclusion, such territories had to have
data for most of the relevant time periods. A few states,
mostly small colonies or ex-colonies, did not have complete
data dating from 1961 or 1971, but if data were available
for most of the period, they were included. Remaining
with the convention that exports are usually better indi-
cators of trade ties than imports, export figures were used
in all cases.

     The derivation of the trading systems was based on
the export pattern with principal markets. For example,
if a country, other than one included as one of the major
centers, had its largest level of exports by value to the
United States, it was considered to be linked with the US
trading system. For the period from 1961 to 1971, if the
United States was the largest market for at least nine of
the ten years, the country or territory was assumed to be
the trading system centered on the United States. For the
period from 1971 to 1976, a country with the United States
as its market for all five years was similarly included in
the US system. If it was connected for four of the five
years, then the flows for 1970 and 1977 (if available) were
checked. If the deviation was only for one year, the

country or territory was included in the trading system. The systems for Japan, Western Europe, and the Soviet Union were constructed using the same procedure.

In addition to countries linked directly to the center of a system, other countries were included in a particular system through less direct links. If a country's major market for either the ten-year or five-year period was already in a trading system, that country was also included in the appropriate system. If country A exported to country B for the 1961-71 period, it was in the trading system of country B. If country C used country A as its major market for those ten years, then it was also in country B's trading system. In the case of states that shifted major markets within a time period, if all of the principal markets were in the same system, the country was included in the system. Thus, in the above example if country C had country B as its major market for four years and country A as its major market for six, it was included in country B's trading system for 1961 to 1971. If, however, two countries traded with each other (that is, were each other's largest markets) in some years and were linked into one of the major systems in other years, they were not included as members of a trading system.

After allocation of countries to the major trading systems, both in terms of direct and indirect ties, there remained a group of countries outside the derived systems. These states and territories either changed from one principal market to another during the time period in question or just had a shifting pattern of export trade. These countries were not placed into any of the systems. Aggregate data for them were used for comparisons with the states in the trading systems and also to provide a complete picture of the roles of the states involved in international trade.

For both time periods data for approximately 150 countries and territories were available, including a few for which data were lacking for a few years near the beginning of a period. These countries and the systems in which they were included are listed in Appendix B. The listing also includes the states that had variable principal markets for their exports in the two time periods. The bulk of the states in both time periods were included in one of the major trading systems.

In addition, to the information on trade links throughout the 15 years, data on total GNP for 1961, 1971, and 1976 and for growth in GNP per capita from 1961 to 1971 and 1971 to 1976 were collected from various issues of the World Bank Atlas. Total export levels were also collected for 1961, 1971, and 1976, as well as the export share accounted for by the principal market. These data permitted a determination of the impact on the economies of the countries in various systems from a concentration of export trade with one major partner and provided an opportunity to assess the structural characteristics of the different trading systems.

THE AMERICAS CONNECTION

For the period from 1961 to 1971, the United States had 28 states in its trading system.* Most of these territories were in the Western Hemisphere, including Canada and 21 others from Latin America and the Caribbean. Of the other six states, Liberia, Israel, and the Philippines had strong links with the United States as a result of historical or political circumstances. The hemispheric connection is reinforced by the fact that only 14 territories in the region were outside the system, including half a dozen island territories in the Caribbean. The major Latin American states not included were Uruguay, Argentina, Paraguay, Bolivia, and Chile, the southernmost states in the hemisphere. Many of these states have had traditional trade ties with Europe. Except for Canada and Israel, the states in the system were developing ones.

A comparison of the US trading system with other groups of countries for the ten-year period indicates that the US partners accounted for approximately one-quarter of the trade and GNP of all the partner countries. The US partners, on average, were larger traders and had larger base economies than the states in the other two groups of

---

*The United States was also the principal market for Japan and the United Kingdom in both time periods, although the percentages of such export trade with the United States have been declining. Since Japan and Western Europe (including the United Kingdom) are considered major trade centers in their own right, they have not been included in the US system. The United Kingdom, in fact, has since shifted to West Germany as its major market.

countries--those trading in other systems and those with variable markets from 1961 to 1971 (see Table 8.1). The partners in the other systems, though smaller economic units, were somewhat more active traders for their size. The countries with variable major markets accounted for a greater proportion of the total GNP than trade, indicating that many countries in this group were less active traders.

Compared to other trading systems, those nations trading with the United States had higher export concentrations. This difference was particularly noticeable when compared to the countries outside all trading systems. The concentration levels were relatively constant for the decade for all three groups; thus, diversification of export markets was not the norm. In 1961, states that remained with the same partners, including the United States, had larger proportions of their GNPs accounted for by the exports to the principal markets. By 1971, however, the US partners had much higher proportions of their GNP devoted to such trade compared to the other two groups.

In terms of average annual per capita GNP growth rates, the countries in the US system were the lowest. Those countries with variable partners showed the highest growth rates. The presence of some of the oil exporters was one reason for this growth. It is also possible that those nations able to switch markets were more likely to have levels of development and industrialization that lead to export expansion or diversification. Although trade concentration with the major market, even though a different market in 1971 compared to 1961, did not decrease noticeably, there may have been less dependence on one or two commodities that were subject to wide price fluctuations. Also, the growth rates of the center nations may have had an impact for those countries that did not switch markets. The GNP per capita growth rate of the United States for this decade was relatively low, being only 3.3 percent. The growth rates for other center nations were generally higher with Japan at 9.4, France at 4.3, Italy at 7.5, West Germany at 3.7, Belgium at 4.1, and the Netherlands at 3.9. The United Kingdom's growth rate of 2.3 was the only one that was lower (World Bank 1975).

Since the countries and territories included in the study ranged from the very small to the very large, the use of simple raw averages of the various measures is misleading. Total GNP also varies greatly for states of the same relative population size. In addition, some

TABLE 8.1
US Trading System, 1961–71

	US Partners (n = 28)	Other Partners (n = 83)	Variable Partners (n = 36)
Percentage of world trade, 1971[a]	25.8	57.6	16.6
Percentage of world GNP, 1971[a]	27.2	47.7	25.1
Average trade levels (millions), 1971	$1,307	$ 983	$ 653
Average GNP (millions), 1971	$8,187	$6,061	$5,784
Unweighted averages			
Trade concentration with partner, 1961	45.0	40.0	32.2
Trade concentration with partner, 1971	44.0	39.2	31.5
Percent of GNP with partner, 1961	7.7	7.9	4.7
Percent of GNP with partner, 1971	11.2	8.1	7.3
Average annual percentage increase in per capita GNP, 1961–71	2.6	2.8	3.3
Weighted by 1971 GNP of partners			
Trade concentration with partner, 1971	50.2	30.5	21.4
Percent of GNP with partner, 1971	8.0	4.1	2.7
Average annual percentage increase in per capita GNP, 1961–71	3.2	3.3	3.3
Weighted by 1971 total trade of partners			
Trade concentration with partner, 1971	52.1	26.8	26.8
Percent of GNP with partner, 1971	12.1	5.3	6.6
Average annual percentage increase in per capita GNP, 1961–71	3.5	3.5	5.4

[a] The trade figures and GNP figures for the states at the centers of the systems (United States, United Kingdom, the Common Market Six, Japan, and the Soviet Union) are not included in total world trade or total world GNP.

SOURCE: Compiled by authors.

countries were more active in terms of trading than others, meaning that occurrences in the world trade regime and relationships with a major market were much more impor- tant. As a result, the averages were weighted, first by partner country GNP and then by the total export volume, to gain a truer comparison.

With both weights, US partners have higher export concentrations and GNP percentages than the other coun- tries. The high levels reflected in part the impact of Canada, the only major developed country in the system, but there was still an obvious concentration of exports. In terms of growth of GNP per capita, the US system com- pared more favorably with the other systems. When GNP was the weight, all three groups had virtually identical growth averages. When weighted by total trade, all coun- tries in the various systems had the same average per capita growth, while the variable partners group was higher. Given the higher growth figures with this last weight, those countries that were more active traders grew faster than those countries less involved in international trade, supporting the idea that increased trade may indeed contribute to growth (Fishlow 1978, p. 26; Rothstein 1977, pp. 45-46). To a lesser extent, those nations that were larger economically also grew at a faster rate than smaller economies, a finding that suggests that developed countries grew faster than developing ones.

For the period from 1971 to 1976, trade partners of the United States continued to be concentrated in the Western Hemisphere. The 33 countries in the system in- cluded Canada and 22 Latin American countries. Again, it was basically the southernmost countries of the hemisphere plus some islands in the Caribbean that were not included. Iceland was the only new developed country in the system. Two important additions to the US system were Taiwan and South Korea, major Asian NICs that had variable principal markets from 1961 to 1971.

Compared to 1971, the US system accounted for ap- proximately the same percentage of world trade but less world GNP. The US partners no longer had the highest trade levels or average GNPs (see Table 8.2). The vari- able partners group accounted for about the same percent- age of world GNP but less trade. This group's percentage of world GNP would have been less but for the presence of the People's Republic of China in the group. Unfortunately, this country could not be included for the first time period

TABLE 8.2
US Trading System 1971–76

	US Partners (n = 33)	Other Partners (n = 83)	Variable Partners (n = 31)
Percentage of world trade, 1976[a]	25.0	65.6	11.4
Percentage of world GNP, 1976[a]	23.7	51.0	25.3
Average trade levels (millions), 1976	$ 3,373	$ 3,402	$ 1,639
Average GNP (millions), 1976	$15,113	$12,895	$17,166
Unweighted averages			
Trade concentration with partner, 1971	42.8	36.6	27.9
Trade concentration with partner, 1976	41.9	35.8	27.6
Percent of GNP with partner, 1971	10.3	7.9	6.2
Percent of GNP with partner, 1976	11.4	10.3	7.7
Average annual percentage increase in per capita GNP, 1971–76	2.5	2.4	3.7
Weighted by 1976 GNP of partners			
Trade concentration with partner, 1976	43.8	23.9	22.3
Percent of GNP with partner, 1976	9.8	6.3	2.3
Average annual percentage increase in per capita GNP, 1971–76	3.9	4.0	4.0
Weighted by 1976 total trade of partners			
Trade concentration with partner, 1976	47.5	24.4	24.3
Percent of GNP with partner, 1976	14.7	10.2	9.2
Average annual percentage increase in per capita GNP, 1971–76	3.7	4.0	4.0

[a] The trade figures and GNP figures for the states at the centers of the systems (United States, United Kingdom, the Common Market Six, Japan, and the Soviet Union) are not included in total world trade or total world GNP.

SOURCE: Compiled by authors.

due to limited data availability.* Its inclusion for the second time period obviously increased the average GNP level of the variable partners group.

In terms of partner concentration in exports, all three groups declined slightly between 1971 and 1976. The percentages of GNP represented by these exports, however, increased in all three cases, reflecting the fact that world trade was increasing faster than world production. The growth rates of the states in the US system now matched those of the partners in the other systems but were well below those of the variable partners group. In this period the US growth rate was closer to many other major industrialized nations in this period: The US rate was 1.6 percent, while West Germany was at 1.9, the United Kingdom at 2.0, Italy at 1.7, and the Netherlands at 2.2. France at 3.4, Belgium at 3.9, and Japan at 4.0 were the only nations with relatively higher growth rates (World Bank 1977). The drops in the averages for all the countries were quite marked compared to the preceding decade, a result of the beginnings of the worldwide economic recession.

When the weighted averages are considered, the concentration of exports to the United States by its partners was even higher. Concentration for states in the other systems dropped by approximately a third, while the variable partners group showed a small drop. In terms of GNP concentration, all three groups dropped with a GNP weight and increased when total trade was taken into account. Since concentration levels were higher with the total trade weight, the larger traders had become more attached to their major markets. While the US partners had the highest GNP concentrations, when total trade and national product were taken into account the gap was even larger. When the growth rates were weighted, the three

---

*There were incomplete trade data and no GNP figures. The Yearbook of International Trade Statistics volumes do not include China, and figures from the Direction of Trade volumes do not contain data on trade between centrally planned economies, a major gap in the figures for China in 1961 when such trade was still present (cf. Smith 1973, p. 217; Mah 1971, p. 24). While figures for this trade are still absent for 1971 and 1976, the generally low volume for this trade permitted the inclusion of China since the missing trade figures were small.

groups were virtually equal, although the US partners lagged slightly behind. For those states in a trading system, growth rates were noticeably higher when GNP and trade were used as weights, although this pattern was not present for the variable partners group in this period.

Some of the differences in the partner groups resulted from the fact that most of the countries in the US system were developing ones. It is quite possible that different patterns could exist for the developing countries in terms of growth, trade concentration, and GNP concentration. Although Lall (1975, p. 808) has argued that developing countries operate in the international trade system much as the developed countries do and that all countries face similar problems to some degree, the developing countries have some special concerns, as noted in the earlier chapters. Additionally, while small industrialized countries are vulnerable to changes in the world trade regime, they do have a greater ability to modify the shocks that can occur from outside events than most of the developing countries (Krasner 1981, p. 133; Rothstein 1977, p. 45). Also, the weighting procedures tended to emphasize trends in the developed countries. As a result of these considerations, the developed countries were removed from the comparisons of the three groups. The UN classification of developed countries was again used, as was the case in Chapter 4. Thus, the nations considered developed in that chapter were excluded, as well as Gibraltar, Malta, and the Faeroes Islands, since the UN classifies them as developed areas. The six Eastern European countries were also excluded since their levels of development are at least roughly comparable to those of Greece or Portugal.

For 1961 to 1971, the developing US partners and variable partners countries were both larger traders and larger economic units, on average, than the states in other systems (see Table 8.3). The trade of the US partners was about as concentrated as that of the other partner countries, while the variable partners group had significantly lower concentrations. There was little change in this regard for any of the groups between 1961 and 1971. GNP concentrations, however, did change. The US partners increased their concentrations as did the variable partners. The countries with other constant markets maintained approximately the same levels. In terms of growth rates,

TABLE 8.3

US Trading System, 1961–71, Developing Countries Only

	US Partners (n = 26)	Other Partners (n = 62)	Variable Partners (n = 33)
Percentage of world trade, 1971[a]	29.0	36.6	34.4
Percentage of world GNP, 1971[a]	32.9	23.1	44.0
Average trade levels (millions), 1971	$ 664	$ 351	$ 619
Average GNP (millions), 1971	$5,021	$1,474	$5,289
Unweighted averages			
Trade concentration with partner, 1961	45.7	43.3	30.9
Trade concentration with partner, 1971	44.1	42.6	31.2
Percent of GNP with partner, 1961	7.9	9.3	4.6
Percent of GNP with partner, 1971	11.4	9.2	7.4
Average annual percentage increase in per capita GNP, 1961–71	2.5	2.5	3.3
Weighted by 1971 GNP of partners			
Trade concentration with partner, 1971	40.5	31.8	22.6
Percent of GNP with partner, 1971	4.9	5.8	3.0
Average annual percentage increase in per capita GNP, 1961–71	2.8	2.3	3.0
Weighted by 1971 total trade of partners			
Trade concentration with partner, 1971	39.2	27.7	28.4
Percent of GNP with partner, 1971	11.8	8.7	7.3
Average annual percentage increase in per capita GNP, 1961–71	3.2	3.3	5.5

[a] World trade and world GNP totals for 1971 incorporate only the figures for the developing countries.

SOURCE: Compiled by authors.

the average growth of the US partners compared favorably with the growth rates of other developing country groups.

With the weighted averages, the countries in the US system had more highly concentrated trading ties. For all groups the larger countries obviously devoted less of their GNPs to their principal market, as reflected in the drops in the weighted GNP concentrations. The larger traders, as evidenced by the total trade weights, had higher concentrations of GNP. As was the case when all countries were included in the comparisons, the countries more involved in world trade had higher average growth rates. Size, as measured by GNP, had a similar effect for the US partners, but not for the other two groups of countries.

For 1971 to 1976, shares of world GNP and trade of the US partners dropped, no doubt reflecting in part higher petroleum prices. The most noticeable increase was in terms of the percentage of the developing countries' total GNP accounted for by the various partners group (see Table 8.4). This increase was also reflected in the average GNP figures of this group. The countries with the United States as their principal market were larger traders than was the case of the other developing countries, although the other partners group was close on this measure. The average trade concentration of the US partners was higher than the other groups, although GNP concentration was only marginally so. Growth rates for all three groups were slightly lower than was the case in the preceding decade.

The weighted averages showed some changes. The US partners no longer had the most concentrated trade or GNP. The higher average growth rates were also more noticeable for the US partners and particularly the other partners group when weights were used. The developing countries trading with Japan and Western Europe thus had better growth in this period than the US partners or those countries with shifting markets. The growth for all the groups was similar with both weights; therefore, there was no indication that the larger economies were growing more or less quickly than larger traders. All other things being equal, however, larger traders and larger economies did have better growth.

TABLE 8.4

US Trading System, 1971-76, Developing Countries Only

	US Partners (n = 30)	Other Partners (n = 64)	Variable Partners (n = 28)
Percentage of world trade, 1976[a]	27.1	55.3	17.6
Percentage of world GNP, 1976[a]	27.7	29.3	43.0
Average trade levels (millions), 1976	$ 2,266	$2,172	$ 1,579
Average GNP (millions), 1976	$10,872	$5,396	$18,074
Unweighted averages			
Trade concentration with partner, 1971	43.1	39.2	26.9
Trade concentration with partner, 1976	42.4	38.9	27.0
Percent of GNP with partner, 1971	10.6	8.8	6.2
Percent of GNP with partner, 1976	11.6	11.5	7.8
Average annual percentage increase in per capita GNP, 1971-76	2.4	2.1	3.2
Weighted by 1976 GNP of partners			
Trade concentration with partner, 1976	35.0	24.4	22.6
Percent of GNP with partner, 1976	6.9	9.7	2.2
Average annual percentage increase in per capita GNP, 1971-76	4.2	4.7	4.0
Weighted by total trade (1976) of partners			
Trade concentration with partner, 1976	38.6	24.9	25.3
Percent of GNP with partner, 1976	14.2	15.2	9.9
Average annual percentage increase in per capita GNP, 1971-76	3.9	4.8	3.9

[a] World trade and world GNP totals for 1976 incorporate only the figures for the developing countries.

SOURCE: Compiled by authors.

145

POLICY ISSUES AND RESPONSES

General characteristics of the US trading system can be seen in the above comparisons. While the aggregation of trading systems in the other partners group obscures possible variations, the following chapters will more clearly delineate their characteristics. The above comparisons indicated that countries in the US system, including the United States itself, faced a set of particular problems or issues when compared with other groups of countries. Some of these issues, and the responses taken, will be discussed below in terms of the four general impacts of the decline of the United States as a world economic actor, the relationship of the United States with developing countries in the Western Hemisphere, responses to NIEO issues, and the choice facing the United States in terms of attempting to maintain free trade or opting for a policy of neo-mercantilism.

From Hegemony to a Regional Trading System

The United States is a former hegemon and a country with a declining share of world trade. Major market losses in the export of manufactures are one symptom of this decline, particularly since manufactures are the major component of world trade. This situation has had some general impacts on its trading system and the countries in it. The United States developed worldwide economic policies for the world trade regime after World War II, relying on the principle of free trade and with little regard to regional characteristics or problems of the Western Hemisphere. The activities of the EC with its association agreements stand in sharp contrast to the approach of the United States, as do some of the efforts of Japan to develop commercial links in parts of Asia and Oceania. As a result, the United States is in a situation of leading a regional trading system that is a residual of a past system that used to be larger.

The United States did have links with some developed countries, with Canada being the largest market for US exports as well as the largest single source of US imports for many years. In addition, Japan and the United Kingdom had the United States as their principal market for the 15 years discussed, reflecting the importance of trade

among industrialized nations. Although the United States
is no longer the largest market for exports from the United
Kingdom, it is likely to remain the most important market
for Japan, particularly since the EC countries maintain
restrictions on Japanese products. Notwithstanding calls
for increased protectionism in the United States, recent
agreements limiting Japanse imports, and increasing Japanese
direct investment in the United States, the primacy of the
United States as a market for Japanese goods is unlikely
to be supplanted in the near future, although there has
been a trend of declining relative importance.

   Related to the trend of increasing regionalization
among the Western Hemisphere countries is the increase of
Japanese trade with other countries, including many within
its own trading system, which is increasing in size (see
Chapter 10). More than a decade ago, Corbet and Streeten
(1971, p. 8) suggested that increasing strains between the
EC and the United States over trade issues might lead the
United States to develop preferential trade links with Western Hemisphere and Asia-Pacific Basin countries. From
today's perspective the possibilities of such links with the
Asia-Pacific Basin must take into account the emergence of
Japan as a leading industrial nation with its own trading
system in this part of the world.

   The fact that the United States was instrumental in
creating the liberal world trade regime after World War II
may make regional cooperation in the Western Hemisphere
more difficult to achieve. As was obvious in the discussion of the arguments surrounding the call for the NIEO,
the regime is perceived to have worked against the interests of the developing countries, a defect that can be
attributed to the United States to at least some degree.
For those states most involved in trading with the United
States, the connection would seem even more obvious since
the major market was the state helping to maintain the
system. Thus, it is not surprising that it was Prebisch
who developed the first detailed call for structural reforms
in the regime and that the dependencia school arose in
Latin America. While dependency theorists have not always
neglected other industrialized countries, their focus has
usually been on the United States. Thus, the past
hegemonic role of the United States, in conjunction with
its strong trade ties with this area, served to spur the
development of two of the political economy perspectives
with prescriptions for changes in the regime.

The United States and the Western Hemisphere
Developing Nations

Not only are the countries in the US trading system
primarily developing ones, but the United States has had a
larger share of its overall trade with the developing states
than other industrialized countries (Deardorff, Stern, and
Greene 1979, pp. 102-03). Exports of US manufactures to
the developing countries, however, have shown greater
relative declines than exports to the developed nations.
Not surprisingly, the performance of US exports of manufactures to the Latin American countries has been better
than average--there has been a smaller market loss
(Mikesell and Farah 1981). This relatively larger concentration of trade with the developing countries, including those in Latin America, has had an impact in a number
of policy areas.
Cooperation between the United States and Latin
America may be more difficult to achieve precisely because
of the predominant US economic role in the region. The
United States is the predominant source of private investment in the area (Lal et al. 1975, p. 2; Morton and Tulloch
1977, p. 206), and it has been suggested that this investment has led to a net capital outflow from Latin
America (Griffin 1978, p. 58). While the net outflow argument has been criticized for ignoring indirect benefits of
private investment and not analyzing all facets of the in-
flow and outflow of capital (Lal et al. 1975, pp. 274-75;
Mikdashi 1976, p. 47; Rothstein 1977, p. 166), the distrust
of US economic activity that remains in Latin America is a
political fact of life. Hollist and Johnson (1979) found
that the concentration of US economic activity plus the
asymmetric nature of economic and political power between
the United States and individual Latin American countries
has led to a noncooperative atmosphere, since the evaluation of these trade and other economic links has been partially negative. It is not surprising, therefore, that
there have been no formal association agreements between
the United States and other Western Hemisphere nations
similar to those concluded between the EC and many developing countries.
The comparisons of per capita growth rates for developing countries did not clearly indicate that countries
in the US trading system suffered in terms of growth.
During the ten-year period under study the developing US

trade partners had growth rates on a par with the other two groups, despite the fact that US growth rates were considerably below those of the other developed states except for the United Kingdom. Yet from 1971 to 1976, when the growth in the United States was nearer that of other developed nations, the weighted average growth of its developing trade partners lagged behind those of developing states in other trading systems. The growth of the US partners would have been lower with the weighted averages but for the presence of some of the Asian NICs and Brazil in the trading system in the second period. These countries have been among the best known developmental "success stories," and their relatively high rates of growth from 1971 to 1976 raised the weighted averages since they were larger economies and larger traders. Moreover, since the countries in the US system were generally more economically advanced compared to the African, Oceanic, and some of the non-oil Middle Eastern and Asian states, a better economic performance might have been expected from the Western Hemisphere countries.

It is possible that one underlying cause of the lower US growth rates was the presence of economic difficulties attendant in the transition of global preeminence to one of regional leadership. It is possible that some of the negative impacts of this transition and the resulting lower growth rates were transmitted to some of the US trade partners. Given the differences in the US growth rates in the two periods and those of the partner countries, the possible negative effects on the US partners may have operated with a time lag. Thus, the lower growth in the United States from 1961 to 1971 led to lower growth rates in the trade partners from 1971 to 1976. It is also possible, however, that other factors, such as domestic economic difficulties in the Latin American countries or economic transition problems resulting from increased industrialization, explain the relatively slower growth of the Latin American nations. Since the export and GNP concentration levels were generally higher for the US partners in both periods, whatever negative impacts existed of the trade association with the United States were probably exacerbated.

One of the responses of the developing Western Hemisphere countries to slower economic growth has been the formation of common markets and free trade associations. The formation of such organizations was one of Prebisch's proposals for strengthening the position of the developing countries in the world economy (Monroe 1975, p. 31). Such groups would effectively aid import substitution for countries within the organizations and create a base for export industries.   Efforts at regional economic coopera- tion were emulations of the successes of the EC, and they had the added incentive of providing a stronger economic bargaining group vis-à-vis the United States.

The Central American Common Market (CACOM), com- prising five countries in the region, was one such cooper- ative effort that was initially successful.   In fact, CACOM provided the most positive example of the economic benefits of cooperation among developing countries (Morrison 1976, p. 40).   Ultimately, Honduras withdrew from the group be- cause it had the smallest economic gains from CACOM and because of political differences with El Salvador (Christou and Wilford 1973, p. 259; Pazos 1973, p. 11).   Current un- settled political conditions in Central America and political differences among the remaining members have probably ended this once promising effort.

The Latin American Free Trade Association (LAFTA) was a looser group consisting of Mexico and the countries of South America.   While the growth of intra-LAFTA trade did not match the gains made by CACOM (Pazos 1973), trade among the members did increase, particularly in manu- factures (Morrison 1976, p. 21).   The gains from the trade, however, largely went to Argentina, Brazil, and Mexico, the three members with the best preexisting industrial bases (Tironi 1980, p. 49).   Attempts to increase trade among the members have been handicapped by disagreements over the inclusion of new products that would not be sub- ject to tariffs within the LAFTA framework and the selec- tion of countries for the establishment of new industries that would profit from access to the larger market of the free trade area.

The fact that Argentina, Brazil, and Mexico had gained the most contributed to the disagreements and led Peru, Colombia, Ecuador, Bolivia, and Chile (later joined by Venezuela) to form the Andean Group.   These countries combined to coordinate their activities and to improve their bargaining position in LAFTA negotiations vis-à-vis the three larger states.   After some initial successes, the Andean group was weakened because of failure to reach agreement on the distribution of benefits and the with- drawal of Chile under the Pinochet regime for political and economic reasons (Rothstein 1977, p. 102).

These efforts at regional economic cooperation have no doubt increased intragroup trade more rapidly than otherwise would have occurred, and they have probably facilitated import substitution for the countries at the aggregate level. These efforts, however, have also epitomized the difficulties that economic associations face in terms of the distribution of gains. Should these groups or new ones achieve additional or greater successes in the future, they can stimulate economic growth for the members. Greater economic cooperation among the developing countries in the Western Hemisphere might also help to maintain the regional trading system by increasing trade among the members. The countries in the southern part of South America that have not been in the US trading system might even be brought into it as a result of greater ties to the present members.

Responses to NIEO Issues

As noted in Chapter 3, the United States did adopt a version of the GSP. Although a relatively recent, and rather reluctant, convert, the United States may have adopted its preference scheme due to the realization that continued opposition to the GSP idea created more ill will among the developing countries, particularly those in Latin America, than the refusal was worth. The various exclusions incorporated into the US preference scheme largely tended to benefit existing US trade partners and worked to the disadvantage of developing countries in other trading systems. US limitations on the extension of the preferences to countries granting reverse preferences or reciprocal privileges to other developed nations were directed at some of the initial EC association agreements negotiated by developing countries. US pressure on this issue even led some Caribbean associate members of the EC to oppose such preferences for European products in the markets of the associates in the 1979 Lomé agreement (Frey-Wouters 1980, p. 31).

The Latin American countries have been among the strongest supporters of the GSP idea. Such support could be at least in part the result of the failure of LAFTA to live up to its expectations. Also, a global preference scheme would end some of the privileged access of the EC associate members to European markets. This last concern is important because many Latin American products are competitive with products from the associate members (Frey-Wouters 1980, pp. 217, 262; Uri 1976, p. 127). Thus, a generalized system would redress this perceived imbalance. In fact, many of the Latin American states would have an advantage with GSP. Their general level of development and the status of many of them as NICs or near-NICs would provide them with a competitive edge over the developing African states and many Asian and Middle East states (Monroe 1975, p. 58; Morton and Tulloch 1977, pp. 69, 175). While the economic situation of these countries led them to a different view of the GSP issue from the early attitude of the United States, the positions in both cases were responses to the perceptions of a less open world economy with reduced market access for their exports.

An area related to the particularistic interest of the US partners in favoring the GSP idea has been the attitude of the Latin American countries toward special aid and treatment for the least developed countries. The United Nations designated approximately 40 states in this category, with the intent of identifying them for special help. The Latin American countries have been opposed to this approach, primarily because Haiti is the only Western Hemisphere nation included in the category (Monroe 1975, p. 121). Thus, special treatment for these countries is seen as coming at the expense of additional foreign aid to themselves. The United States has not been in conflict with its trade partners on this policy issue since the countries so identified are generally ones with very strong ties to other developed nations, often a former colonial power such as France or the United Kingdom. The areas are also of limited strategic or military importance in most cases.

A number of specific commodities of importance for the Western Hemisphere trading system are worthy of note. Sugar is an important export for many of the Caribbean islands, as well as the Philippines, and most of the producers rely on US purchases (Fox 1971, p. 169). The 1974 attempt to renew the sugar program maintained by the United States with quotas for various countries, however, failed in Congress due to domestic concerns and what has been considered the lack of priority given to Latin American concerns (Mingst 1980, pp. 11-12). Coffee and bananas are two other agricultural commodities important to some Latin American countries and dependent upon the US market. In the area of nonagricultural commodities, petroleum exports from Venezuela and Ecuador and refined products from Trinidad and Tobago and the Netherlands Antilles are major trade items. Bauxite exports to the United States, and Canada in some cases, are another important commodity. Jamaica, Surinam, and Guyana exported the bulk of their production to North America, and they have been important members of the bauxite producers group.

While trade between the United States and its partners in other commodities was being carried on in the system, the broader world market is more relevant in terms of the issues involved. Although security of supply for various commodities, including petroleum, has been an ongoing concern for the United States, it has been subordinated to other goals (Krasner 1978). Also, since the United States also functions as a commodity exporter, it has not been as concerned with this issue as have resource-poor developed areas, such as Western Europe and Japan.

Free Trade or Protectionism in
the United States?

The United States faces a decision in terms of opting for continued support of free trade or shifting to neo-mercantilism to counter such practices abroad. After World War II, the United States lead in creating and upholding a free trade system, and the idea of free trade became an important element of foreign economic policy. "At the moment the United States lacks the institutions and the belief system to operate effectively in a mercantilist world" (Russet 1981-82, p. 55). This commitment to free trade and its attendant perceptual background have made US responses to a changing world trade regime more difficult to formulate. The ultimate response, whatever its nature, will be vitally important to its trading partners.

Past support for the idea of free trade can be seen in the tariff structure of the United States. US tariff levels are generally the lowest among the industrialized countries (Meyer 1978, p. 113; Monroe 1975, p. 23). Only Norway and Switzerland have had lower average tariffs, and in only 6 of 22 industrial categories has the US average tariff been above the world norm (Deardorff, Stern, and Greene 1979, p. 85). The United States is facing considerable domestic pressures to protect declining industries and save domestic jobs. No democratic system can ignore public pressures for protectionism (Calleo and Rowland 1973, p. 104), particularly in the face of similar practices abroad. But the choice is not simply one between free trade and protectionism with domestic groups on only one side of the issue. While such protective measures as orderly marketing arrangements and voluntary export restraints have been negotiated, it is not clear that protectionism will triumph as a trade policy.

Protectionism may well be an unwise policy for the United States. In an overview of the impacts of tariff reductions, Deardorff, Stern, and Greene (1979) found that the United States would gain in terms of overall employment from most multilateral reductions. Domestic industries would be provided with cheaper inputs (imports) and would thus become more competitive internationally. Greater competitiveness would lead to greater production and more employment. While the above is generally valid, certain industrial sectors would not share in the gains and would suffer losses (pp. 96-97), and it could not be assumed that all firms, even in an individual sector that gained, would benefit (p. 97). Thus, there are likely to be countervailing domestic pressures for protectionism and free trade.

In countries in the early stages of industrialization, consensus on either free trade or protectionism is easier to achieve among domestic producers. Most of the basic industries are at the same level of development in terms of competitiveness, both domestically and abroad. In countries such as the United States that have passed this stage, industries are in a wide variety of competitive positions, thus preventing any agreement over the desirability of an open trade regime or a restricted one (Kurth 1979). Domestic pluralist politics within the United States combine with fragmented decision-making centers in Congress, the presidency, and bureaucratic agencies to make agreement difficult. Thus, it is often difficult to determine an optimum policy, let alone implement one. Some industries face major foreign competition and desire protection. Others export heavily and prefer free trade. Yet other industry groups cannot even adequately determine whether or not they would gain more from free trade or neomercantilism given the mix of goods that they produce. Thus, neither protectionism nor free trade is necessarily favored by a summation of particularistic interests in the

United States (Krasner 1978, p. 19; Krasner 1979, p. 492; Lipson 1982, pp. 420-21; McKeown 1984, p. 218). Given these variable domestic pressures, the resulting mix of selective protectionism and continuing pursuit of free trade in the United States is understandable.

A special aspect of the debate between free trade and protectionism has been the competition for domestic manufactures markets and international markets from the NICs. At the end of the 1960s, the United States was the largest aggregate market for manufactures from the developing countries (Morrison 1976, p. 20).* Among the NICs, many of the Latin American nations, Hong Kong, and the Philippines, as well as Taiwan and South Korea from the mid-1960s, were in the US system, with the resulting pressure on domestic firms. The manufactures from the Latin American NICs may also be in worldwide competition with the United States, since the export mix of Brazil, Mexico, and Argentina was found to be generally similar to that of the United States (Boatler 1978). Domestic pressure has been effective in leading to voluntary restraints and various forms of quotas. The problem is likely to continue in the future given the countries in the US system. Among the developing countries it is the export of manufactures from the Asian and Latin American countries that are growing at the same rate as the exports of manufactures worldwide, while such exports from African states have grown much more slowly (Lipson 1982, p. 427; Morrisor 1976, p. 18; Morton and Tulloch 1977, p. 158). Even this issue, however, reflects the presence of differences among domestic groups. Some industries in the United States have gained markets in the NICs as a result of their industrialization (and exporting), while other industries have lost sales to NIC exports (Krasner 1979, p. 506). Thus, heightened protectionism could lead to decreased export markets for some US manufactures.

Another response to neomercantilist practices and pressures from competition abroad has been foreign investment by US firms. Such investment is also subject to free trade and protectionist arguments since it is seen as

---

*Morrison used a different, more restrictive group of products for manufactures categories (cf. pp. 91-92). Thus, his results do not agree in all respects with the results discussed in Chapter 5.

the export of jobs. Faced with market losses, firms have created subsidiaries to protect their market positions in various parts of the world (Calleo and Rowland 1973, p. 169; Evans 1977; Lal et al. 1975, pp. 22-23; Michalet 1982, p. 39; Monroe 1975, pp. 45-46). While this type of activity does not directly facilitate trade, it does so indirectly via trade among the subsidiaries and the parent company, perhaps ultimately to the benefit of the United States. Such actions may be appropriate for individual firms, but it is not clear that they will negate regionalism in international trade, and they may even reinforce it, thus hindering US efforts to maintain an open world trade regime. It should be noted that European and Japanese firms have increasingly invested in the United States so that the investment flow, with consequent losses or gains, is a two-way street. Probable reasons for investment in the United States include the same idea of protecting market shares and perhaps diffusing protectionist sentiment in the country. In terms of economic benefits, the balance sheet is difficult to calculate for any country since there remain many arguments about the gains and losses that occur with direct investment.

GLOBALISM OR REGIONALISM?

The future course of action for the United States is a relatively open one, but there are limits to the available choices. Opting for continued free trade to the extent possible is in many respects the easiest choice since it represents continuation of the status quo and existing attitudes. Domestic support for the option does exist among some economic sectors. Free trade may also be essential for a US leadership role, even at a reduced level, in the international system. The present regional trading system is even likely to persist, as other countries are attached or remain attached to other trading systems. It would still be a residual system and may continue to suffer some of the disadvantages noted above. Protectionism would require a more formal connection with the Latin American countries, a possibility with political problems and potential liabilities as a result. It is unlikely that the Latin American countries in all cases would forgo the possibilities of receiving greater trade benefits from other developed countries unless the United States was willing to grant offsetting advantages. Ultimately, since the United States is both a world and a regional leader, there will be some form of dualism, although the degree of emphasis on the global versus the regional role may vary and it is not presently evident which will be considered more important. Such dualism may not provide the best of both worlds, but it may avoid the worst of either.

9   Western Europe and Africa

The formation and subsequent enlargement of the EC with its "implicit, if not explicit, regionalism and protectionism" marked a significant event in the history of the world trade regime in the post-World War II era. The EC has played a key role in the development of regional trading blocks; furthermore, it is the "prime exemplar" of such a trading bloc (Barraclough 1980, p. 58). The importance of the trading links between Western Europe and other areas of the world lies in both the trading relationships of the countries involved and their impacts on the world trade regime in general. Western Europe has become an increasingly important factor in world trade since its recovery from World War II. The EC itself has come to account for a larger proportion of world trade than either the United States or Japan, even when intra-EC trade is excluded. Trade has also been more essential to the economies of the EC states than it has been for the United States (Frey-Wouters 1980, p. 6; Vaitsos 1982, p. 173) or the Soviet Union, which has been a less active trader than its economic size would indicate. Thus, of the world's four major trading systems, the Western European center has clearly been the largest trader in absolute terms, with trade playing a much more important role for many of the nations involved.

A TRADING SYSTEM BY DESIGN

EC trade has been characterized by increasing integration among the members and by the fact that such integration was, to a large extent, consciously developed.

Since the formation of the Common Market in 1959, the trade of the original six members has come to be concentrated with each other. In those cases when the principal market had been some other state their largest trading ties have since shifted to another member (cf. Green and Lutz 1978, chap. 4). Similarly, by 1979, the reorientation of British export and import trade had progressed to the point that West Germany had replaced the United States as the United Kingdom's largest trade partner, while Denmark and Ireland still retain the United Kingdom as their principal market. Thus, trade integration continued after the enlargement of the EC. For the periods under study it is necessary to talk of the Western European trading systems in the plural, since the United Kingdom was not linked to an EC state as its principal market, although this distinction became a historical one in 1979.

The EC was formed, and has since expanded, based on a number of treaties. Currently, ten European countries are full members. EC agreements have given associate membership to many states, thus linking them economically to the Common Market. The first Yaoundé Convention signed in 1963 gave 18 former French, Belgian, and Italian African colonies the status of associate members. These associate members had certain rights and privileges compared to non-members and nonassociates. With the conclusion of the second Lomé Convention in 1979, 46 developing countries in Africa, the Caribbean, and the Pacific (hence the usual collective designation as the ACP states) had attained this status. In addition, most of the few remaining small colonial holdings and overseas departments of the European members have also in effect been included within the EC framework. Special association agreements or trade agreements with ten European countries, Israel, and seven other countries bordering the Mediterranean have also been negotiated (cf. Matthews 1977, p. 11). The agreements with Spain and Turkey now envision the possibility of eventual full membership.

The accession of the United Kingdom to full membership greatly expanded the EC links with other nations. Denmark and Ireland followed their principal market into the EC. Also, most of the members of the British Commonwealth that had not previously attained associate status gained it with the British entry. The industrialized Dominions and the Asian members of the Commonwealth, including the Crown Colony of Hong Kong, however, were not granted this status. Thus, the nations linked to the EC, either as full members, associate members, or by special trade agreements, have been considerable. The extension of these ties and the Common Market preferences that have gone with them have led to a situation where almost half of the world's total trade has been contained within some type of special EC arrangement (Monroe 1975, pp. 44-45).

EUROPE AND THE ACP STATES

From 1961 to 1971, two European trading systems existed—one centered on the United Kingdom and the other on the original members of the EC. During this period the nations in these two trading systems were largely concentrated in Europe and Africa, and in Asia to a lesser extent, accounting for a total of 59 states. Of these states, 11 were in Europe, 27 in Africa, 8 in Asia, and 4 in Oceania. The remaining nine members were in the Western Hemisphere, all of them small island territories and some of them still colonies or overseas departments. The overall geographic focus of the two trading systems was thus largely Eurafrican in nature.

As can be seen in Table 9.1, the countries in these systems were in large measure smaller territories in terms of GNP when compared with the partners in other systems and the states that were not in any trading system. While the European partners had the lowest average GNPs, they were somewhat larger traders than the variable partners group of states. Their trade concentration levels fell by about 5 percent in ten years, after being initially high, so that by the end of the period their average level was less than that of the countries in other systems. A similar decline occurred in GNP concentrations, a trend contrary to the one occurring worldwide as represented by the higher GNP concentrations for the other two groups of countries. The average growth rate for the ten-year period was the lowest of the three groups, reflecting in part the presence of many of the least developed African states in the trading systems.

The weighted comparisons show a different picture. The industrialized states, 11 in Europe, as well as New Zealand and South Africa, that were in the systems had the largest effects on the weighted measures. Trade and GNP concentration were lowered and were equivalent to the

TABLE 9.1
Western European Trading Systems, 1961–71

	Western European Partners (n = 59)	Other Partners (n = 52)	Variable Partners (n = 36)
Percentage of world trade, 1971[a]	31.6	51.8	16.6
Percentage of world GNP, 1971[a]	22.7	52.2	25.1
Average trade levels (millions), 1971	$ 759	$1,396	$ 653
Average GNP (millions), 1971	$3,758	$9,684	$5,784
Unweighted averages			
Trade concentration with partner, 1961	43.3	39.0	32.2
Trade concentration with partner, 1971	38.8	42.2	31.5
Percent of GNP with partner, 1961	9.1	6.5	4.7
Percent of GNP with partner, 1971	7.9	10.1	7.3
Average annual percentage increase in per capita GNP, 1961–71	2.4	3.2	3.3
Weighted by 1971 GNP of partners			
Trade concentration with partner, 1971	23.4	40.9	21.4
Percent of GNP with partner, 1971	4.3	5.8	2.7
Average annual percentage increase in per capita GNP, 1961–71	3.1	3.3	3.3
Weighted by 1971 total trade of partners			
Trade concentration with partner, 1971	22.5	42.0	26.8
Percentage of GNP with partner, 1971	5.2	8.8	6.6
Average annual percentage increase in per capita GNP, 1961–71	2.8	3.8	5.4

[a] The trade figures and GNP figures for the states at the centers of the systems (United States, United Kingdom, the Common Market Six, Japan, and the Soviet Union) are not included in total world trade or total world GNP.

SOURCE: Compiled by authors.

variable partners group. The weighted growth rates, however, were still behind the other two groups, particularly when total trade was the weight. While the larger traders in the European systems did have better growth rates, as was the case with all countries, the impact of size was not as great. Greater involvement in trade and a larger economy did aid growth somewhat, indicating that it was the smaller, less developed states in the European systems that had the lowest per capita growth rates.

The countries with European nations as their principal markets fell into three groups that can be compared with each other. Thirty-one of the 59 states were in the system centered on the United Kingdom. This group included most of the Western Hemisphere territories, three in Oceania, and more than half of the European states. Within the EC (the Common Market Six) system, France was the principal market for 19 developing countries or territories, overwhelmingly African in composition. Collectively, the other EC countries served as principal markets for a few European countries and scattered developing states. The different compositions of these trading systems were reflected in the differences on the various measures used for comparison, as displayed in Table 9.2. The French partners exhibited the lowest trade and GNP averages by far, the highest concentration levels, and the poorest growth performances. The other EC group generally had the opposite trends. The GNP and trade levels were high enough to raise the total EC weighted averages above those of the states in the UK trading system. In terms of the various measures, weighted and unweighted alike, the territories trading with the United Kingdom fell between the French group and the other EC group.

From 1971 to 1976, the trading systems of the European countries retained the same geographic characteristics as in the preceding period. Of the 55 countries in the systems, 10 other European countries were included, as well as 29 from Africa, 3 in Asia, and 4 in Oceania. Nine of the territories were in the Western Hemisphere, with seven of these again being small Caribbean territories. There were some shifts of major markets, however, as the trading system of the United Kingdom declined from 31 to 24 states. The number of states linked to France was relatively stable, while the other EC countries accounted for 13 states as opposed to 9 in the preceding decade.

TABLE 9.2
Comparison of Western European Trading Systems, 1961-71

	UK Partners (n = 31)	Common Market Six Partners (n = 28)	French Partners (n = 19)	Other Common Market Partners (n = 9)
Percentage of world trade, 1971	15.8	15.8	2.2	13.6
Percentage of world GNP, 1971	10.5	12.2	2.6	9.6
Average trade levels (millions), 1971	$ 723	$ 798	$ 161	$ 2,142
Average GNP (millions), 1971	$3,295	$4,271	$1,311	$10,518
Unweighted averages				
Trade concentration with partner, 1961[a]	34.4	53.1	68.9	19.7
Trade concentration with partner, 1971[a]	37.3	40.5	47.3	26.3
Percent of GNP with partner, 1961	8.1	10.2	12.7	4.7
Percent of GNP with partner, 1971	8.4	7.3	7.7	6.4
Average annual percentage increase in per capita GNP, 1961-71	2.4	2.3	1.9	3.1
Weighted by 1971 GNP of partners				
Trade concentration with partner, 1971[a]	25.0	21.9	38.4	17.6
Percent GNP with partner, 1971[a]	5.1	3.7	4.2	3.5
Average annual percentage increase in per capita GNP, 1961-71	2.8	3.4	1.7	3.8
Weighted by 1971 total trade of partners				
Trade concentration with partner, 1971[a]	25.2	19.8	35.1	17.4
Percent of GNP with partner, 1971[a]	6.1	4.3	6.9	3.9
Average annual percentage increase in per capita GNP, 1961-71	2.5	3.2	1.5	3.5

[a] Concentration levels are for trade with the principal market only, not the Common Market as a whole.

SOURCE: Compiled by authors.

The countries linked to these European markets had lower average GNPs than those in other systems and the variable partners group (see Table 9.3). As their average trade levels indicate, they were smaller traders than the countries in other systems, although somewhat larger traders than the variable partners group. By 1976, their average trade and GNP concentrations had dropped below those of the states in other systems. While the countries in the other systems had increasing trade concentrations for this period, the countries in the European systems had declining trade concentrations. Their GNP concentrations did rise, but not as dramatically as was the case for countries in other trading systems. The trade diversification combined with increasing GNP concentration came about as a result of world trade increasing more rapidly than world productivity, so that the smaller percentage of trade to the principal market managed to represent a larger portion of GNP. The average growth rates were markedly lower, and they were less than half of the growth rates of the variable partners group.

With the weighted averages the growth rates were higher for all three groups, again indicating that larger traders and larger economic units grew more rapidly. The rates for the countries in the European systems did remain lower than those for the other two groups of countries. Concentration levels for trade and GNP were also much lower. The developed countries in the systems, with their larger trade and GNP levels, had much more diversified export markets, particularly when compared to those of countries in the other trading systems, a fact evident from the comparison of the weighted averages for the three sets of countries.

Again there were some distinct differences among the partners of the various European markets. On average, the French partners were smaller traders with relatively small economies, high concentration levels of both types, and very low growth (see Table 9.4). In contrast, the other EC group contained the largest traders and economies. These states had lower concentration levels and better growth. For the EC as a whole, however, the combination of these two disparate groups led to unweighted averages that were similar to the averages for the states in the British system. With the weighted averages, all groups had similar trade concentration levels, and the GNP concentrations were also reasonably close for the various groups

TABLE 9.3
Western European Trading Systems, 1971–76

	Western European Partners (n = 55)	Other Partners (n = 61)	Variable Partners (n = 31)
Percentage of world trade, 1976[a]	27.4	61.2	11.4
Percentage of world GNP, 1976[a]	26.6	48.1	25.3
Average trade levels (millions), 1976	$ 2,216	$ 4,456	$ 1,639
Average GNP (millions), 1976	$10,168	$16,553	$17,166
Unweighted averages			
Trade concentration with partner, 1971	39.0	37.8	27.9
Trade concentration with partner, 1976	34.5	40.3	27.6
Percent of GNP with partner, 1971	8.3	9.0	6.2
Percent of GNP with partner, 1976	9.4	11.7	7.7
Average annual percentage increase in			
per capita GNP, 1971–76	1.8	3.1	3.7
Weighted by 1976 GNP of partners			
Trade concentration with partner, 1976	18.4	36.7	22.3
Percent of GNP with partner, 1976	4.3	9.1	2.3
Average annual percentage increase in			
per capita GNP, 1971–76	3.1	4.5	4.0
Weighted by 1976 total trade of partners			
Trade concentration with partner, 1976	19.9	35.9	24.3
GNP concentration with partner, 1976	6.6	13.7	5.9
Average annual percentage increase in			
per capita GNP, 1971–76	2.9	4.4	4.0

[a] The trade figures and GNP figures for the states at the centers of the systems (United States, United Kingdom, the Common Market Six, Japan, and the Soviet Union) are not included in total world trade or total world GNP.

SOURCE: Compiled by authors.

165

TABLE 9.4
Comparison of Western European Trading Systems, 1971–76

	UK Partners (n = 24)	Common Market Six Partners (n = 31)	French Partners (n = 18)	Other Common Market Partners (n = 13)
Percentage of world trade, 1976	12.4	15.0	3.4	11.6
Percentage of world GNP, 1976	10.1	16.5	5.8	10.7
Average trade levels (millions), 1976	$2,298	$ 2,152	$ 838	$ 3,971
Average GNP (millions), 1976	$8,859	$11,181	$6,762	$17,300
Unweighted averages				
Trade concentration with partner, 1971[a]	40.2	38.1	45.1	28.3
Trade concentration with partner, 1976[a]	35.6	33.7	40.5	24.2
Percent of GNP with partner, 1971[a]	7.7	8.7	9.3	8.0
Percent of GNP with partner, 1976[a]	10.7	8.5	9.9	6.6
Average annual percentage increase in per capita GNP, 1971–76	2.1	1.6	0.4	3.0
Weighted by 1976 GNP of partners				
Trade concentration with partner, 1976[a]	18.3	18.4	18.4	18.4
Percent of GNP with partner, 1976[a]	5.1	3.9	2.7	4.5
Average annual percentage increase in per capita GNP, 1971–76	2.2	3.7	4.4	3.3
Weighted by 1976 total trade of partners				
Trade concentration with partner, 1976[a]	19.4	20.4	22.4	19.7
Percent of GNP with partner, 1976[a]	5.8	7.2	6.5	7.4
Average annual percentage increase in per capita GNP, 1971–76	2.2	3.5	3.8	3.4

[a] Concentration levels are for trade with the principal market only, not the Common Market as a whole.

SOURCE: Compiled by authors.

166

Average growth rates were higher with the weights for the Common Market partners, although not for the countries in the UK trading system. For the British trading partners larger size or more active involvement in world trade did not lead to higher growth rates. The marked improvement for the French partners reflected the fact that from 1971 to 1976 France was the largest export market for Spain in addition to 17 developing states. This improvement was largely due to the fact that Spain had a relatively high per capita GNP growth rate of 5.1 percent that naturally raised the overall average greatly.

For the 15 years from 1961 to 1976, the Western European trading partners did not compare well with countries in other trading systems in any respect. They were more active traders to some extent, but they had smaller economies. Their exports were somewhat more diversified, particularly by 1976. In regard to growth rates, however, their performance was poor. The comparison of separate European trading systems indicated that the system of the United Kingdom was responsible for the lower growth rates. The EC partners, even when the low growth averages for the French partners were included, compared much more favorably with the averages for the countries in the other trading systems. The variable partners group showed higher growth rates compared to the European systems, as had been the case for the US system.

The Western European trading systems were compared to the other systems and variable partners group with only the developing states of the world included, as was done in Chapter 8. The two European systems included a significant number of developed states, whereas Canada was the only large developed economy in the Western Hemisphere system. The developing countries in the Western European systems in 1971, in contrast to other developing states, were very small traders and small economies (see Table 9.5). The states exporting to the United Kingdom were somewhat larger traders but smaller economies than the EC partners, but compared to the other systems and the variable partners groups, the small size of the European partners was readily apparent. The 24 states linked to the Common Market countries included the 19 states linked to France as a principal market, all of which were developing states that had even lower average trading levels than the UK partners (see Table 9.2).

TABLE 9.5

Western European Trading Systems, 1961-71, Developing Countries Only

	Western European Partners (n = 46)	Other Partners (n = 42)	Variable Partners (n = 33)	UK Partners (n = 22)	Common Market Partners (n = 24)
Percentage of world trade, 1971[a]	19.9	45.7	34.4	11.0	8.9
Percentage of world GNP, 1971[a]	13.9	42.1	44.0	6.0	7.9
Average trade levels (millions), 1971	$ 258	$ 646	$ 619	$ 298	$ 220
Average GNP (millions), 1971	$1,197	$3,973	$5,289	$1,073	$1,311
Unweighted averages					
Trade concentration with partner, 1961[b]	47.5	40.2	30.9	35.4	58.6
Trade concentration with partner, 1971[b]	42.3	43.9	31.2	40.1	44.3
Percent of GNP with partner, 1961[b]	10.0	7.7	4.6	8.5	11.3
Percent of GNP with partner, 1971[b]	8.5	11.3	7.4	9.0	8.0
Average annual percentage increase in per capita GNP, 1961-71	1.9	3.0	3.3	1.9	2.0
Weighted by 1971 GNP of partners					
Trade concentration with partner, 1971[b]	31.7	38.7	22.6	25.0	36.7
Percent of GNP with partner, 1971[b]	5.7	5.2	3.0	6.4	5.1
Average annual percentage increase in per capita GNP, 1961-71	1.5	2.9	3.0	1.1	1.9
Weighted by 1971 total trade of partners					
Trade concentration with partner, 1971[b]	27.2	35.2	28.4	23.4	31.9
Percent of GNP with partner, 1971[b]	8.1	10.9	7.3	8.4	7.6
Average annual percentage increase in per capita GNP, 1961-71	1.1	4.2	5.5	0.3	2.0

[a] World trade and world GNP totals for 1971 incorporate only the figures for the developing countries.

[b] Concentration levels are for trade with the principal market only, not the Common Market as a whole.

SOURCE: Compiled by authors.

The developing countries in the European trading systems as a group had declining trade and GNP concentrations unlike the other two groups. Within the individual systems, however, the states linked to the United Kingdom were increasing their export concentrations, while the countries linked to EC countries were in a period of export diversification. Since many states in the system were associate members of the Common Market, the trade was often going to other members of the EC, a possibility less open to the members of the British trading system in this period. The countries in both the British and EC trading systems had low growth rates compared to those of developing states in the other trading systems and in the variable partners group.

Some differences became apparent with the weighted averages. The trade concentration levels of the European partners were lower than for the other partners group, and the GNP concentration was roughly the same (being somewhat higher with the GNP weight and lower with the total trade weight). The states in the British system were less reliant in trade terms on the market of the United Kingdom, although they still had a larger percentage of GNP committed to that trade, a situation reflecting their role as more active traders. The weighted growth rates of the Western European partners were still low compared to those of the other groups of developing countries. The averages for the countries in the UK trading system were particularly low.

For 1971–76, the developing countries in the Western European systems as a group were more similar to developing countries in other systems than had been the case in the previous decade. The 16 states in the British system, however, were extremely small economic units and small traders (see Table 9.6). In fact, both 1976 averages were below the 1971 averages for the 22 states in the British system in the previous decade. Obviously, the larger developing economic units had either shifted to other systems or to variable markets. The concentration levels for the developing states that were in trading systems, either Western European or others, were similar in this period, but average growth rates were again low for the countries in the European systems and particularly so for the EC partners. The low unweighted averages for this period for the 17 developing French partners lowered the overall EC averages.

TABLE 9.6
Western European Trading Systems, 1971-76, Developing Countries Only

	Western European Partners (n = 43)	Other Partners (n = 51)	Variable Partners (n = 28)	UK Partners (n = 16)	Common Market Partners (n = 27)
Percentage of world trade, 1976[a]	14.2	68.2	17.6	1.5	12.7
Percentage of world GNP, 1976[a]	13.0	44.0	43.0	1.4	11.6
Average trade levels (millions), 1976	$ 832	$ 3,357	$ 1,579	$ 230	$1,189
Average GNP (millions), 1976	$3,576	$10,151	$18,074	$1,106	$5,099
Unweighted averages					
Trade concentration with partner, 1971[b]	42.8	38.6	26.9	46.0	41.0
Trade concentration with partner, 1976[b]	38.2	41.6	27.0	42.2	35.9
Percent of GNP with partner, 1971[b]	9.1	9.6	6.2	8.3	9.7
Percent of GNP with partner, 1976[b]	10.4	12.5	7.8	12.3	9.2
Average annual percentage increase in per capita GNP, 1971-76	1.5	2.8	3.2	2.1	1.2
Weighted by 1976 GNP of partner					
Trade concentration with partner, 1976[b]	21.0	32.1	22.6	25.5	20.5
Percent of GNP with partner, 1976[b]	5.6	9.1	2.2	6.8	5.4
Average annual percentage increase in per capita GNP, 1971-76	3.5	4.7	4.0	1.2	3.7
Weighted by 1976 total trade of partner					
Trade concentration with partner, 1976[b]	23.9	30.6	25.3	29.7	23.3
Percent of GNP with partner, 1976[b]	10.9	15.7	9.9	9.6	11.0
Average annual percentage increase in per capita GNP, 1971-76	3.9	4.6	3.9	1.6	4.2

[a] World trade and world GNP totals for 1976 incorporate only the figures for the developing countries.
[b] Concentration levels are for trade with the principal market only, not the Common Market as a whole.

SOURCE: Compiled by the authors.

The weighted averages indicated that the smaller states had depressed the growth figures for the European partners. The larger traders and larger economies among the EC partners did have higher growth rates, although there was an opposite trend for the British partners. Given the fact that there were no large traders in this group, however, this latter trend was not particularly contradictory to the worldwide trend favoring growth among larger traders and larger economies. The trade of the EC partners had less concentrated trade with their principal market than was the case for the other partners group. They also had slightly lower growth rates. Compared to the variable partners group, no particular pattern appeared since concentration levels and growth rates varied, depending on the weight. In general, when compared to the other two partner groups, the European partners had slightly lower growth rates, greater GNP concentrations, and similar levels of trade concentration.

The preceding discussion illustrates that the developing countries in the Western European systems generally had not fared as well as the other developing countries. Their growth rates, particularly for the French and British partners, were usually lower than the other groups. The US partners, by way of comparison, had higher growth rates in the 1961–71 period and higher or equivalent growth (depending on the weight) from 1971 to 1976. The developing countries in all other systems, including the US system, also performed better in terms of growth. The small economic size and the lower levels of trade of many of the countries in the Western European systems may have proven to be a handicap to growth, a conclusion confirmed by the general finding that greater trade and economic size were associated with better growth rates. The improvement for the EC partners in the second five-year period might be a positive sign for the countries involved. Since the developing countries that had the United Kingdom as their principal market consisted of very small territories, they may face continuing growth problems.

REGIONALISM AND PROTECTIONISM IN THE
WESTERN EUROPEAN TRADING SYSTEMS

The largely Eurafrican trading systems discussed above exemplify the trend toward regional trading blocs.

In addition to the different geographic focus of these systems compared to the US system, they included both industrialized and developing states that were connected to the principal European markets. The regionalism in the case of the EC has been buttressed by a whole series of treaty arrangements culminating with the admission of the United Kingdom. Although the former Commonwealth preferences that existed in the case of the United Kingdom shared the attribute of formal arrangements, they did lack a regional focus. Such regionalism and various kinds of protectionism have had effects on all the states in the trading systems, as well as other countries, industrialized and developing alike, outside the European systems.

The Developing Countries in the Trading Systems

Most of the developing states in the European trading systems have been linked to their principal markets by formal documents. Since such economic links were undertaken by conscious choice rather than through the operations of the international marketplace, a determination of the advantages and costs of such arrangements becomes important. The developing countries have obviously expected greater gains to occur from association than would have existed had they remained outside the structure of the EC. The additional associate members indicate that leaders in these developing countries have seen such a connection as an advantageous one.

A very noticeable pattern in Tables 9.5 and 9.6 is that the growth rates of the developing countries in both European systems were below those of the developing states that were in other trading systems and that had variable principal markets. This finding might indicate that the maintenance of the formal trading links with the European markets worked to the disadvantage of the developing states involved. While there can be little doubt as to the poor relative growth performance of these states, such low growth could also have reflected the initial low levels of development in the African states compared to those in countries in Latin America or Asia. The NICs that have displayed the most rapid growth have been in these latter two areas, not Africa, and the NICs have been in other trading systems or in the variable partners group.

The fact that the European trading systems contained many of the least developed nations in the world contributed to the poor growth averages between 1961 and 1976. The per capita growth rates for the African states were also lower because the African region has had some of the highest rates of population increase. Such rapid population growth often directly hinders economic growth and lowers the rate of GNP per capita increases (cf. Stockwell and Laidlaw 1981, chap. 3). Thus, while a neocolonialist would argue that the poor economic base resulted from past colonial practices, or a neo-Marxist could claim that past capitalist exploitation created the poor base, the poorer economic performance still becomes less surprising given such constraints as rapid population increase. Ultimately, the proof of the value of formal association can only be determined by ascertaining whether growth would have been better without association. Such a calculation is, of course, essentially impossible to make in any definitive fashion.

If association was designed to even more closely link some developing states to European markets or to provide these states with greater market opportunities (implicitly at the expense of the other developing countries), its success has been limited. The associate members have remained heavily dependent on European markets, although as Tables 9.5 and 9.6 indicate, they are less dependent on any single market. The diversification that has occurred has most often been in exports to other EC members (Matthews 1977, p. 49; Ouattara 1973, p. 529). Trade expansion between the associate members and European markets has not occurred as rapidly as hoped. In fact, trade between the ACP countries and the EC has not expanded as rapidly as trade between the EC and other developing areas (Dolan 1978, p. 372; Feld 1976, p. 107). This situation would seem to indicate that even with associate membership, opportunities have been lost to other developing states.

While the ACP states have indeed lost some ground in a relative sense in European markets, it is possible that association status was still advantageous. Association agreements could have prevented even greater trade losses. The associate members, most of which achieved independence about 1960, had trade links that had been protected while they were colonies. As colonies, they had already received subsidies in some cases or enjoyed favorable tariff considerations. If these states had entered the world trading system and been forced to compete without the associate status, the relative decline of trade with the EC could have been even greater (Frey-Wouters 1980, pp. 182-83; Matthews 1977, p. 47). In effect, the initial levels of trade between the colonies and Europe could have been artificially high. Thus, the slower growth of ACP trade with European markets reflected an adjustment to a different and new position in the world trade regime.

Primary commodities have been an important component of trade in the European systems for both the European markets and the developing countries. The European nations have a greater concern with trade in raw materials than has been the case for the United States or the Soviet Union. Like Japan, the industrialized European countries are resource poor (Serfaty 1981, p. 16; Vaitsos 1982, p. 174). As seen in Chapter 4, European countries, such as West Germany, Switzerland, and Italy, relied on manufactures for more than 85 percent of their exports in 1978, while others, such as the United Kingdom, France, Belgium/Luxembourg, and Sweden, were near or over 80 percent in the same year. These figures are a reflection of the lack of raw materials in many, though not all, European countries. The developing countries in the trading systems, on the other hand, are exporters of primary commodities, so they have naturally been concerned with trade in these products. Unlike the NICs in Latin America and Asia, they lack diversified export mixes. Also, their relatively small economic size and levels of trade would tend to make them less influential in producer associations with a few exceptions such as the position of Zambia and Zaire, which are two of the four founding members of the Intergovernmental Council of Copper Exporting Countries (CIPEC).

Given the scarcity of natural resources, the European nations have been interested in world commodity trade both in terms of price and in terms of assured access to needed raw materials. Critics have seen the association arrangements as an effort to control supplies of raw materials (Dolan 1978, p. 389; Frey-Wouters 1980; Galtung 1973, p. 59; Green 1980). Although the Yaoundé and Lomé Conventions dealt with other issues than access to raw materials, they have indeed facilitated such access. Efforts have been made to favor exploitation of sources of raw materials by European companies, and the second Lomé Convention included provisions for giving European firms preferential opportunities for developing raw materials at the expense of Japanese and American companies (Mytelka and Dolan 1980, p. 237). While helping to meet European needs for primary commodities, these efforts have also tended to maintain the concentration of ACP export trade with European markets (Twitchett 1980, p. 150).

Some concessions were made to the developing EC associates in return for access to raw materials. The European countries have been willing to pay somewhat higher prices for some commodities and have given more aid as specified in the various Lomé and Yaoundé agreements. The first Lomé Convention created a stabilization fund (STABEX), continued in the second Lomé Convention, that was designed to limit price fluctuations for some products and to provide some security of supply (Frey-Wouters 1980, p. 54). To date, the STABEX system has been primarily applied to agricultural products, although the associate members have been pressing for the extension of the principles to mineral commodities as well. It has proven to be useful in terms of stabilizing prices for some products (Persaud 1980, pp. 95-99) and thus at least has met one of the goals often sought by developing countries that rely on commodity exports.

On the whole, as with other aspects of association, the developing members have probably gained in the short-term from this trade-off between access and price. The possibility of higher long-term costs does remain. Association could lead to a situation of dependence and the resulting economic distortion that dependency-neocolonial theorists argue exists in such a relationship. Similarly, free trade advocates would argue that it has led to trade contrary to the ideas of comparative advantage and has ultimately limited the trade of the EC associates.

The Prevalence of Protectionism
and Neomercantilism

Neomercantile and protectionist practices have been common in all the EC countries. In varying degrees these practices have been directed at other industrialized countries outside the agreement structure of the EC, the NICs, and the developing countries, including at times the EC associate members. Such protectionism may have increased the size of the EC trading system by encouraging other countries to enter formal agreements to alleviate some of the disadvantages that they were facing in terms of market access or price stability for primary commodities.

The EC countries have been sensitive to competition for some domestic manufacturing industries that come from other industrialized states. The creation of the Common Market itself, of course, established a basic level of protection for industries within the common tariff barriers. As noted in Chapter 8, the European countries in general have usually had higher tariff barriers than the United States; thus, this common tariff was of some importance. A direct result of this situation was the formation of the European Free Trade Association (EFTA) by countries that opposed the protectionism inherent in the EC. The applications of the United Kingdom for membership have been another indication of the disadvantages of being outside the EC. The other original EFTA members have since joined the EC or signed special agreements with it. Interestingly enough, these countries have since modified their former criticism of protectionism in the EC (Matthews 1977, p. 95).

A variety of protectionist measures have been utilized by the EC countries to protect domestic industries. These methods, such as quotas and subsidies, have been effective against the exports of developing and other developed countries. In the case of the developed countries, the EC has been particularly concerned with competition from Japan. While there is no Community-wide policy, various EC members have retained restrictions on Japanese imports, and they did not extend GATT principles to Japan, even when pressured to do so by the United States (Calleo and Rowland 1973, pp. 197, 212). The concern with Japanese competition has taken some extreme forms, as demonstrated in a news report of December 1982 detailing the French requirement that all imports of Japanese video recorders clear customs at the inland post at Poiters. The post had a small staff, which was not augmented, thus effectively preventing the Japanese products from being available in French stores during the peak Christmas period.

The European states have also reacted to competition from manufactures from the NICs (Seers 1980a, p. 312; Wionczek 1980, pp. 169-70). The European countries have negotiated voluntary export restraints and other limitations on imports threatening domestic production. Textiles, an important export item for the NICs, as was seen in Chapter 5, are just one example. The negotiation of the Multi-

Fibre Textile Agreements of 1974 and 1977 laid voluntary limits on the exports of the developing nations in certain product areas. The exclusion of the Asian members of the Commonwealth from EC associate status was another example of protectionism. In effect, associate status was conferred on those states and territories that were least competitive with weaker domestic industries (Vaitsos 1982, p. 186). In general, domestic political pressures in the disturbed economic conditions of the 1970s have resulted in levels of protectionism that are to the clear disadvantage of the developing states both inside and outside the association agreements (Franko and Stephenson 1981, p. 199; Frey-Wouters 1980, p. 115; Seers 1980b, p. 16; Twitchett 1980, p. 170), although the associate members have had some buffers against the adverse impacts.

Neomercantilism has also been present in the area of agricultural products. The Common Agricultural Policy and subsidies to farmers have limited imports from developed and developing nations. Agricultural exports by the United States to the EC have been effectively limited, as US farmers cannot undersell European farmers in most cases. New Zealand's agricultural exports have also suffered since the admission of the United Kingdom as an EC member (Mahler 1981, pp. 488-89). In fact, by 1979 the United States was close to replacing the United Kingdom as the major market for New Zealand's exports. The developing countries have also lost potential markets as a result of such protectionism. The ACP states have gained somewhat by guaranteed markets and STABEX, but while they are treated better than other developing states, they are not treated as well as the domestic European producers (Twitchett 1980, p. 168).

Even some of the advantages are more apparent than real. In good crop years in Europe the EC associates do retain their share of the domestic European market, but the subsidized European agricultural products then appear in the international market, ultimately often at the expense of the exports of the associate members. For example, although quotas provided the EC associates with export opportunities at a guaranteed price for sugar in the late 1960s and early 1970s, surpluses from the subsidized European sugar beet farmers entered the world marketplace and drove down world prices at the expense of developing country exporters, including many of the associate members (Mahler 1981, p. 478). In this way the gains made in the European market by the ACP countries may be offset by losses in the world market. The only consistent advantage to the ACP states may be the stable market and price in Europe which they acquired as a result of associate membership and the possibility that nonassociated developing states are hurt even more by European surpluses.

AN ENLARGED COMMON MARKET?

The formation of the Common Market in 1959 greatly affected world trade, a process continued by expansion and the system of trade agreements since concluded. Any extension of EC trade arrangements or expansion of full membership could have additional impacts on the world trade regime and the present regional trading systems. An enlargement of the EC would create problems for the present members if the new entrants are presently outside the present framework. When Spain, Portugal, or Turkey, for example, become full members as envisioned, their exports would gain a competitive edge compared to some of the ACP states. The Mediterranean products of these three states would gain vis-à-vis the exports of the North African associate members. Other ACP states in many cases would face competition in the areas of fruits, vegetables, and textiles (Twitchett 1980, p. 173). Since these three countries already have trade agreements with the EC directed toward full membership, closer association would be difficult to prevent, notwithstanding adverse impacts on some of the associate members.

Large numbers of new associate members from the developing countries are probably unlikely. The Asian countries, such as Hong Kong and Singapore, previously intentionally excluded, are unlikely to be offered EC associate status. Latin American states lack the specific links from the colonial periods of many of the present associates, and the ACP states would oppose any lessening of their present advantages, particularly as the Latin American countries might be very effective competitors. The ACP countries have made active efforts in the past to avoid the extension of general privileges to the developing countries at the expense of the preferences that they presently enjoy (Dolan 1978, pp. 387-88; Mytelka and Dolan 1980, p. 246).

Overall, it appears that the EC system of agreements has achieved a size that will continue for the immediate future. The system ultimately requires some limitation since universal membership would defeat the advantages of joining the EC or having associate status. Some continuation of market shifts in the world could be present, such as the shifting trade of Oceanic territories outside the ACP group toward other trading systems, as is the case for New Zealand. Although new trends could always appear, any major reorientations are unlikely. So long as regionalism remains a major factor in the world trade regime, the EC will likely constitute an impediment to an open trading regime, rather than a base from which a modified open trading regime can be established.

10 Japan and the Asia-Pacific Basin

Japan is a trading nation that has global connections. Its economic interaction with the outside world, which is rather extensive and expanding, has been largely with the world's major trading centers, such as the United States and the EC countries. For this reason it is somewhat misleading to consider Japan within the context of a specific region, such as Asia or the Pacific Basin. Nevertheless, an analysis of the trade patterns in the 1960s and 1970s shows that Japan has become the leader of a distinct trading system that might be termed the Asia-Pacific Basin. Although some members of this trading system come from outside the region, as in the other trading systems, most of them are located in the Asia-Pacific region defined broadly. The present chapter will discuss the nature of the emerging Asia-Pacific Basin community first and then the pattern of the Japanese trading system and Japan's role in the regional trade.

PACIFIC BASIN TRADE IN PERSPECTIVE

The Asia-Pacific Basin represents one of the most dynamic regions in the world; economic growth and international trade in the region have increased in the two decades from 1960 to 1980 at rates not experienced elsewhere in the world (Krause and Sekiguchi 1980a). The region could thus become the world's most viable economic center in the 1980s. The Pacific Basin region, defined broadly, includes the countries bordering on the Pacific: Australia, New Zealand, the United States, Canada, the ministates of the South Pacific, the Latin American states, and the East Asian and

Southeast Asian nations. A subarea of the Pacific Basin is the Asia-Pacific Basin, which, for the purpose of the present study, consists of the three main areas--East Asia, Southeast Asia, and Oceania--including Australia, New Zealand, Japan, China, South Korea, Taiwan, Hong Kong, and the five Association for South East Asian Nations (ASEAN) of Indonesia, Malaysia, the Philippines, Singapore, and Thailand.*

Advantages for the Pacific and Asia-Pacific Basin

The economic growth potential of the Pacific Basin has several advantages over that of other world regions (Tokuyama 1981, pp. 53-54). First, the region embraces the world's major food-producing and -exporting countries. Because the region experienced rapid population increases in the past, the capacity for food production and food imports will help assure political stability in the region, creating an environment for continuous economic growth. Southeast Asia is the world's leading rice-producing area, and some of the countries, like Thailand, are major rice exporters. The United States, Australia, and Canada are the world's major food-producing and -exporting countries, accounting for 90 percent of the global wheat shipments. The region, therefore, has the necessary ingredients for excellent performances both in the food-producing and export sectors and in the manufacturing production and export sectors.

The Pacific Basin's second advantage is its abundance of natural resources. Australia, with rich coal deposits and 15 percent of the world's total uranium deposits, is an important energy supplier. Oil deposits have been discovered on the continental shelf in the East and South China Seas, and oil and natural gas are produced and exported by Indonesia and Brunei (Harrison 1977). Forests are plentiful, as are iron ores and nonferrous metals. If supplies of these and other resources are fully developed to meet demand, and coupled with adequate investment capital and technology, a powerful economic base could be created for the industrialization of the entire region.

---

*Brunei joined ASEAN in 1984.

Still a third advantage is the presence of two of the world's leading economic and technical powers. Due to their dynamic economies and large population bases, the United States and Japan have been the sources of technical innovation and new product lines in manufacturing; they also make up two of the largest, most affluent, and most sophisticated markets in the world. Market creation through trade expansion and mutual investment would thus encourage and sustain the economic development of the Pacific Basin (Benjamin and Kurdle 1984).

The more important fourth advantage is the region's positive attitude toward the North-South economic problem. The ASEAN countries have emerged to become a cohesive economic bloc in the 1980s, maintaining active economic ties with the outside world (Crone 1983). Their development policies have generally been based more on cooperation with the developed countries than has been the case with many other developing countries. Thus, the possibility is present for a mutually beneficial economic interaction between the advanced industrialized countries and the developing ASEAN countries in the Pacific Basin. Compared with other developing regions of the world where the situation is more precarious, political and economic conditions in the Asia-Pacific region also seem more stable in a relative sense. Increased trade in the 1970s is both a reflection of and contributing factor to this stability.

Japan and the Trade Pattern in the Pacific Basin

The United States and Japan, and Canada to some extent, are obviously the key trading nations for the Pacific Basin since they are the major industrialized nations and they are linked by virtue of their geographic location. The trade of the United States and Canada with Pacific Basin countries, in fact, has been increasing faster than their trade with countries bordering the Atlantic. US exports to the ASEAN countries in 1978, for example, were 3.4 times higher than in 1972. In the same period US exports to Hong Kong rose by a factor of 3.3, to South Korea by 4.3, to Taiwan by 3.7, and to Japan by 2.6 (Tokuyama 1981, p. 54). Overall, trade between the United States and East Asia, including Japan, doubled between 1975 and 1979. In 1979, the United States provided 18.4 percent of Japanese imports and took 25.6 percent of Japanese exports, while Japan provided 12.7 percent of total US imports. Japan was thus second only to Canada as a US trading partner in terms of volume. Japan has also become the second largest trading partner for Canada, after the United States, assuming the position formerly held by the United Kingdom.

Japanese exports to world markets were very substantial in a recent decade, totaling $24 billion in 1971, $67.3 billion in 1976, and $151.5 billion in 1981. Of these exports more than half were to the Pacific Basin countries, including the United States and Canada--65.5 percent of total exports in 1970, 50.5 percent in 1975, and 56.8 percent in 1980. Although less than exports to these developed countries, Japanese exports to the Asian neighbors have also been substantial. Exports to the Asian NICs and ASEAN countries accounted for approximately 20 percent of Japan's world exports in the 1970s--11.5 percent to Asian NICs in 1970, 9.8 percent in 1975, and 12.1 percent in 1980, as compared with 9.4 percent to ASEAN countries in 1970, 10.5 percent in 1975, and 10.0 percent in 1980.* Japanese exports to China in the 1970s, although relatively small as a proportion of total trade, were also substantial. China was the market for 2.1 to 4.0 percent of Japanese exports and was the source of 1.3 to 3.1 percent of Japanese imports in the 1970s. With the entrepot trade through Hong Kong, China as a trade partner probably constituted approximately 5 or 6 percent of Japanese imports or exports in the 1970s.

Japan's trade with the Asian countries has dramatically increased in the post-World War II years, thereby displacing former European colonial powers and surpassing the United States by a large margin (Hellmann 1975, p. 29). Nevertheless, trade with its Asian neighbors in the region was not as extensive in the 1970s as it was in the pre-World War II years. The substantial Japanese trade since World War II has flowed in different patterns than it did in the prewar years. Japan's Asian neighbors, for instance, accounted for 50.3 percent of Japanese exports in 1913 and 63.1 percent in 1936. The same countries provided 51.9 percent of Japanese imports in 1913 and 53.2 percent in 1936 (Lockwood 1954, p. 395). A larger proportion of Japanese exports in the 1970s, as

---

*Singapore is included in both the ASEAN and Asian NIC figures.

already noted, went to the developed rather than to the developing countries. In this respect Japan was not dissimilar to other major developed free market economies, which also exported primarily to industrialized and industrializing states. Imports, on the other hand, came primarily from developing countries, reflecting the need for raw materials and petroleum for Japanese industry.

THE JAPANESE TRADING SYSTEM

The Japanese trading system between 1961 and 1971 overlapped the Asia-Pacific Basin trading system. Using the same method of identifying trade partners as in Chapter 8, seven nations were included in Japan's trading system in the 1960s. Two of them were Arab countries in the Middle East (Saudi Arabia and United Arab Emirates), three were Oceanic countries or territories (Australia and Papua-New Guinea), and two were in Asia (Thailand and Ryukyus). In 1971 the Japanese trading system had increased its membership to 15. In addition to the five already in the system (Saudi Arabia, UAE, Australia, Thailand, and Papua-New Guinea), ten were added in 1971, including six in the Middle East and North Africa (Iran, Jordan, Kuwait, Lebanon, Oman, Somalia), two in Southeast Asia (Brunei and Indonesia), and two in Oceania (British Solomons and Gilberts).

The Japanese trading system from 1961 to 1971 was thus centered in the Asia-Pacific Basin with an extension into the Middle East. The Japanese trading partners, as indicated by their average trade levels, were larger traders than countries in other trading systems or the variable partners group (see Table 10.1). The average unweighted trade concentrations were similar to countries in other trading systems and lower than the variable partners group. Average GNP concentrations went from being relatively low in 1961 to being quite high in 1971. The growth rates for the limited number of Japanese partners were quite high in relation to the other countries.

The weighted averages for these ten years displayed some differences. Trade concentration levels were lower for the larger traders and larger economies in the Japanese system as evidenced by the decline in the levels with the weights applied. GNP concentrations remained higher than was the case for the other groups, but the disparity

TABLE 10.1
Japanese Trading System, 1961–71

	Japanese Partners (n = 7)	Other Partners (n = 104)	Variable Partners (n = 36)
Percentage of world trade, 1971[a]	7.0	76.4	16.6
Percentage of world GNP, 1971[a]	5.9	69.0	25.1
Average trade levels (millions), 1971	$1,419	$1,041	$ 653
Average GNP (millions), 1971	$7,100	$6,563	$5,784
Unweighted averages			
Trade concentration with partner, 1961	40.7	41.3	32.2
Trade concentration with partner, 1971	42.3	40.3	31.5
Percent of GNP with partner, 1961	6.5	8.0	4.7
Percent of GNP with partner, 1971	12.8	8.7	7.3
Average annual percentage increase in per capita GNP, 1961–71	6.2	2.5	3.3
Weighted by 1971 GNP of partners			
Trade concentration with partner, 1971	28.1	36.1	21.4
Percent of GNP with partner, 1971	5.4	5.1	2.7
Average annual percentage increase in per capita GNP, 1961–71	3.9	3.2	3.3
Weighted by 1971 total trade of partners			
Trade concentration with partner, 1971	26.0	35.4	26.8
Percent of GNP with partner, 1971	8.7	7.3	6.6
Average annual percentage increase in per capita GNP, 1961–71	5.4	3.3	5.4

[a] The trade figures and GNP figures for the states at the centers of the systems (United States, United Kingdom, the Common Market Six, Japan, and the Soviet Union) are not included in total world trade or total world GNP.

SOURCE: Compiled by authors.

185

was not as marked as had been the case with the simple averages. Unlike the other trading systems considered earlier, growth rates in the larger economies and larger traders did not raise the average growth for the system as a whole.

Of the countries in the Japanese trading system from 1971 to 1976, some of the Middle Eastern members were indirectly connected to Japan through reliance on other members as their principal markets. A number of countries in the variable partners group had developed ties with Japan toward the end of the period and the years after it. Malaysia had shifted to Japan as its major market, a trend with every appearance of continuing. Exports from the People's Republic of China to Japan were also increasing. In some years Japan displaced Hong Kong as the principal market for China. During the 1970s, Japan and Hong Kong were roughly equal in terms of serving as a market for Chinese exports, indicating that Hong Kong's former role of entrepot for Chinese trade might be declining.

In this second period the Japanese partners were active participants in the world trade regime. The percentage of world trade that they accounted for was double their percentage of world GNP (see Table 10.2). Their average trade concentrations were similar to those of partners in other systems, although the average increased slightly between 1971 and 1976. GNP concentrations remained higher than for the other two groups, as would be expected with their relative trade and GNP levels. The unweighted growth rate was higher than for the other partners group and equal to that of the variable partners group.

The weighted averages displayed a different pattern from the preceding decade. The Japanese trade concentrations declined relative to the other two groups, but the GNP concentrations increased. The growth rates in this period were higher with the weights, indicating that it was the Japanese partners with larger economies and that were larger traders that had had the higher rates of growth. This change was in keeping with the findings of the previous chapters. It could have reflected the presence of new members, such as Kuwait and Oman, in the system in this period. The increase in petroleum prices in the 1970s would also have raised the growth rates of the OPEC members of the trading system and thus the system average as a whole.

TABLE 10.2
Japanese Trading System, 1971–76

	Japanese Partners (n = 15)	Other Partners (n = 101)	Variable Partners (n = 31)
Percentage of world trade, 1976[a]	23.5	65.1	11.4
Percentage of world GNP, 1976[a]	11.6	63.1	25.3
Average trade levels (millions), 1976	$ 6,952	$ 2,865	$ 1,639
Average GNP (millions), 1976	$16,176	$13,132	$17,166
Unweighted averages			
Trade concentration with partner, 1971	36.7	38.6	27.9
Trade concentration with partner, 1976	37.8	37.5	27.6
Percent of GNP with partner, 1971	10.0	8.4	6.2
Percent of GNP with partner, 1976	13.3	10.2	7.7
Average annual percentage increase in per capita GNP, 1961–71	3.8	2.3	3.7
Weighted by 1976 GNP of partners			
Trade concentration with partner, 1976	28.3	30.5	22.3
Percent of GNP with partner, 1976	10.6	6.8	2.3
Average annual percentage increase in per capita GNP, 1971–76	4.9	3.8	4.0
Weighted by 1976 total trade of partners			
Trade concentration with partner, 1976	25.7	32.8	24.3
Percent of GNP with partner, 1976	15.1	10.2	9.2
Average annual percentage increase in per capita GNP, 1971–76	4.8	3.6	4.0

[a] The trade figures and GNP figures for the states at the centers of the systems (United States, United Kingdom, the Common Market Six, Japan, and the Soviet Union) are not included in total world trade or total world GNP.

SOURCE: Compiled by authors.

The comparison of only the developing countries in
the three groups did not change the unweighted averages
for the members of the Japanese trading system since Australia was the only developed member. The Japanese partners remained active and large traders between 1961 and
1971 (see Table 10.3). Trade concentrations were similar
to the developing countries in other systems, but the GNP
concentrations of the Japanese partners started low and
finished high in comparison with the other two groups.
With the weighted averages, trade concentrations declined,
but the GNP concentration was still high. The growth
rates did not decline with the total trade weight, and they
declined much less with the GNP weight compared to the
unweighted average than had been the case for the system
as a whole.

From 1971 to 1976, the Japanese partners were extremely active traders compared to the other groups of developing states (see Table 10.4). The unweighted trade
concentrations were equivalent to the other partners group,
but GNP concentrations were noticeably higher. The unweighted average growth rate was higher than the other
two groups, particularly the other partners group. The
results with the weighted averages showed declines in
trade concentrations for the Japanese partners to the level
of the variable partners group. The GNP concentrations
were still the highest for the Japanese partners. The average growth rates were even higher with the weights;
thus, there was an indication that in this period larger
economic size and involvement in the world trade regime
facilitated growth. The growth rates of the developing
members of the Japanese trading system were again easily
the highest of the three groups of developing countries.

The Japanese trading system differed from the other
trading systems in two particular respects. The Japanese
developing partners generally had better weighted growth
rates than developing states in the other trading systems
and the variable partners group. This finding was not
surprising compared to the Western European systems inas-
much as the Asian and the Middle Eastern members of the
Japanese trading system were generally more economically
advanced than many of the African states. This difference
existed, however, for the Latin American countries in the
US system and the countries with shifting markets. A number of NICs were in the US trading system and the variable
partners group, and this last group also included a number

TABLE 10.3

Japanese Trading System, 1961–71, Developing Countries Only

	Japanese Partners (n = 6)	Other Partners (n = 82)	Variable Partners (n = 33)
Percentage of world trade, 1971[a]	7.9	57.7	34.4
Percentage of world GNP, 1971[a]	3.3	52.7	44.0
Average trade levels (millions), 1971	$ 782	$ 418	$ 619
Average GNP (millions), 1971	$2,175	$2,547	$5,289
Unweighted averages			
Trade concentration with partner, 1961	44.2	44.0	30.9
Trade concentration with partner, 1971	44.8	42.9	31.2
Percent of GNP with partner, 1961	7.1	9.0	4.6
Percent of GNP with partner, 1971	14.2	9.5	7.4
Average annual percentage increase in			
per capita GNP, 1961–71	6.7	2.2	3.3
Weighted by 1971 GNP of partners			
Trade concentration with partner, 1971	29.0	37.4	22.6
Percent of GNP with partner, 1971	8.4	5.1	3.0
Average annual percentage increase in			
per capita GNP, 1961–71	5.9	2.4	3.0
Weighted by 1971 total trade of partners			
Trade concentration with partner, 1971	23.9	34.0	28.4
Percent of GNP with partner, 1971	14.1	9.5	7.3
Average annual percentge increase in			
per capita GNP, 1961–71	8.0	2.6	5.5

[a] The trade figures and GNP figures for the states at the centers of the systems (United States, United Kingdom, the Common Market Six, Japan, and the Soviet Union) are not included in total world trade or total world GNP.

SOURCE: Compiled by authors.

TABLE 10.4

Japanese Trading System, 1971-76, Developing Countries Only

	Japanese Partners (n = 14)	Other Partners (n = 80)	Variable Partners (n = 28)
Percentage of world trade, 1976[a]	36.3	46.1	17.6
Percentage of world GNP, 1976[a]	14.1	42.9	43.0
Average trade levels (millions), 1976	$ 6,509	$1,448	$ 1,579
Average GNP (millions), 1976	$11,831	$6,323	$18,074
Unweighted averages			
Trade concentration with partner, 1971	37.3	40.9	26.9
Trade concentration with partner, 1976	38.1	40.4	27.0
Percent of GNP with partner, 1971	10.4	9.2	6.2
Percent of GNP with partner, 1976	13.9	11.1	7.8
Average annual percentage increase in per capita GNP, 1971-76	3.9	1.9	3.2
Weighted by 1976 GNP of partners			
Trade concentration with partner, 1976	25.6	30.8	22.6
Percent of GNP with partner, 1976	12.8	6.8	2.2
Average annual percentage increase in per capita GNP, 1971-76	6.1	3.9	4.0
Weighted by 1976 total trade of partners			
Trade concentration with partner, 1976	24.5	33.3	25.3
Percent of GNP with partner, 1976	16.4	13.7	9.9
Average annual percentage increase in per capita GNP, 1971-76	5.1	4.0	3.9

[a] The trade figures and GNP figures for the states at the centers of the systems (United States, United Kingdom, the Common Market Six, Japan, and the Soviet Union) are not included in total world trade or total world GNP.

SOURCE: Compiled by authors.

of OPEC members. The other major distinction was that the Japanese partners were among the most active traders in the world relative to their GNP levels, as shown by their percentages of world trade and world GNP. Thus, the Japanese trading system as a whole provided support for the idea that greater involvement in world trade facilitated growth and perhaps development as well.

POLICY ISSUES IN THE ASIA-PACIFIC BASIN

Japan's Role in the Trading System

In spite of Japan's global trade links, the Japanese role in intra-Asia-Pacific Basin trade has, as previously noted, become extensive in recent years--a reflection of Japan's geographic location and sociocultural status as an East Asian country. Since World War II Japan's participation in the intra-Asian trade has gradually increased to the point where Japan's exports to Asian developing countries increased, between 1971 and 1980, from 26.3 to 33.9 percent of Japan's total and imports from 32.0 to 53.9 percent of the total. As Asia's leading industrial economy and trading nation, Japan's position in Asia-Pacific trade is paramount, as is the prospect of Japan playing a catalyst role in the Pacific Basin trade in the future (Okita 1979).

Discussion on policy issues relative to Japan as the leading trading nation in the Asia-Pacific region may be grouped in three areas--Japanese trade dependence, Japanese competition with its trading partners, and Japanese economic adjustment and adaptation.

Japan is a trading nation that exports manufactured products to world markets in return for imports of fuel and raw materials. In sharp contrast to its traditional role of insularity in the feudal days, export has become a way of life for the Japanese in modern times. As the world's second largest industrial economy, the degree of Japan's dependence on foreign sources of raw material is dangerously high. Its paucity of domestic natural resources has meant that Japan must purchase primary and agricultural commodities from abroad (Sanderson 1978). This vulnerability has led the Japanese to a national preoccupation with "economic security." In the 1970s Japan became particularly sensitive to the rise in raw material prices and the oil crisis that raised the price for energy.

Japan's dependence on imported raw materials is well known. Nearly 100 percent of critical primary commodities, such as iron ore and petroleum, and high percentages of other materials and agricultural commodities, such as wheat and soybeans, are imported (Hellmann 1975, pp. 30-31; JEI Report, July 2, 1982). Japan has an acute sense of insecurity vis-à-vis overseas supply of raw materials and food commodities. Maintaining food self-sufficiency at least in rice production, although with high economic costs, has been a national policy in the post-World War II years (Sanderson 1978). Japan has adopted certain policy measures to protect itself from the vulnerability in the supply of raw materials and fuels. These measures have included substitution of materials, substitution of suppliers, stabilization of suppliers, flexible foreign policy initiatives, and domestic economic programs to meet externally induced shortages. On the agricultural trade issue Japan has pursued a policy of protectionism by imposing restrictions on the import of foods. Its policy is sustained by the pressure of strong farm organization and interest groups in Japan (Talbot and Kihl 1982).

Given the importance of foreign trade for the country, Japan has not been sufficiently active in maintaining and preserving a world trade regime based on liberal trade practices. Since Japan must export in order to import raw materials, the country should be in the forefront of maintaining and promoting a global liberal trade regime. As agricultural trade disputes between the United States and Japan illustrate, however, Japan has not done enough according to some critics, who attach symbolic significance to Japanese concession on agricultural trade issues and on removing import restrictions on cherries, oranges, and beef (Castle ahd Hemmi 1982).

Japan has also practiced protectionism in industrial sectors according to some critics. Meiji Japan encouraged target industries by setting up factories under state ownership and then selling them to private interests once they became viable. Postwar Japan continued to encourage basic industry, largely through tax and credit policies that allowed Japan to remain competitive in world markets. Without this kind of support, which allows Japan to produce inexpensive steel, the prices of Japanese automobiles sold abroad, for example, would be much higher (Hofheinz and Calder 1982, p. 179; Hadley 1981, pp. 267-71). The Ministry of International Trade and Industry (MITI) and Japan's

External Trade Organization (JETRO) have provided active guidance to the export-oriented industries to capture overseas markets.

Japan has used protectionism as a means rather than an end in itself in its overall trade policies. Its trade policy in the past, for instance, was heavily geared to protect infant industries until they become strong enough to be competitive in world markets. For this purpose the Japanese government often extended subsidies and supports to such key industries as steel, petrochemicals, shipping, and semiconductors (U.S. GAO 1979, 1982).

Japan's trade competition with the Asian NICs in third countries has become a contentious issue. Asian NICs have emerged as serious Japanese competitors for markets in the developed countries, especially in the export of labor-intensive manufactures, such as textiles, clothing, and travel goods (Okumura 1981, pp. 262-69). As some of the NICs have enhanced the industrial structures of their economies in recent years, they have become competitive with Japan in world markets for heavy industrial goods as well, cutting into such capital-intensive industrial sectors as shipbuilding, steel products, and electric appliances. Further, since these rapidly growing and dynamic East Asian NICs are most anxious to export more of their own manufactured products to Japan, they are unhappy with the Japanese reluctance to open its market to their manufactured exports.

Japan's trade partnership with the People's Republic of China is another problem area for Japan. Since the normalization of diplomatic relations in 1972, and especially since the 1977 signing of the Treaty of Friendship and Commerce, China has become an important trade partner that is rapidly falling into the Asia-Pacific Basin trading system. Since 1981, however, the earlier euphoria on China trade has proven to be an illusion for the Japanese as China reassessed its four modernization policy goals by scaling down the initial agreement for the massive infusion of Japanese loans for investment that were to be paid by increasing exports of Chinese petroleum and coal. Initial expectations regarding the potential of Chinese purchases of Japanese technology have not worked out and proved to be too optimistic (JEI Report January 4, 1980; November 14, 1980; July 16, 1982).

The Japanese government adjustment assistance has typically been undertaken by MITI in the industry con-

cerned. Adjustment policy goals typically include the promotion of either hoarding or abolition of excess capacity
and the reorientation of the industry in new directions.
Although primarily targeted to assist small- and medium-
sized enterprises, as in the Textile Industry Acts, more
established and viable industries have also come under
government protection in recent years, as witness the 1978
Structural Depression Act (Yamazawa 1981). Under this act
the government provided assistance to those manufacturing
industries severely affected by the growing international
competition. The 11 manufacturing industries so designated
included electric furnace steel making, ferro-silicon manufacturing, aluminum smelting, synthetic fiber making, spin-
ning, ammonia and urea fertilizer production, phosphatic
acid production, vinyl chloride production, paper board
making, and shipbuilding (Yamazawa 1981, p. 437).

Flexible industrial policies have been the instrument
for enabling Japanese competitiveness in world marketplaces
and the key to the apparent success of Japan in world
trade (U.S. GAO 1979, 1982). Japan's industrial policies
have changed significantly over time in response to changes
in both international and domestic economies. The Japanese
approach to industrial adjustment, for instance, has been
to develop specific industries with good world market prospects and shift resources from weak industries. Specific
measures under this flexible policy have thus included supporting growing industries, such as computer, aircraft, and
robotics, and assisting declining industries, such as shipbuilding and textile, to adjust. Also, the Japanese government has generally ensured selected industries' access
to inexpensive capital, as in the case of the steel, auto,
and shipbuilding industries in the 1950s and 1960s and
electronics and machinery industries in the 1970s (Hofheinz
and Calder 1982, p. 179).

The flexible Japanese industrial policies of adaptation have been aimed at assuring success and high growth.
The emphasis of government support has shifted from heavy
industries in the early years after World War II to sophisticated technological products in the 1980s. Industries
were assisted in developing and diffusing technologies
throughout the economy that would contribute to high value
added through increased productivity and resource conservation. Such government assistance has been especially evident in the computer, robotics, and aircraft industries.
Japan has also successfully assisted its less competitive

industries in adjusting to declines as a result of such factors as rising labor costs, sluggish world demand, foreign competition and import restrictions, and increased raw materials and energy costs (U.S. GAO 1982). Although the financial support for industrial development has been coupled with extensive controls over trade and capital flows in Japan, the government has basically encouraged mechanisms that use incentives rather than the control of business activities (Rapp 1975; U.S. GAO 1982).

Greater Regionalization of Trade?

Regional trade blocs, whether or not desirable, have been in existence for some time. Regionalization of trade could herald and unleash "Balkanization" of world trade, conjuring up an image of incessant and escalating trade wars among the major trading nations. In the context of the Pacific Basin trade, including the Asia-Pacific region, this trend of regionalization was facilitated by the end of US hegemony and Japan's emergence as an economic force in world trade (Krause and Sekiguchi 1980b, 1980c). The changes in the economic interaction in the Pacific Basin were affected by four world crises in the 1970s--the breakdown of the international monetary system, the 1972-74 rise in raw materials prices and commodity boom, the 1974 oil crises, and the worldwide recession and resultant weak economic recovery (Krause and Sekiguchi 1980a).

A variety of nations constitute the membership of the present trading system in the Pacific Basin, including raw materials producers, petroleum exporters, industrialized states, and newly industrializing economies (that have relied on Japan for capital goods). The economies of these countries are dynamic when compared with those of the countries in other trading systems. The Japanese trading partners, for example, demonstrated greater growth on virtually every measure that was used than countries in other trading systems or the ones that had variable markets. The growth rates for the Japanese partners were noticeably higher than those for members of the US trading system or the Western European systems. Japan itself has consistently outperformed other countries in terms of domestic growth and has risen to the status of a major world economic power.

The overall dynamism of the Japanese trading system may be explained in two ways. It is possible that vitality of the Japanese market attracted the faster growing nations. On the other hand, the countries most closely involved in trading relationships with the Japanese market might have made economic gains as a result of their ties with such a dynamic principal market. In either case, the economic gains of all the countries involved, particularly when compared to other areas, is one factor that may facilitate further integration and perhaps even a widening of the trading system.

Regional economic integration in Asia in the future is thus feasible. Certain negative and positive factors, however, would inhibit or facilitate the process of trade cooperation and economic integration in the Asia-Pacific region. The negative factors are largely psychological and historic. Japan, as a defeated nation in World War II, was admitted into GATT in 1955 and the OECD in 1964 with the strong backing of the United States, in spite of some initial objection by the European countries (Gilpin 1971, pp. 62-63; Saxonhouse 1977). Economic recovery and rapid growth in the post-World War II years were possible through active Japanese participation in the liberal trade regime through trade expansion in the export of manufactured products. As a successful trading nation Japan would have the least incentive to sacrifice this current status if such participation in an Asia-Pacific Basin trade bloc would entail negative trade-offs. In fact, there is a strong Japanese fear of rejection if they were suddenly to be excluded from the club of Western industrial countries (Scalapino 1977; Sato 1977; Saxonhouse 1977). Japan, in fact, has tried hard to avoid "playing favorites" with Asian neighbors to dispel any misunderstanding by the Western countries.

Many Asian countries share similar psychological inhibition toward an Asia-Pacific regional community in which Japan plays an active role. Small Asian countries' fears of Japanese economic presence and aggressive moves have been real and undeniable. Japan's overpowering economic role in the region is largely feared, and its economic expansion has been strongly resisted by other Asian countries in the name of resisting a resurgence of Japanese economic imperialism. An example is Singapore's attitude toward Japan's expansive role in Asia and resulting encouragement of Western countries' economic presence in the area as a counterweight and balance to Japan. This anti-Japanese sentiment is widely shared by other Southeast Asian and

East Asian countries. A Japan-dominant Asia-Pacific Basin trading system conjures up for many Asian nations the imperial Japanese scheme of a Greater East Asia Co-Prosperity Sphere that was advanced before and during World War II (Jo 1968). Despite the positive-sounding imagery of a Pan-Asian movement, Japan proved to be more than the first among equals, and other Asian nations were made to play a subservient role in fulfilling the Japanese ambition of an Asian empire.

The objective reality of increasing economic interdependence among the Asian countries, however, may counterbalance the psychological and historic inhibitions toward a process of economic regionalism in the Asia-Pacific area. There exist obvious complementaries between the resource-poor developed countries like Japan, the resource-rich developed countries like Australia, and developing countries like the ASEAN members (Drysdale 1978). As Asia's leading industrial power, Japan desperately needs to secure resources and raw materials, and only the resource-rich countries in Asia and the Pacific Basin are in a position to ensure security of supply. Moreover, as Asia's leading trading nation, Japan also needs markets for its products. Other developed and developing Asian countries need the latest technology and markets from Japan to achieve their policy goals of development through trade expansion. On this complementarity of expected mutual benefits between Japan and other Asian countries, the firm foundation for an evolving process of economic interaction in the Asia-Pacific region could be erected.

From the Japanese perspective, the formation of a regional community for promoting trade and economic cooperation is the best guarantee for the national goal of resource security. Both bilateral and multilateral channels have been utilized in attaining these policy objectives. Bilaterally, Japan has negotiated with the resource-rich Asian countries for long-term commodity agreements. The 1978 Japan-China barter agreement is a case in point. Under this agreement China agreed to provide Japan with petroleum and coal in exchange for Japan's delivery of $10 billion worth of high-quality steel and other industrial products. The amount was subsequently scaled down as China failed to fulfill its part of the agreement (JEI Report, July 16, 1982). A multilateral arrangement, involving Japan, host countries in Asia, and Western multinationals, has also been suggested as a means of ensuring resource security for Japan, and for the Pacific Basin area, on a long-term basis (Kojima 1978, p. 521; Ozawa 1979).

Regional Integration via PAFTA and OPTAD?

As for the plans and proposals for the formation of regional bodies and institutions for trade promotion and cooperation in the Pacific and Asia-Pacific area, two specific examples may be cited. The first plan was a proposal for the formation of a Pacific Free Trade Area (PAFTA) in the 1960s (Allen 1968; Kojima 1968, 1971). The second plan proposed the formation of Organization of Pacific Trade and Development (OPTAD) in the 1970s (Drysdale 1968; Drysdale and Patrick 1979; U.S. Congress 1979). Other suggestions, which are variations of these proposed plans, have also been put forward, such as the Pacific Summit Conference, to promote trade and economic cooperation in the region (Trade Policy Research Centre 1983).

The creation of a Pacific trading community has enlisted serious support from several quarters and has now entered the arena of academic and political debate. The realization that there are common interests among the Pacific Basin countries that such a grouping might promote, as well as common dangers that it might help to avoid, has given the proposals plausibility. At the same time, events in the outside world, such as the energy crises in the 1970s, provided further stimulus to Japanese consideration of the subject.

The growth of intraregional trade in the Pacific Basin during the 1970s has provided the basis for discussion as to the possible formation of a Pacific trade organization similar to the EC and the EFTA in Western Europe. Kiyoshi Kojima (of Hitotsubashi University in Japan) provides a vew of a typical protagonist on the subject. His thesis, in capsule summary, is that although trade among the developed countries in the Pacific Basin has been growing rapidly, it has not grown as fast as intra-European trade since the formation of the EC. Because the Pacific countries have at least as great a potential for economic development as Europe, close cooperation among them should be sought in order to realize that potential. If this cooperation were achieved and a PAFTA arrangement established, then the group of developed countries, including the United States and Canada, could associate the develop-

ing countries in the Asia-Pacific Basin with increased prosperity that mutual free trade would confer and by according them aid, investment, and trading privileges. Each
country in isolation might be reluctant to grant these benefits on the scale required because of a lack of resources
or because one country could not face alone the structural
consequences to its own economy of the industrial development of those countries (Kojima 1968; Allen 1968, pp. 40-41).
Thus, the common-front approach through PAFTA would, at
least in theory, make all the participating countries real
and potential winners in the positive-sum game of trade
cooperation.

In presenting the idea of PAFTA, Kojima has also
explored some alternatives. He has acknowledged, for instance, that the best choice for Japan would be freedom of
trade with all countries of the world. This choice would
be dictated by the dual pattern of trade with developed
and developing countries, by Japan's own industrial capacity, and by its geographic situation. A further global
tariff reduction hardly seems practicable for many years
to come, and would, in any case, likely stop far short of
complete free trade. He was firmly of the opinion, therefore, that Japan could not afford to be isolated commercial-.
ly in a world that, despite multinational trade agreements,
seemed to be moving toward the formation of restrictive
trade blocs. In the circumstances likely to confront Japan,
the most prudent Japanese policy would be a free trade
area composed of the developed Pacific Basin countries and
the developing countries in Asia and South America (Kojima
1968; 1971, pp. 71-73).

PAFTA would thus lead to an expansion of intra-
area trade. But the distribution of gains between the developed countries in the Pacific Basin, once PAFTA was set
up, would be so unequal that an agreement could scarcely
be reached. Moreover, it would have a massive effect on
the income distribution of its members, by forcing a restructuring and readjustment of domestic industries. Manufacturing industries, such as the automobile sector, would
resist the pressure of international competition that such a
measure of free trade area in the Pacific Basin would entail, as would the farmer groups, which would feel threat-
ened.

The proposal for PAFTA, as advanced by Kojima,
received attention in the Japanese business community and
an official sanction by the Japanese government (Wionczek

1980, pp. 171-72). Japanese Foreign Minister Takeo Miki, for instance, spoke on the subject of Asia-Pacific Policy and Japan's Economic Cooperation in 1967 at a monthly meeting of Japan's influential Keizai Doyukai (Committee for Economic Development). Miki also delivered a speech on the same topic at the Conference for the Development of Southeast Asia, held at Manila in April 1967. Since then a series of Pacific Trade and Development conferences has been held almost annually with economists from many of the Pacific Basin countries participating--Tokyo in 1968, Honolulu in 1969, Sydney in 1970, Ottawa in 1971, Tokyo in 1973, Mexico City in 1974, Auckland in 1975, Thailand in 1976, San Francisco in 1977, Canberra in 1979, Seoul in 1980, Vancouver in 1981, and so on. The papers and proceedings of these conferences--focusing on such wide-ranging topics as direct foreign investment, technology transfer, and trade and employment--have been published (see, for example, Krause and Patrick 1978).

If PAFTA was to be a loose EFTA-type association of trading nations in the Pacific Basin, OPTAD was likewise to be a loose but more coordinated OECD-type arrangement, primarily for the benefit of the industrialized countries but with a tie to the developing countries in the region. Theoretically, OPTAD could become a prototype for an EC-type, but stronger, organization providing a common market for Asia. Realistically, however, the chance of such a body coming into being is small.

OPTAD was initially proposed by Peter Drysdale of Australia in the late 1960s with support appearing elsewhere later (Drysdale 1968; Drysdale and Patrick 1979). The US House Subcommittee on Asian and Pacific Affairs of the Committee on Foreign Affairs held public hearings on the subject of the Pacific Community in 1979. Senator John Glenn, as chairman of the US Senate Asia-Pacific Subcommittee of the Committee on Foreign Relations, also commissioned the Library of Congress to initiate a study on the feasibility of such an organization (Drysdale and Patrick 1979). OPTAD's broad objectives, as envisioned by its proponents, were to provide a more "effective safety-valve" for trade disputes and economic grievances among the member countries; to stimulate investment and aid flows from developed to developing Pacific nations; to serve as a forum for consultation and dialogue on long-term development issues for the region; and to provide a more secure framework for an economic alliance among the Asian and Pacific nations (U.S. Congress 1979, pp. 43-44). Thus, the initial PAFTA idea presented by the Japanese business and academic circles has come to attract broader attention by academic and government circles in Australia and the United States.

One of OPTAD's professed benefits is to solve resource and trade problems for the developed countries in the Pacific Basin. Such an arrangement, however, is more the concern of the larger nations, and more attention seems to be required on the trade and investment problems peculiar to the smaller countries in the region (Drysdale 1978, p. 660). The Pacific Resources Bank, initially proposed by Drysdale, for instance, is potentially useful as a means to handle riskier investments. But there is no reason why the existing commercial banks and financial institutions cannot do the business transactions along the lines suggested in the OPTAD plan (Drysdale 1978).

To make OPTAD successful, US leadership and participation seem essential. However, an OPTAD-type scheme is not presently high on the US government's priority list, and the necessary incentive or preconditions for its formation do not seem to exist from the standpoint of the United States. The US government is more preoccupied with such salient policy issues as the ongoing trade disputes with Japan (on automobile exports and agricultural trade), and unless such problems can be handled more effectively by a proposed scheme an OPTAD-type plan will not receive the necessary government blessing and public support in the United States. Moreover, the economic perspective that an OPTAD-type proposal represents needs to be balanced with broader considerations of US foreign policy objectives in Asia that reflect both geopolitical and security interests.

US participation in the OPTAD-type arrangement may also be perceived by its allies in Europe, Africa, and Latin America as "some form of attention lapse or even discrimination" against their respective regions (Drysdale 1978, p. 660). As a great power the United States has responsibilities to protect and promote both regional and global interests. Balancing of global and regional interests, although not necessarily conflicting, will inevitably be required in the US calculation of the possible participation in an OPTAD-type body in the Pacific. In short, political economy considerations of balancing the domestic and foreign policy concerns are needed before any scheme for a regional trade organization or economic integration will materialize in the Pacific Basin area. The United States will also have to balance trade concerns, as noted in Chapter 8, between those represented in its own Western Hemisphere trading system and that of broader global concerns.

THE FUTURE OF REGIONAL TRADE EXPANSION

Japan has pursued a neomercantile policy in world trade in modern times. Unlike traditional insularity in Tokugawa Japan, exports have since become a way of life, enabling the Japanese to attain and enjoy a higher standard of living. In this transformation the Japanese government has played an active and interventionist role in the economy by exercising a guiding role in export expansion. It is remarkable that, despite the Confucian bias against commerce and trade in the old days, export operation and expansion in modern Japan have taken place with official sanction (Sato 1977). The mercantile or neomercantile philosophy is reflected in the idea that trade policy is an integral part of the national economic policy, which in turn underlies national strength and prosperity. Japan's foreign economic policy in the post-World War II era that advocates the preserving of a system of free and liberal trade is, in turn, based on the considerations of this mercantile or neomercantile philosophy.

The challenge lies in dealing with the dynamic change that results from trade expansion in the Pacific Basin. In spite of economic disruptions in the 1970s, as evidenced by the four world crises noted above, the Asia-Pacific Basin region promises to become one of the most dynamic and rapidly growing areas in the world economy. With Japan's emergence as an economic force in the region, coupled with the rise of Asian NICs, the real challenge is to devise institutional mechanisms and procedures for promoting regional cooperation in such a way that creative potential for the area will continue to be fulfilled in the years ahead. The nature and form of such a regional cooperative body is not yet clear. If participation is limited to a handful of developed countries, largely excluding the developing countries in the region, such restrictive practices could exacerbate further fragmentation and regionalization of world trade. If the arrangement encompasses all countries in the region and wider participation from other areas, such as the Western Hemisphere, however, the cooperative body in the Pacific Basin might continually serve as an opportunity and catalyst for a more open trading system on a worldwide basis (Hong and Krause 1981; Trade Policy Research Centre 1983).

11　The Soviet Union and the Centrally Planned Economies

The Soviet Union's trading system, while relatively small in terms of nations included, did account for a meaningful portion of the world economic product and included most of the centrally planned economies for which trade data were available. To a certain extent, the Soviet Union and the Eastern European countries are in a different category from the other trading systems discussed in this volume, because of their ideological and political similarities. The USSR and its trading partners, however, did represent a significant subset of actors in the world trade regime, and it is a subset that fits comfortably within the context of increasing regionalism in the world trade regime. This particular case of regionalism developed in part because of dissatisfaction with the structuring of the world trade regime after World War II, including the hegemonic position of the United States.

While the trading practices of the centrally planned economies are different, the countries in question still affected the world regime and were in turn affected by it. In recent years discussion of East-West trade has focused attention on these interactions. There has been debate among some theorists, including neo-Marxists, as to the extent the centrally planned economies actually participate in the world trade regime. It has been argued that these countries are, in effect, independent of the world system since most of their interactions are with each other. They have been seen as constituting an autonomous system that only interacts with the larger world system for nonessential trading exchanges (Szymanski 1983). The opposing view has been that, although the centrally planned economies are quite different in their interactions with each other, they cannot totally escape the regime that is dominated by capitalist countries, with all the disadvantages that such a regime is assumed to have (Borrego 1983). Also, world trade occurs in a market setting, and the centrally planned economies must function in that context, notwithstanding their differences with capitalist states (Chase-Dunn 1983b; Galtung 1973, p. 82; Lindblom 1982, p. 325).

Two distinct trading practices of the centrally planned economies should be noted. First, although trade in dollar figures was available and used for delineating the system, exact dollar amounts can be misleading. Trade among the centrally planned economies is based on non-convertible currencies. Nonconvertible currencies have the major advantage of insulating the domestic economic plan from external influences (Dernberger 1968, p. 207). For purposes of trade, the values of good A and good B are negotiated, and some unit of account is used. While such trade is converted to dollars on the basis of official exchange rates, either good A or good B could be greatly undervalued or overvalued. Thus, while exact dollar volumes may be misleading, the general magnitude of trading links does remain indicative of membership in the trading system. This problem did not exist for trade between the centrally planned economies and the free market economies since world prices are used as a medium exchange and values are expressed in convertible currencies.

A second phenomenon of trade among the centrally planned economies is bilateralism. Each country attempts to balance its trade with the others. Such bilateralism is a direct consequence of nonconvertible currencies since there is no utility in holding the currency of another centrally planned economy (Holzman 1968, p. 286). Bilateralism also explains the use of barter agreements by various centrally planned economies. Bilateralism can also be useful in terms of fulfilling the various national plans. While these two characteristics are important in terms of evaluating the impacts of trade links and effectively valuing the real worth of trade, the general magnitudes of trade links could still be used to indicate the extent and characteristics of the Soviet trading system.

A SYSTEM OF DEVELOPED COUNTRIES

Not surprisingly, Soviet trade ties were strongest with the other centrally planned economies. From 1961 to

1971, the six Eastern European members of the Council for Mutual Economic Assistance (CMEA or, more frequently, COMECON)--Poland, East Germany, Czechoslovakia, Hungary, Romania, and Bulgaria--all had their principal ties with the Soviet Union, which is also a member of COMECON. Yugoslavia, though not a member of COMECON, was also in the trading system. The only other states included were Cuba, Afghanistan, and Egypt. The presence of these three states was not surprising. Cuba, also considered a centrally planned economy and a member of COMECON, was isolated in the Western Hemisphere and dependent on the Communist countries as markets for its sugar. Geographic proximity accounted for Afghanistan, and diplomatic and military ties in the face of the ongoing Middle Eastern disputes explained Egypt's presence.

It is possible that the Asian centrally planned economies may also have been in the system. Unfortunately, complete trade data were not available for Mongolia, North Korea, and North Vietnam, nor for the People's Republic of China, in the first period. Although China did reorient its trade away from the USSR after the Sino-Soviet split of the 1950s, Mongolia has clearly been within the economic orbit of the Soviet Union since the 1920s (Murphy 1966) and is a member of COMECON, as is Vietnam. Of the ten nations for which data were available, the seven European states in the trading system could be considered developed. As a result, only a comparison of the full trading systems including both developed and developing countries was undertaken, as three developing states provided an inadequate base for a developing country comparison of different trading systems.

The most obvious difference from a comparison of the Soviet system with other groups was the presence of relatively large economies that traded much less than their size would indicate (see Table 11.1). The large GNP average reflected the inclusion of the Eastern European nations whose average absolute GNP and trade levels were much greater than the averages for the other two groups. The smaller percentage of world trade that they accounted for indicated that they were less involved in trade. Their concentration of trade was equivalent to the variable partners group and less concentrated than that of the countries in other systems. Given their lesser propensity to trade, the lower GNP concentration levels were not

TABLE 11.1
Soviet Trading System, 1961-71

	Soviet Partners (n = 10)	Other Partners (n = 101)	Variable Partners (n = 36)
Percentage of world trade, 1971[a]	16.4	67.0	16.6
Percentage of world GNP, 1971[a]	22.6	52.3	25.1
Average trade levels (millions), 1971	$ 2,325	$ 940	$ 653
Average GNP (millions), 1971	$22,115	$5,060	$5,784
Unweighted averages			
Trade concentration with partner, 1961	34.1	42.0	32.2
Trade concentration with partner, 1971	34.0	41.0	31.5
Percent of GNP with partner, 1961	--[b]	8.6	4.7
Percent of GNP with partner, 1971	4.2	9.4	7.3
Average annual percentage increase in per capita GNP, 1961-71	2.8	2.8	3.3
Weighted by 1971 GNP of partners			
Trade concentration with partner, 1971	34.7	36.0	21.4
Percent of GNP with partner, 1971	3.7	6.1	2.7
Average annual percentage increase in per capita GNP, 1961-71	3.3	3.3	3.3
Weighted by 1971 total trade of partners			
Trade concentration with partner, 1971	34.9	34.6	26.8
Percent of GNP with partner, 1971	4.1	8.2	6.6
Average annual percentage increase in per capita GNP, 1961-71	3.4	3.5	5.4

[a] The trade figures and GNP figures for the states at the centers of the systems (United States, United Kingdom, the Common Market Six, Japan, and the Soviet Union) are not included in total world trade or total world GNP.

[b] No figures available for sufficient countries in 1961.

SOURCE: Compiled by authors.

unexpected. The growth figures for the countries in the Soviet trading system were equivalent to those for the countries in other systems.*

The weighted averages provided a somewhat different picture. With both the GNP and trade weights, the countries in the Soviet trading system had approximately the same levels of export concentration as the countries in other trading systems. This equivalence is particularly noteworthy given the fact that the trading partners were primarily developed countries. The Soviet partners still had lower GNP concentrations, reflecting their less active involvement in trade in general. The growth rates of the Soviet partners were also on a par with the growth rates of countries in other systems. Overall, the countries in the Soviet trading system displayed characteristics similar to those of countries in the other systems.

The Soviet trading system remained relatively stable for the 1971-76 period. Trade data for East Germany were not available, but the other nine members of the system remained the same. By 1979, however, the Soviet Union had been replaced as Egypt's major market due to the changing diplomatic orientation of that country. Afghanistan will obviously retain such economic ties in the foreseeable future. The countries in the Soviet system continued to be somewhat smaller traders for their size in this period, but the difference was not nearly as marked as it had been in the previous decade (see Table 11.2). The trade concentration levels were closer to those of the countries that were in other trading systems, and they actually increased from 1971 to 1976 in contradistinction to average downward movements in the other two groups of countries. GNP concentrations were on the increase, a reflection of the greater role that trade was playing in these economies. While absolute levels of East-West trade were increasing in this period, relative exports to the Soviet Union were keeping pace with this increase. The unweighted growth figures indicated that the countries in the Soviet system were faring well compared to other countries.

---

*Marer (1979, pp. 252-53) noted a number of reasons for a tendency to inflate or exaggerate growth figures among the Eastern European countries. As a result, caution must be exercised for the comments on growth in this chapter.

TABLE 11.2
Soviet Trading System, 1971-76

	Soviet Partners (n = 9)	Other Partners (n = 107)	Variable Partners (n = 31)
Percentage of world trade, 1976[a]	11.2	77.4	11.4
Percentage of world GNP, 1976[a]	12.4	62.3	25.3
Average trade levels (millions), 1976	$ 5,503	$ 3,216	$ 1,639
Average GNP (millions), 1976	$29,052	$12,220	$17,166
Unweighted averages			
Trade concentration with partner, 1971	33.6	38.8	27.9
Trade concentration with partner, 1976	35.4	37.8	27.6
Percent of GNP with partner, 1971	4.3	9.0	6.2
Percent of GNP with partner, 1976	9.0	10.7	7.7
Average annual percentage increase in per capita GNP, 1971-76	4.0	2.3	3.7
Weighted by 1976 GNP of partners			
Trade concentration with partner, 1976	31.4	30.0	22.3
Percent of GNP with partner, 1976	6.1	7.6	2.3
Average annual percentage increase in per capita GNP, 1971-76	5.0	3.8	4.0
Weighted by 1976 total trade of partners			
Trade concentration with partner, 1976	30.5	30.0	22.3
Percent of GNP with partner, 1976	8.0	12.0	9.2
Average annual percentage increase in per capita GNP, 1971-76	4.9	3.8	4.0

[a] The trade figures and GNP figures for the states at the centers of the systems (United States, United Kingdom, the Common Market Six, Japan, and the Soviet Union) are not included in total world trade or total world GNP.

SOURCE: Compiled by authors.

When the weighted comparisons were used, the trading concentrations and GNP concentrations remained closer to those of countries in other trading systems than was the case in the preceding decade. These weighted growth rates were the highest of the three groups, and they were on a par with the higher growth rates found for the Japanese trading partners for the same period. It is possible that the increased trade may have been a contributory factor to this high growth. The higher weighted growth averages also indicated that the three developing countries in the system were not sharing in this performance. Again, as with other trading systems, the larger and richer states would appear to have been faring somewhat better.

The results for both periods indicated that the nations in the Soviet trading system had over time become more similar to those of other trading systems. Trade was increasing as a portion of GNP, as it was for the world as a whole, and export reliance on the principal market also remained high. Growth rates in this second period were very high for the countries as a group when weights were used, indicating that the Eastern European countries were faring well economically in a period of Western recession. Overall, at least on the basis of the above comparisons, the Soviet trading system began to look more like the other trading systems.

ISSUES AND RESPONSES

Despite similarities to other trading systems, there remain some differences in the system encompassing the Soviet Union and the Eastern European nations. Some of the issues are different from those confronting the countries in other systems or those not in any system, yet other issues and problems are similar in broad outline to those found in the other trading systems. One series of issues that has arisen in one form or another has resulted from the Soviet economic and political position of dominance, or hegemony if you will. Even issues that have been similar to concerns of other countries in trading systems have often been affected by this basic structural consideration. Thus, the relationships involved with the question of Soviet dominance in its various manifestations will be discussed first; then the interactions of these countries with the rest of the world trade regime will be considered.

The Question of Soviet Dominance

The strong economic ties between the Soviet Union and the other centrally planned economies did not develop as a natural economic phenomenon. They were, in effect, constructed in a conscious effort to reorient trade away from former partners. Mongolia, in the 1920s, was the first example of this practice (Murphy 1966, pp. 43–51 and especially pp. 89–91). In the case of Eastern Europe, a similar change occurred. Before World War II, the trade of Eastern Europe was primarily directed westward, and there was relatively little trade with the Soviet Union (Clark 1980, p. 9; Smith 1973, p. 197). After the establishment of Communist governments, the trade was redirected on the Mongolian pattern toward the Soviet Union. Direct trade ties have since been reinforced by a wide range of other economic linkages. Perhaps the best demonstration of the importance of these economic links, including trade, has been the fact that the Soviet Union has attempted to strengthen them in the aftermath of political and economic disturbances, such as those in Hungary, Czechoslovakia, and Poland (Evanson and Lutz 1983; Graziani 1981, p. 68).

This reorientation of trade was not surprising given the international climate after World War II. The prewar Soviet goal under Stalin had been as much economic independence or autarky as possible in order to eliminate the risk of Western capitalistic manipulation of economic links to the disadvantage of the Soviet Union (Dernberger 1968, p. 215; Hudson 1972, pp. 83–84; Smith 1973, p. 16; Simai 1981, p. 125; Szymanski 1983, pp. 65–66; Toma 1979, p. 132; Turpin 1977, p. 10). This goal, of course, was also one of the reasons for the relatively small levels of prewar trade between the USSR and Eastern Europe. After the war it was logically extended to the new Communist states in the region. Limiting trade with the West limited the potential for economic disruption, and it also tied these countries more firmly to the USSR and each other (Holzman 1976, p. 125; Levine 1968, p. 259; Smith 1973, p. 26; Toma 1979, p. 132). The new governments also undertook heavy industrialization programs and even as much individual autarky as possible in emulation of the Soviet experience, which also had the impact of limiting trade ties between them and accentuating their links to the Soviet Union (Marer 1979, pp. 262–63). The ensuing reliance on internal resources resulted in the relatively low trading levels of these nations in 1961 and 1971.

The lower levels of trade in the early years did not prevent Eastern European vulnerability to Soviet economic pressures given the concentration of the existing trade. Unlike the other trading systems, however, the Soviet system was characterized by a major market that exchanged raw materials for manufactures from the trading partners (Bornstein 1981, p. 202; Chase-Dunn 1983b, p. 279). The more industrialized Eastern European nations, such as East Germany and Czechoslovakia, in particular traded manufactures for raw materials, including fuels. Vulnerability still existed since many of the manufactured products were designed to Soviet specifications, and they were either nonusable or noncompetitive in other markets (Graziani 1981, p. 72; Holzman 1976, p. 66; Marer 1979, p. 272). As a consequence, the Soviet market was as critical for Eastern European manufactures as the US market was for sugar from various Caribbean producers. In addition, many Eastern European factories were geared to receive Soviet raw materials, and they could not easily shift to alternative sources of supply (Brzezinski 1967, pp. 477-78; Clark 1980, p. 13). The fact that the economies in question were all under state planning exacerbated the vulnerability, since the withholding of key inputs to the state plan could have been extremely disruptive, particularly when there is limited flexibility to seek alternative sources (Holzman 1976, p. 65).

Although the Eastern European countries have been noticeably reliant on Soviet trade links, this trade dependence does not necessarily create a situation of dependency. Some dependency theorists have argued that the contextual situation is significantly different so as to make dependency concepts inapplicable (Duvall 1978, p. 58; Fagen 1978, pp. 297-300; Gantzel 1973, p. 210; Stehr 1977). And, although the Eastern European nations are economically reliant in various ways, it is far from clear that the Soviet Union has used its position in an economically exploitive fashion. In the first years after World War II, the Soviet Union did extract economic advantages from the Eastern European and Asian countries, such as the dismantlement and removal of industrial plants, but since that time there is no distinctive pattern. In the 1960s, there were indications, though no conclusive evidence given the difficulties with pricing intrabloc trade, that the Soviet Union was actually paying higher costs in economic terms as a result of trade with the other centrally planned economies (Chase-Dunn 1983b, pp. 278-79; Clark 1980, p. 19; Holzman 1976, p. 86). In fact, it was possible that the terms of trade were running against the Soviet Union. In the 1970s, however, there was a possibility that the trend reversed itself and that it was the Eastern European countries that faced declining terms of trade (Abonyi 1983, p. 189; Bornstein 1981, pp. 203-04). The terms of trade figures for the European centrally planned economies from 1970 to 1978 in Table 6.2 provide support for this possibility. Over longer periods of time, however, there remains no clear evidence that the Soviet Union has economically exploited these nations.

Exploitation is only one danger from economic dependence on another state, with political compliance being a second possibility. Clark (1980, p. 28) argued that while both economic and political reasons can lie behind attempts to create dependency, in the case of Eastern Europe, Soviet political goals were placed ahead of economic profits. Thus, while there was not necessarily any economic exploitation, there has been political domination (Chase-Dunn 1983b, p. 278), and the economic vulnerability of these countries plays a role in that domination. The economic vulnerability and the potential for political domination are enhanced by the prevalence of bilateral trading relationships within the bloc since an individual country's bargaining position vis-à-vis the Soviet Union is weakened further because of less opportunity to act in concert with the other states (Abonyi 1983, pp. 188-89; Dernberger 1968, p. 206).

Placing political goals ahead of economic benefits would explain the tendency toward the periods of variable terms of trade for the centrally planned economies. The Soviet leadership chose to forgo the economic benefits in order to maintain good relationships with local elites (Holzman 1976, p. 103). These local elites have thus been strengthened, as well as rewarded (Abonyi 1983, p. 189; Graziani 1981, p. 69). Since these elites were maintained in power and rewarded for their efforts on behalf of the Soviet Union, it is not difficult to see a similarity between them and the elites supposedly used by Western capitalists to maintain influence in the developing countries (Ray, 1973, p. 9).

> Command planning, which in effect is controlled
> by the penetrated elite, is the cornerstone
> of this model of political control and remains
> the key structure through which East Euro-
> pean economies are conditioned and national
> and regional imbalances reflecting Soviet
> interests are maintained. (Abonyi 1983,
> p. 187)

All the contours of Soviet influence are not clear, although economic dependence is hardly the only weapon available to Soviet leaders. There do seem to be, however, at least some potential similarities between the Soviet trading system and the capitalist ones.

The creation of COMECON provides a good example of the dominant position of the Soviet Union. From the beginning, the organization was seen as providing both a defense against Western capitalism and a means of more closely integrating the members with the Soviet economy and to a lesser extent with each other. Unlike the Common Market, where at least some of the members are roughly equal, COMECON provides a setting for the one large economy to establish economic patterns and integrate the smaller economies into these patterns (Abonyi 1983, p. 184; Bornstein 1981, p. 202; Grotewold 1979, p. 19). As a result, the local leaders in Eastern Europe have not been wholehearted advocates of increased COMECON integration (Bracewell-Milnes 1976, p. 273; Bornstein 1981, pp. 206-07), as have not the Asian centrally planned economies, which have refused to join, except for Vietnam in 1979.

The effort to integrate even more closely the member states by creating "economic regions" crossing state borders with specialized economic tasks generated Romanian opposition to further integration, which would have increased economic vulnerability to the Soviet Union by further removing domestic economies from the control of national leaders. For Romania it also would have meant that industrialization plans would have been postponed or limited since its role was to be a producer of agricultural products and raw materials. The success of Romania in objecting to this plan and actually decreasing its economic ties with COMECON may illustrate the importance of politics over economics. The Romanian leadership was permitted to pursue a course of economic deviation, at least in part because the domestic politics were seen to be ultraorthodox in nature. Unlike Czechoslovakia in 1968, there were no threats to the primacy of the Communist party, which retained strict domestic controls.

Interactions with the World Trade Regime

It is impossible to answer the question clearly as to whether or not the centrally planned economies are part of the world trade regime or a separate system, since ultimately an answer requires a specification of a minimal level of necessary interaction. But comparisons of trading systems do provide some insights. Trade between the centrally planned economies and the countries of the West has increased, particularly in the 1970s, but the proportion of trade with the Soviet Union remained at the same levels. While export reliance on the Soviet market has remained relatively constant, GNP concentration has increased since trade has become more important. As a result, the Eastern European countries are more involved in the wider system, even though they have not managed to reduce their reliance on the Soviet Union. Although the increased trade with the West has increased the centrally planned economies' integration into the world system, for better or worse, it has not led to great changes in the characteristics of the trading system itself.

The Soviet trading system clearly lacked a component of developing nations, at least ones for which data were available. The centrally planned economies have principally traded among themselves, with the industrial West providing most of the remainder of their trade. The developing countries provided a very small portion of their trade (Monroe 1975, p. 29; Simai 1981, p. 135; Smith 1973, p. 17), although there were obvious exceptions, such as Egypt in the years covered. The lack of trade with the developing countries might account for the observed fact that the Soviet Union has shown little interest in the issues surrounding the call for a New International Economic Order (Anell and Nygren 1980, p. 106; Lindblom 1982, p. 332). One reason for a lack of such trade is historic. Soviet autarky between the wars limited such trade, and Eastern European levels of development left relatively little scope for trade with developing countries. The presence of the old colonial empires also left limited opportunities for trade between developing areas and many other parts of the world.

Growth and development have been important to members of the Soviet trading system, and the countries have demonstrated at least average performance in the first period and relatively rapid growth in the second. This growth has been taken to demonstrate the superiority of trade among the centrally planned economies as opposed to capitalist trade. It has been argued further that another advantage of these trading relationships (and economic systems in general) is that the lesser developed countries have grown faster than the more developed ones, whereas in the capitalist West economic strength becomes more concentrated in the more industrialized countries (Chase-Dunn 1983a, p. 45; Simai 1981, p. 126). In fact, East Germany and Czechoslovakia, as the most advanced industrial states in COMECON, have apparently lost in terms of trade benefits from intrabloc trade (Bracewell-Milnes 1976, p. 178). Greater growth in the least advanced countries apparently did occur from 1950 to 1970, including greater growth on the part of the Soviet Union (Graziani 1981, p. 73), which was less industrialized than either East Germany or Czechoslovakia. Indeed, the largest gainers over time have been Bulgaria and Romania, the two least developed COMECON members.

From 1961 to 1971, when the less developed centrally planned economies did advance faster, the growth of the countries in the system was on the average equivalent to that of nations in the other systems. Growth did lead to greater equality, a potentially desirable outcome, but the growth was not greater. This tendency of greater growth in the least developed economies was not present in the second period (World Bank 1977), when all the countries grew at approximately the same rate. Yet this period was the one when growth rates were the highest. Thus, it is not at all clear that the efforts toward a more egalitarian distribution of economic benefits were more promotive of general growth, although there was no indication that growth was hindered.

The growth of the centrally planned economies from 1971 to 1976 deserves additional comment. There are a number of possible causes, all of which no doubt had some impact. First, the Eastern European economies were more open to trade and closer to the level of trade indicated by their portion of world GNP. If greater trade does indeed lead to growth, the general increase in trade would help to explain the growth. And since these countries had formerly been relatively inactive traders, immediate gains may have been particularly noticeable once trade increased. Such gains, however, might indicate short-term benefits rather than a long-run trend, and recent economic difficulties in Eastern Europe may indicate less rapid growth in the future. Decreasing emphasis on replicating Stalinist heavy industrialization in all states may have helped, since more specialization of production could also have enhanced domestic growth possibilities. COMECON integration would also permit additional specialization of effort as well, although such multilateral integration has been hindered by problems associated with nonconvertibility and bilateralism (Bornstein 1981). Both deemphasis of heavy industry and COMECON integration would have helped growth by permitting economies of scale and taking advantage of latent comparative advantage opportunities.

Emphasis on intrabloc trade and COMECON economic relationships has created some economic problems. Although there are obvious political advantages to this type of trade, it has limited the potential economic benefits to the members by excluding most of the world. Also, as a type of customs union, it has undoubtedly diverted trade from more beneficial avenues, particularly for the Eastern European economies because they are smaller (Holzman 1976, pp. 73-74). The political input from Eastern Europe into the original decisions on trade orientations, moreover, has been relatively limited. Thus, there may have been economic costs, although a Marxist or neo-Marxist could logically argue that the economic and political costs of nonintegration into the world economic system are outweighed by the dangers from capitalist economic penetration.

East-West trade is related to all these concerns, and there has obviously been some feeling that the dangers have lessened. Also, it is possible that one reason for the Soviet Union being more open to East-West trade has been the perception of economic losses suffered in intrabloc trade (Bornstein 1981, p. 196). East-West trade presents new problems. Such trade hinders central planning because some inputs are outside the control of the central government. Importing Western technology provides for future advances, but the imports require a corresponding increase in exports to pay for the new goods and services. In Poland, for example, exports of basic agricultural commodities were designed to provide hard currency for Western technological imports. The Western recession in the 1970s, however, hurt the market for Polish exports, thereby limiting the ability to pay (Fallenbuch 1981, p. 351). The resulting economic difficulties played a key role in domestic disturbances in subsequent years, and the foreign debt has left the Polish leadership subject to exactly the kinds of outside pressures that autarky was designed to avoid in the first place. Thus, imports of technology will only work if they become self-generating in terms of continuous supply to the domestic economy and provision of a surplus for export.

Increased East-West trade has probably gained greater favor among the Eastern Europeans for a number of reasons, notwithstanding the potential problems. First, the trade can ease some of the difficulties from previous economic decisions, such as the one to develop all heavy industry sectors in all states (Abonyi 1983, p. 197). Second, although Hungary has managed internal economic reforms effectively, trade with the West provides an alternative to domestic economic changes that could be risky to implement for political and economic reasons (Bornstein 1981, pp. 191-96). Third, trade provides one means to help contain domestic dissatisfaction that might appear with stagnating growth (Russet 1981-82, p. 43). Fourth, trade diversification could lessen vulnerability to Soviet pressures. Given the greater support for increased trade in Eastern Europe, it is not surprising that the Soviet Union has been less than enthusiastic about such a process and has become more desirous of maintaining its position of dominance in the area (Holzman 1976, p. 204).

THE SOVIET TRADING SYSTEM IN THE FUTURE

The Soviet trading system will probably continue to follow patterns of regional concentration in the future as in the past and thus remain similar in that respect to the other trading systems. The Soviet Union will remain the dominant state in the system since it has the political, economic, and military resources sufficient to this purpose. As long as trade is concentrated with other developed nations, it is unlikely that the Soviet Union will become more involved in the debates in international forums surrounding the developing countries and the idea of a new international regime or even develop markedly greater trading ties with the developing states. The trends discernible from 1961 to 1976 would indicate that the system will be somewhat more open to trade with the rest of the world. The negative impacts from the Western recession and the economic pressure that was applied linked to political actions, such as martial law in Poland and the presence of Russian troops in Afghanistan, will probably prevent any dramatic increases in such trade. In effect, to the Soviet leadership the advantages of autarky may have been reemphasized, although the economic advantages of trade with the rest of the world will also remain. How the Soviet Union and the Eastern European countries will ultimately deal with this question of relative autonomy versus greater integration in the world trade regime will continue to be an issue for both the leadership of the Soviet Union and the indigenous leaders in Eastern Europe.

PART IV Perspectives on World Trade

12   Conclusion

The preceding chapters have presented relevant information not only on various aspects of the world trade
regime but also on the varying impacts of world trade in
particular types of commodities as well as in specific geographic regions. Many of the findings and analyses were
valuable for the additional insights on trade conflicts and
policy issues that they generated, both at the global level
and in the context of particular countries or groups of
countries.

Rather than attempt to summarize all of the pertinent
substantive findings and insights, the present chapter will
focus on three conceptual themes that stand out and that
may substitute as a summary of this volume. The first of
these three themes is policy relevant and, more specific,
it deals with the effect on domestic economic growth of
participation in world trade. Chapters 8 through 11 in
particular considered the global role of foreign trade in
domestic economic growth, and this trade-growth connection
will be considered in overview. The second theme deals
with the interactions between the structure of the prevailing trade patterns and the trade regime and trade policies
undertaken by countries or groups of countries. This sec-
tion will also consider in broad strokes the policies related
to the regional trading systems that have emerged. The
third theme concerns the possible future of the world trading system, including the directions that trade patterns
might take in light of the discussions in the previous chapters. While necessarily speculative in some ways, perspectives on the future of trade and trading systems are a
logical extension of the preceding analyses.

TRADE AND DOMESTIC ECONOMIC GROWTH

An overview of the major trading systems, as well as the countries that had variable principal markets, has provided data that are applicable to a number of aspects of domestic economic growth in different countries. It was not particularly surprising that the countries in the Japanese trading system displayed the greatest average economic growth, given the dynamism and economic growth of the industrialized market that was at the center of the system. By this criterion, the EC trading system members would also have been expected to display higher growth rates than they actually did. As Chapters 8 and 9 showed, however, the EC partners did not experience growth rates that were noticeably greater than those of the members of the US trading system. The latter system was centered on a nation that had relatively poor economic growth and experienced other economic difficulties in periods under consideration. While the potential impact of basic levels of economic development was noted in Chapter 9, it might still have been expected that the trade linkages with the EC would have led to higher relative growth.

A more important finding, and a possible explanation for the rapid economic growth of the countries in the Japanese trading system, was the fact that countries that were more active in trade experienced higher economic rates. While economic growth is not necessarily development, higher per capita growth rates are more likely to be associated with greater economic development than low growth rates. The unweighted and weighted growth rates for countries in trading systems, as well as those countries with variable major markets (summarized in Table 12.1), show that both larger economic size and larger trade volumes tended to enhance growth--both for countries in trading systems and those outside them, as well as for both developed and developing countries. The larger economic size and larger trade volumes of the nations in the US trading systems, as compared to the Western European trading partners, would thus partially explain the better growth performance of the states in the US trading system.

As can be seen, when the economic growth rates were weighted by GNP, the larger economic units did have better growth rates in most cases. The higher weighted growth rates in the averages for all countries (developed and developing), particularly from 1971 to 1976, reflected

TABLE 12.1

Comparison of Unweighted and Weighted Growth Rates

	Unweighted	Weighted by GNP	Weighted by Total Trade
1961–71			
Developed and developing countries in trading systems (n = 111)	2.8	3.3	3.5
Developed and developing countries that changed principal markets (n = 36)	3.3	3.3	5.4
Developing countries in trading systems (n = 88)	2.5	2.6	3.2
Developed countries that changed principal markets (n = 33)	3.3	3.0	5.5
1971–76			
Developed and developing countries in trading systems (n = 116)	2.5	4.0	3.9
Developed and developing countries that changed principal markets (n = 31)	3.7	4.0	4.0
Developing countries in trading systems (n = 94)	2.2	4.4	4.5
Developing countries that changed principal markets (n = 28)	3.2	4.0	3.9

SOURCE: Compiled by authors.

the presence of the developed states, countries that are large in an economic sense given their relatively high per capita GNP levels, which lead to larger GNPs even with smaller populations. The relationship of higher growth with economic size still generally held for only the developing countries as well, although the differences were not as great and were actually reversed for the variable partners group of states in the 1961–71 period, where the unweighted growth rates were slightly higher. The possibility of a positive impact on economic growth resulting from larger size would also suggest that larger domestic markets, either in the form of a large domestic population base or through measures increasing economic cooperation, could have relevance for growth potential, including economic growth in the developing countries.

In terms of the impact of weighting by involvement in trade, Table 12.1 also reveals that differences exist between the two time periods. From 1961 to 1971, trade volume was more important than economic size in contributing to the domestic economic growth of a country, since the total trade weight was always associated with higher growth rates than the weight utilizing the economic size of the states. Thus, although larger economic units naturally were likely to have larger volumes of total trade, there was additional benefit from the fact that a country was an active trader regardless of its size. As a result, the idea that participation in international trade tends to improve the chances for greater economic growth was supported by the results of the analyses of previous chapters and by the averages shown in Table 12.1. From 1971 to 1976, both size and trade involvement had approximately equal impacts, given the similarity of the two sets of weighted growth rates. Thus, in this latter period, involvement in trade was as beneficial as large size, but not more so.

The overall conclusions are that economic growth is favored by an active trading posture by a country that possesses a larger economy, a description that fits most of the developed countries and is also reasonably appropriate to many of the NICs. Further, even smaller countries appear to gain economically by being involved in the world trade regime; thus, trade, on average, has had positive economic impacts regardless of size. Finally, a larger domestic economy, even with relatively smaller levels of trade, also tends to have beneficial impacts, on average, for growth rates. Overall, however, the association between economic size and growth is much less consistent than the association of trade with growth.

A notable fact about the variable market group of countries was the relatively low level of involvement in trade relative to economic size. This group of states in both time periods always accounted for a smaller portion of world trade than overall world GNP. The countries in this group, however, were often not smaller economies, particularly when compared to the Western European systems that had a number of very small developing states; therefore, the advantages of size and large absolute volumes of trade were still present to some degree, as seen in the higher weighted growth rates.

No one reason can be adduced for this tendency of relatively lower propensities to trade. The variable market group of countries was a rather disparate one that included a few developed states, NICs and near-NICs, oil exporters, and other developing states. The lower levels of trade may partly explain the fact that the weighted averages for per capita GNP growth of this group of countries actually dropped to or below the averages for the states in trading systems in the 1971-76 period after being considerably higher from 1961 to 1971 (see Table 12.1).

REGIME, STRUCTURE, AND POLICY

There were some very important interactions among the world trade regime, the structure of the trading relationships among nations, and a variety of policy issues that have affected individual countries and groups of states, whether they be countries in the regional trading systems or other distinguishable subsets of trading nations. The issues that are relevant to these areas and their interactions have had important influences on patterns of world trade, and they will also have effects on the future of international trading relationships. In addition, these relationships have already had a number of political impacts that will continue in the future.

Although the preceding discussions did not consider the developing countries as a separate group of trading states in most cases, this group of states, or subsets of states that included many developing countries, did have a particular set of problems. Many of these difficulties could be ascribed to the trade regime and the types of

trade linkages that exist. Perceptions that the trade regime had negative impacts on their economies have led to
expressions of dissatisfaction by many developing countries,
as was clearly apparent in some of the views included in
the discussion of the various political economy perspectives
on world trade in Chapter 2. Many of the provisions of
various NIEO documents reflect the pervasiveness of such
dissatisfaction among many developing countries with respect to the regime and the prevailing pattern of world
trade. The call for a NIEO clearly was a manifestation of
a joint policy effort on the part of the developing states
actively involved in the work of the Group of 77 and
UNCTAD. The various NIEO documents have prescribed a
number of policy changes and structural reforms that are
deemed essential for the future economic welfare of the developing states.

Some of the most important policy recommendations
put forward for changes in the existing situation include
proposals to provide price stabilization, to improve the
terms of trade of the developing countries, to create GSP
schemes, to form organizations of commodity exporters, and
to generate greater trade links among the developing
states. Some changes in the conduct of trade have occurred. While the GSP schedules adopted by the developed
nations are incomplete and are not common to all industrialized states, they can serve as a starting point for
future modifications. Some cooperative efforts among commodity exporters for products other than petroleum have
proven to be workable and to have provided benefits for
the participants. The EC did establish its STABEX fund,
even though there were limits in its coverage. Additional
proposals have at least been included on the international
agenda for subsequent debate and deliberation, whereas 20
years ago they were not even major topics of discussion.
Thus, while these policy suggestions or NIEO demands have
not yet led to major substantive changes in the world trade
regime and its structures, they at least have the potential
for inducing policy changes in future years.

The developing countries have also exerted pressure
for greater attention to the problems of world food and hun-
ger and the establishment of a world food security system.
While not all developing countries have been concerned with
these issues, especially those that are self-sufficient or
food exporters, it is primarily the developing countries
that suffer the most in times of worldwide food shortages

and high prices. Some of the developing states are most
likely to face (or continue to face) the possibility of famine
and starvation in the future. While food issues have received less attention recently than was the case in the
1973-74 crisis, there has been some regularity brought to
trade in foodstuffs, even though it has often been arranged
through the mechanisms of bilateral agreements. Other suggestions for providing greater regularity in food trade in
effect suggest that greater integration of such trade with
the trade regime should exist.

As noted in Chapter 7, food trade occurs in a relatively different context than trade in most other products.
Large numbers of nations, for example, practice agricultural protectionism because they are more concerned with
the consequences of being forced to import food and with
the difficulties that domestic farmers face when confronting
foreign competition. Greater regularity for food trade
would bring foodstuffs into line with the flow of other commodities that are traded internationally. Integration of
food trade with other types of trade might be in the context of the freer movement of foodstuffs than is presently
the case.

Manufactured products have often been associated
with much of the dissension surrounding world trade issues. The advanced developed states have been keenly
competitive, both for individual domestic markets and foreign ones. Even the transnationalization of production processes and greater integration of production facilities in
different states did not lessen but, rather, noticeably ag-
gravated this competition. The developed states have also
become increasingly concerned with competition from the
NICs. Various restrictions on trade in manufactures continue to exist, and nontariff barriers have been increasingly used instead of straightforward customs duties to limit
the intrusion of foreign products into domestic markets.

Trade in manufactures has also set the NICs somewhat
apart from the other developing countries. The NICs as a
group have gained the most from the prevailing structures
and trade patterns, even if they have not benefited as much
as might have been possible under a different set of regime
structures. The NICs have been favored by the prevalent
trading patterns compared to most other developing states
in at least some respects; consequently, their trade policies have been different from those of the other developing
states in regard to their involvement in the calls for the
reform of the international economic system.

The interactions between the structure of the trade regime and the formation of regional trading systems, as noted in the preceding four chapters, have led to a number of specific issues and policies that are, to greater or lesser extents, particular to given systems. The various trade issues discussed in these chapters have in some cases been policy responses advanced by members of a given trading system to wider global trading patterns. Other policies have dealt with issues that were of particular importance for states or a subset of states within a given trading system. The emergence of both types of issues was to be expected within a world trade regime where regional patterns of trade have become increasingly prominent, and the presence of both types of issues will continue to persist as long as the present regional trade links remain as prevalent as they have been.

The four major regional trading systems can be seen as a result of very significant policy responses made by individual countries to the trading regime and global trading patterns. Each of the four systems discussed in Part III reflected a somewhat different set of policy responses on the part of the states at the centers as well as the other members of the trading systems. The Soviet system clearly reflected distrust of the present structures of world trade, as well as a perception of the possible dangers that may result from greater involvement in global trade. While the centrally planned economies in Eastern Europe, as well as the Soviet Union itself, have all recently become more involved in world trade, the system as a whole still remains the most autarkic. In addition, the experience of Poland in the 1980s after more active involvement with the Western economies may have demonstrated some potential disadvantages that can result from such involvement. Ultimately, it would seem that greater integration of the centrally planned economies in global trade would probably require either a diminishing of world political tensions or changes in the norms and principles of the trade regime.

The Western European and Japanese trading systems have evolved as a result of policy responses by advanced industrial nations to a different set of policy concerns. Because of domestic scarcities, both Japan and Western Europe have expressed a greater concern for access to and assured supplies of a variety of raw materials. The United States and Canada, in contrast, have been less concerned with access, since their economies are much less reliant on foreign sources for many primary commodities, and they also export a variety of raw materials. In general, raw materials are not a primary concern for the Soviet Union and the few developing countries in the Soviet trading system. The Soviet Union itself is a major exporter of many types of primary commodities. Resource scarcities tended to provide much of the impetus for the broad network of EC association agreements. Specific provisions of these trade and economic agreements thus provide evidence of how important the issue of access to raw materials is to the EC countries. The potential arrangements for trade groupings in the Pacific Basin, as well as the provisions of the China-Japan trade agreement that were discussed in Chapter 10, also displayed Japan's real concern for ready access to raw materials.

Policies on the level of economic cooperation, and even regional integration in some senses, have varied among the four trading systems. The EC and its treaty network represent the highest level of economic cooperation within a trading system. The economic integration in Western Europe, the establishment of the STABEX fund, the guaranteed markets for some products from the associate members, and the preference given to European companies in some types of natural resource extraction--all represent important cooperative arrangements. The Soviet trading system has also included a variety of cooperative efforts in trade and economic areas. The joint effort in the construction of the natural gas pipelines from Siberia to Eastern Europe is just one recent example. The Soviet Union did attempt to make COMECON a framework for even greater economic cooperation and integration, particularly with the proposal to create economic regions that cut across state boundaries. This effort at greater integration, however, has not been noticeably successful, partly because of some opposition by Eastern European governments and partly because of the need to maintain external links for a continuing influx of technology, capital, and imports from the West.

The Japanese and US trading systems have generally displayed much lower levels of economic cooperation and few attempts at economic integration between the center state and the other members. Both Japan and the United States, as noted in Chapters 10 and 8, respectively, have had to face distrust stemming from the history of their past involvement in the regions where their present trade partners are concentrated. The record of political, military, or economic domination has left a residue of ill-feeling that hinders regional economic cooperation. Japan has entered into some cooperative agreements with neighboring states and has encouraged the movement of declining industries to nearby Asian countries. As the correlations in Chapters 4 and 5 demonstrated, this effort has been successful to at least some extent. There has also been some consideration in Japan of forging more formal links between itself and the other nations in the Asia-Pacific Basin region. In contrast, the United States has not engaged in any major regional formal cooperative efforts. It is not surprising, therefore, that the US trading system is perhaps the most loosely structured of the four systems.

Western European economic integration can also be seen as a specific policy response undertaken by the European countries. The EC has provided a domestic market of a size that is competitive with that of the United States. When the EC was originally formed, the United States was the chief competing industrialized state, although the economic achievements of Japan have since placed that country in a similar position. Western European economic integration has resulted in considerable advantages for manufactures, the chief products and exports of the EC nations. It has also provided major advantages for agricultural interests within the EC by providing a market protected by the CAP. With the enlargement of the EC from six to ten states, the domestic market has become larger than that of the United States or Japan, providing the advantages that exist with economies of scale and the potential for research and development activities that are aided by the presence of a large market.

The varying makeup of the four regional trading systems in terms of the types of member countries also affected some policies instituted by various countries. The system centered on the Soviet Union was unique in consisting primarily of developed states. The Western European trading systems were the other ones to have a major component consisting of developed nations. The US and Japanese trading systems, on the other hand, consisted primarily of the major industrialized markets and the developing countries that were linked with them. These latter two systems were the ones that included NICs that were in trading systems (with other NICs being in the variable

partners group). Thus, while the Western European countries, the United States, and Japan have had concerns with
competition from the NICs, as demonstrated by various recent protectionist measures, the existence of strong trading
relationships between developed nations and the NICs is
perhaps more difficult to reconcile, especially when a
major industrialized state is the principal market for a
large number of other developed states. This possible
incompatibility was perhaps most clearly demonstrated by
the decision of the EC not to grant associate membership
status to the Asian Commonwealth territories.

The US trading system, as well as the Japanese one
to some extent, may be seen as a response less to regional
and more to global trade issues. These two trading systems have emerged in many respects in response to patterns
of trade that have naturally evolved in reaction to the
formation of the EC and the extension of treaty arrangements that encompass the ACP states and other European
and Mediterranean countries. The resulting stronger ties
between the EC states and the associate members have naturally facilitated closer trade links among the remaining
states in the world, except for the centrally planned economies. It has also led to greater concern for the trade
links and for trade interactions among the states in the
other trading systems. These concerns were evident in the
proposals for OPTAD and PAFTA. Also, while the EC system is by no means a totally closed one, it does grant
preferential treatment to the states in the system in a
number of respects compared to outsiders, although some
critics of the EC network would argue that the developing
states inside the system are also losers. Thus, Japan and
the United States have been forced to devote more attention
to their mutual trade as well as their respective trade with
the developing countries in the Western Hemisphere, Oceania,
and Asia. The developing countries that are not associate
members of the EC have also had to be attentive to potential markets in the non-European industrialized countries
as well as to markets among themselves. The formation of
CACOM, LAFTA, and ASEAN, the three best known trade associations among the developing countries, and probably the
three that have had the best results in different time periods, reflected an interest in promoting trade links among
subsets of developing countries, none of which had EC associate status, and hopes for gaining greater benefits from
participation in trade.

The countries included in the US and Japanese trading systems did reflect the interactions between the centers of the systems and their relationships with Western Europe. While all the developed nations, particularly the free market economies of the West, trade among themselves, and such trade is important for all of them, trade outside the regional systems is more important for the United States and Japan. Japan and the United States are thus central markets with greater global trade concerns. As noted in Chapter 8, the US trading system was something of a residual one, while the Japanese system has obviously been growing. Given the economic links between Japan and North America, further coalescence between the two systems is possible, particularly since trade between Japan and North America has increased relative to trade between North America and Western Europe. US–Japanese competition for trade with various Asian, Oceanic, or Western Hemisphere states, however, is another possibility. Thus, new economic and trade policies may be more likely to appear in the future as responses to changing patterns in world trade more for the countries in these two trading systems than for the countries in the Western European and Soviet trading systems.

THE UNCERTAIN FUTURE OF THE WORLD TRADING SYSTEM

The world trading system in the 1960s and 1970s was associated with unprecedented global prosperity and benefits to the countries participating in international trade. The evolution of the international economic order that sustained the world trading system must therefore be placed in its proper historic context in the belief that the past is prelude to the future. In the era after World War II an extraordinary and unexpected explosion of world production was largely responsible for trade expansion, and industrialization, and particularly the export of manufactures, provided the base for trade and economic expansion (Lewis 1978, pp. 32–34; Lipson 1982, pp. 421–23). In partaking of the benefits of this global economic prosperity through trade expansion, the industrialized countries experimented with new policy instruments and a new strategy for domestic economic growth. A strategy of export-led industrialization, rather than a strategy of import substitution, was

successfully adopted by the Western industrialized countries, a strategy later emulated by the NICs.

The slowdown in world economic growth in the 1980s,
however, will not only reduce the rate of growth of international trade but may also change its composition in the
years ahead. The abolition of trade restrictions on manufactured imports was a blessing to advanced industrialized
nations, such as the EC countries, and also to many developing countries that subsequently became NICs in the 1970s
and 1980s. The return of trade protectionism in the developed countries coupled with a worldwide economic recession,
however, has posed a serious threat to the viability of developing countries as traders and also to their domestic
economic development. The rise of protectionism thus poses
a serious challenge and threat to the maintenance of an
open and liberal trade regime that has been associated
with the unprecedented economic prosperity in the post-
World War II years.

Since world economic prosperity and trade expansion
were inexorably linked in this period, successful macro-
economic politics of growth and expansion pursued at the
national level in the industrial countries may well be essential to continued global prosperity and trade expansion.
Historically, however, the world economy has followed a
pattern of cyclical rise and fall, and world trade has also
reflected this familiar pattern. The year 1929, for example, was a turning point in the international economy that
had repercussions for the world trading system. The Great
Depression was particularly hard on the tropical countries
and ultimately gave rise to their coordinated efforts seeking international commodity agreements as well as attempts
to industrialize via the import substitution strategy (Lewis
1978, p. 26). This historic experience of the 1930s and the
1940s is relevant for the concerns about the rising neomercantilist tendencies and associated protectionist practices
in the world trading system in the 1980s.

Although economic gains from trade are undeniable,
power and influence derived from trade are often over-
looked (Hirschman 1945 [1969]), and the connection between
economic welfare and political power, therefore, needs to be
better understood. From a political economy point of view,
it is obvious that a dominant trading country will attempt
to shape its trading patterns. Trade relations between
large and small states are inherently not symmetrical, just
as political relations between powerful and weak states are

asymmetrical. If trade autonomy and interdependence are a necessary virtue, trade dependence and dominance are a necessary evil. This asymmetry is one explanation for the emergence of regional trading systems, although the hegemonic role that the United States provided in the post-World War II era sustained a relatively open world trading system and trade regime that were global in their orientation. As noted in the initial chapter, however, this hegemony has weakened in recent years.

The international trading system established in 1948 under GATT was aimed at restoring some semblance of order in international trade by promoting the position that the trade policies of signatory countries would adhere to a set of basic principles, which in brief were nondiscrimination, liberalism, stability, and transparence (readily seen and openly established) of trade barriers (Lipson 1982, p. 452; Trade Policy Research Centre 1983, p. 91). Liberalism has meant, in principle, letting markets rather than government intervention determine the allocation of resources and reducing restrictions on imports (such as tariffs) to facilitate a steady expansion of trade. The GATT rules of international trade were not designed to achieve free trade as such, since the right of the signatory members to protect against possible injury from foreign competition was also recognized. The few general principles of liberal trade in GATT were limited by a collection of loopholes, such as Articles 6, 11, 12, 16, 19, 14, and 28. Although a series of multilateral trade negotiations, held in seven rounds thus far, have been conducted on the principle of reciprocal bargaining on trade issues, principles of nondiscrimination have been seriously eroded as a result of the appearance of a multitude of discriminatory trade practices that are permitted by GATT rules.

On balance, the accomplishments of GATT have been mixed, since both liberal trade has been encouraged and protectionist trade policies have been tolerated. The world has thus witnessed the emergence of a "managed" trading system, as government intervention has expanded and governments have yielded to domestic protectionist measures (Page 1981, p. 18). Governments have also increasingly relied on bilateralism rather than multilateralism in trade negotiations. Government intervention has also taken the form of sectoral protectionism, rather than comprehensive programs of protection applied throughout the domestic economy (Lipson 1982). The consequences of this protectionism, noted in many of the preceding chapters, have been increases in trade disputes, the emergence of competing trade blocs, and fragmentation in the world trading system.

The world trading regime in the 1980s, in light of the preceding developments, is less a body of fundamental rules binding governments in the interest of promoting international economic order. There has been erosion in the liberal world trade regime, although the GATT system has not collapsed as such (Lipson 1982, p. 455). Trade under GATT rules does increasingly represent a series of political deals, and even permanent negotiations, among states with conflicting mercantile interests. A return to bilateralism and sectoralism, as opposed to multilateralism and industry-wide general agreements on trade, poses a serious challenge to and crisis for the concept of an open, liberal trading system. It has been estimated that only one-third to one-half of the total world trade actually flows in liberal channels, with the remainder subject to quantitative restrictions or other managed arrangements, such as bilaterally concluded VER or OMA agreements, and the trend in this direction has been on the rise since 1974 (Tumlir 1982, p. 29). If an open and liberal trading system is an ideal, a tilt toward a protected and restricted pattern of trade has been a trend that has been in vogue, especially since 1974.

Given severe competition in the world marketplace, protectionist measures have become prevalent and trade disputes are also growing. Such measures affect not only trade among the industrialized countries but trade between the NICs and the industrialized states. Both the EC proposal to limit the importation of grain substitutes from the United States and the commission of the EC's proposal for a new trade policy against "unfair" trading practices are manifestations of such protectionist tendencies. The growing inclination of the United States and the EC to try to solve economic problems by means of government aid and subsidies, as in the case of steel and agricultural exports to third countries, are also cases in point. US efforts to impose its antitrust laws on matters of fair trade outside its territorial boundaries have been met by threats by European countries to retaliate by enacting legislation that would prohibit domestic firms from complying with demands to observe such US laws. Moreover, protectionist tendencies in the developed nations will hinder the prospects of the developing countries for economic growth and export expansion. Since export earnings are essential for many developing countries, whose foreign debts are high and domestic savings generally low, these protectionist practices constitute a potentially severe hardship and are decried as unfair trade practices.

The challenge to the future world trade system and its participants, therefore, lies in renewing a commitment to the maintenance of an open and liberal trading system and a commitment to revitalizing the machinery for liberalizing trade. At the same time there is a need to provide an opportunity for economic growth and development for all the countries participating in world trade. International trade has obviously facilitated economic growth in the past, but opportunities to participate and gain from trade need to be made available to all countries that desire to be involved in trade, perhaps most particularly to the least developed ones. How to reverse the trend from an "inward-looking" to an "outward-looking" trading system, thereby stemming the retreat toward protectionism and trading blocs, constitutes a major challenge facing the world trade regime in the immediate future.

Appendix A

Two- and Three-Digit SITC Level Manufactures

SITC Code	Description
013	Canned meat
032	Canned fish
04	Processed cereal products
11	Beverages
122	Tobacco manufactures
431	Processed vegetable and animal oils
51	Chemical elements, compounds
52	Mineral tar and crude chemicals
53	Dyes
54	Medicines and pharmaceuticals
55	Perfume
56	Manufactured fertilizers
57	Explosives, fireworks
58	Plastic materials
59	Chemicals NES (not otherwise specified)
61	Leather manufactures
62	Rubber manufactures
63	Processed wood products
64	Paper and pulp products
65	Textiles
66	Cement and construction materials
67	Iron and steel
68	Other metals
69	Metal manufactures NES
71	Nonelectric machinery
72	Electric machinery
73	Transport equipment
81	Plumbing, heating, and lighting fixtures
82	Furniture
83	Travel goods (luggage)
84	Clothing
85	Footwear
86	Instruments
89	Miscellaneous manufactures

Appendix B

Countries in Trading Systems

1961-71

United States (n = 28)

Canada	Guyana (British Guiana)	Trinidad and
Bahamas	Haiti	Tobago
Brazil	Honduras	Venezuela
Colombia	Jamaica	Burundi[a]
Costa Rica	Mexico	Ethiopia
Dominican Republic	Netherlands Antilles	Liberia
Ecuador	Nicaragua	
El Salvador	Panama	Hong Kong
French Guiana[a]	Peru	Israel
Guatemala	Surinam	Philippines

United Kingdom (n = 31)

Denmark	Uruguay	People's Democratic
Faeroes Islands	Windward Islands[a]	Republic of
Finland		Yemen (Aden)
Ireland	Gambia	Cyprus
Malta	Kenya	Kuwait
Portugal	Malawi[a]	Sri Lanka
	Mauritius	Yemen
Barbados	Mozambique	
Bermuda	Nigeria	Fiji
Bolivia	Sierra Leone	New Zealand
Greenland	South Africa	Western Samoa
Leeward Islands[a]	Tanzania	

France (n = 19)

Guadeloupe	Dahomey	Senegal
Martinique	Gabon	Togo
	Ivory Coast	Tunisia
Algeria	Malagasy Republic	
Cameroons	Mali	South Vietnam
Central African	Morocco	
Republic	Niger	New Hebrides[a]
Chad	Reunion	

Other EC (n = 9)

Austria	Congo-Brazzaville	Iraq
Greece	Rwanda	Macao
Sweden	Zaire	
Switzerland		

Japan (n = 7)

Saudi Arabia	Australia	Ryukyus
Thailand	New Guinea	
United Arab Emirates[a]	Papua	

Soviet Union (n = 10)

Bulgaria	Romania	United Arab
Czechoslovakia	Yugoslavia	Republic (Egypt)
East Germany		
Hungary	Cuba	Afghanistan
Poland		

Other (n = 7)

Paraguay (to Argentina)	Brunei[a] (to Malaysia)
	Malaysia (to Singapore)
Equatorial Guinea[a] (to Spain)	Nepal[a] (to India)
Rhodesia[a] (to Zambia)	Singapore (to Malaysia)

Variable Partners (n = 36)

Gibraltar	Portuguese Guinea	South Korea
Spain	Somalia	Laos
	Sudan	Lebanon
Argentina	Uganda	Oman
Belize (British	Upper Volta	Pakistan
Honduras)	Zambia	Qatar
Chile		Syria
	Bahrain	Turkey
Angola	Burma	
Djibouti	Taiwan	Naru[a]
Ghana	India	New Caledonia
Guinea	Indonesia	Solomon Islands[a]
Libya	Iran	
Mauritania	Jordan	

1971–76

United States (n = 33)

Iceland	French Guiana	Venezuela
	Guatemala	
Bahamas	Haiti	Burundi
Belize	Honduras	Ethiopia
Bolivia	Jamaica	Uganda
Brazil	Mexico	
Canada	Netherlands Antilles	Bangladesh
Colombia	Nicaragua	Hong Kong
Costa Rica	Panama	Israel
Dominican Republic	Peru	South Korea
Ecuador	Surinam	Philippines
El Salvador	Trinidad and Tobago	Taiwan

United Kingdom (n = 24)

Denmark	Guyana	Mauritius
Faeroes Islands	St. Lucia	Mozambique
Ireland	St. Vincent	Sierra Leone
Norway		South Africa
Portugal	Angola	Tanzania
Sweden	Gambia	
	Ghana	Cyprus
Dominica	Guinea-Bissau	Fiji
Greenland	Malawi	New Zealand

France (n = 18)

Spain	Central African Republic	Morocco
		Niger
Guadeloupe	Gabon	Reunion
Martinique	Ivory Coast	Senegal
	Malagasy Republic	Upper Volta
Benin (Dahomey)	Mali	
Cameroons	Mauritania	French Polynesia
		New Caledonia

Other EC (n = 13)

Austria	Paraguay	Togo
Greece		Tunisia
Switzerland	Congo (Brazzaville)	Zaire
	Equatorial Guinea	
Argentina	Libya	Iraq
		Turkey

Japan (n = 15)

Somalia

Iran
Jordan
Kuwait
Lebanon

Oman
Saudi Arabia
United Arab Emirates
Brunei
Indonesia
Thailand

Australia
Gilberts[a]
  (Kiribati)
Papua-New Guinea
Solomon Islands

Soviet Union (n = 9)

Bulgaria
Czechoslovakia
Hungary
Poland

Romania
Yugoslavia

Cuba

Egypt

Afghanistan

Other (n = 4)

Nepal (to India)
Maldive Islands[a] (to Sri Lanka)

Singapore (to Malaysia)
Seychelles[a] (to Pakistan)

Variable Partners (n = 31)

Finland
Gibraltar
Malta

Barbados
Bermuda
Chile
Uruguay

Algeria
Djibouti
Guinea
Kenya

Liberia
Nigeria
Sudan
Zambia

Bahrain
Burma
People's Republic of
  China
India
Macao
Malaysia
Pakistan

Qatar
Sri Lanka
Syria
South Vietnam
Yemen Arab
  Republic
  (North Yemen)

Naru
New Hebrides
  (Vanatu)
(Western) Samoa
Tonga

---

[a] Data available for only part of the time period.

Bibliography

Abonyi, Arpad. 1983. "Eastern Europe's Reintegration."
In Socialist States in the World-System, ed. Christopher
K. Chase-Dunn, pp. 181-201. Beverly Hills, Calif.:
Sage.

Adler, F. Michael. 1970. "The Relationship Between the
Income and Price Elasticities of Demand for United
States Exports." Review of Economics and Statistics,
Vol. 52, No. 3, pp. 313-19.

Allen, G. G. 1968. Japan's Place in Trade Strategy:
Larger Role in Pacific Region. London: Moore House.

Alschuler, Lawrence R. 1976. "Satellization and Stagnation
in Latin America." International Studies Quarterly,
Vol. 20, No. 1, pp. 39-82.

Anell, Lars, and Birgitta Nygren. 1980. The Developing
Countries and the World Economic Order. London:
Frances Pinter.

Arrighi, Giovanni. 1970. "International Corporations,
Labor Aristocracies, and Economic Development in
Tropical Africa." In Imperialism and Underdevelop-
ment: A Reader, ed. Robert I. Rhodes, pp. 220-67.
New York: Monthly Review.

Ashby, Lowell D. 1968. "The Shift and Share Analysis:
A Reply." Southern Economic Journal, Vol. 34, No. 3,
pp. 423-25.

_____. 1964. "The Geographic Redistribution of Employ-
ment." Survey of Current Business (October), pp.
13-20.

Balaam, David N. 1981. "Asian Food Systems: Structural
Constraints, Political Arenas, and Appropriate Food
Strategies." In Food Politics: The Regional Conflict,
eds. David N. Balaam and Michael J. Carey, pp. 106-42.
Totowa, N.J.: Allanheld, Osmun.

Balassa, Bela. 1981. The Newly Industrializing Countries
in the World Economy. New York: Pergamon.

_____. 1978. "The 'New Protectionism' in the Interna-
tional Economy." Journal of World Trade Law, Vol. 12,
No. 5, pp. 409-36.

_____. 1977. "'Revealed' Comparative Advantage Re-
visited: An Analysis of Relative Export Shares of the
Industrial Countries, 1953-1971." Manchester School of
Economic and Social Studies, Vol. 45, No. 4, pp. 327-44.

Baldwin, Robert E. 1981. "North America." In The Political Economy of New and Old Industrial Countries, ed.
Christopher Saunders, pp. 240-60. London: Butterworth.

Barongo, Yolamu R. 1980. Neocolonialism and African Politics: A Survey of the Impact of Neocolonialism on
African Political Behavior. New York: Vantage.

Barr, Terry N. 1981. "The World Food Situation and
Global Grain Prospects." Science, Vol. 214 (4 December),
pp. 1087-95.

Barraclough, Geoffrey. 1980. "The EEC and the World
Economy." In Integration and Unequal Development:
The Experience of the EEC, eds. Dudley Seers and
Constantine Vaitsos with Marja-Liisa Kiljunen, pp. 57-
71. New York: St. Martin's.

Baumgartner, T., and T. R. Burns. 1975. "The Structuring of International Economic Relations." International
Studies Quarterly, Vol. 19, No. 2, pp. 126-59.

Benjamin, Roger, and Robert T. Kurdle. 1984. The Industrial Future of the Pacific Basin. Boulder, Colo.:
Westview.

Bhagwati, Jagdish N. 1977. "Introduction." In The New
International Economic Order: The North-South Debate,
ed. Jagdish N. Bhagwati, pp. 1-24. Cambridge, Mass.:
MIT Press.

Blake, David H., and Robert S. Walters. 1983. The Politics of Global Economic Relations, 2nd ed. Englewood
Cliffs, N.J.: Prentice-Hall.

Boatler, Robert W. 1978. "Comparative Advantage: A Division Among Developing Countries." Inter-American Economic Affairs, Vol. 32, No. 2, pp. 59-66.

Bodenheimer, Susanne. 1971. "Dependency and Imperialism:
The Roots of Latin American Underdevelopment." In
Readings in U.S. Imperialism, eds. K. T. Fann and
Donald C. Hodges, pp. 155-81. Boston: Porter Sargent.

Bornschier, Volker. 1982. "World Economic Integration
and Policy Responses: Some Developmental Impacts."
In The New International Economy, Sage Studies in
International Sociology, 26, eds. Harry Makler, Alberto
Martinelli, and Neil Smelser, pp. 59-77. Beverly Hills,
Calif.: Sage.

Bornstein, Morris. 1981. "East-West Economic Relations and Soviet-East European Economic Relations." In The Soviet Economy: Continuity and Change, ed. Morris Bornstein, pp. 1193-215. Boulder Colo.: Westview.

Borrego, John. 1983. "Metanational Capitalist Accumulation: Reintegration of Socialist States." In Socialist States in the World-System, ed. Christopher K. Chase-Dunn, pp. 111-43. Beverly Hills, Calif.: Sage.

Bracewell-Milnes, Barry. 1976. Eastern and Western European Economic Integration. New York: St. Martin's.

Brandt, Willy. 1980. North-South: A Program for Survival. Cambridge, Mass.: MIT Press.

Brzezinski, Zbigniew K. 1967. The Soviet Bloc: Unity and Conflict, rev. and enlarged ed. Cambridge, Mass.: Harvard University Press.

Calleo, David P., and Benjamin M. Rowland. 1973. America and the World Political Economy: Atlantic Dreams and National Realities. Bloomington: Indiana University Press.

Caporaso, James M. 1981. "Industrialization in the Periphery: The Evolving Global Division of Labor." International Studies Quarterly, Vol. 25, No. 3, pp. 347-84.

_____. 1978. "Dependence, Dependency, and Power in the Global System: A Structural and Behavioral Analysis." International Organization, Vol. 32, No. 1, pp. 13-43.

Cardoso, Fernando Henrique. 1982. "Development Under Fire." In The New International Economy, Sage Studies in International Sociology, 26, eds. Harry Makler, Alberto Martinelli, and Neil Smelser, pp. 141-65. Beverly Hills, Calif.: Sage.

Carlsson, Bo, and Lennart Ohlsson. 1976. "Structural Determinants of Swedish Foreign Trade: A Test of the Conventional Wisdom." European Economic Review, Vol. 7, No. 2, pp. 165-74.

Castle, Emery N., and Kenzo Hemmi. 1982. "Overview." In U.S.-Japanese Agricultural Trade Relations, eds. Emery N. Castle and Kenzo Hemmi, pp. 1-14. Baltimore: Resources for the Future.

Chase-Dunn, Christopher K. 1983a. "Socialist States in the Capitalist World-Economy." In Socialist States in the World-System, ed. Christopher K. Chase-Dunn, pp. 21-55. Beverly Hills, Calif.: Sage.

_____. 1983b. "The Transition to World Socialism." In
Socialist States in the Capitalist World-System, ed.
Christopher K. Chase-Dunn, pp. 271-96. Beverly Hills,
Calif.: Sage.

_____. 1982. "The Uses of Formal Comparative Research
on Dependency Theory and the World System Perspective."
In The New International Economy, Sage Studies in In-
ternational Sociology, 26, eds. Harry Makler, Alberto
Martinelli, and Neil Smelser, pp. 117-37. Beverly
Hills, Calif.: Sage.

_____. 1975. "The Effects of International Economic De-
pendence on Development and Inequality: A Cross-
National Study." American Sociological Review, Vol.
40, No. 6, pp. 720-33.

Christou, G., and W. T. Wilford. 1973. "Trade Intensifi-
cation in the Central American Common Market."
Journal of Interamerican Studies and World Affairs,
Vol. 15, No. 2, pp. 249-64.

Clark, Cal. 1980. "Dependent Development: A Socialist
Variant." Paper read at annual meeting of the Ameri-
can Political Science Association, August, Washington,
D.C.

Cochrane, Willard W. 1979. "International Commodity Man-
agement as a Policy Problem for the United States: The
Grains Case." In The New International Economic Order:
A U.S. Response, ed. David B. H. Denoon, pp. 143-83.
New York: New York University Press.

Cohen, Stephen D. 1977. The Making of United States International Economic Policy: Principles, Problems, and
Proposals for Reform. New York: Praeger.

Collier, David (ed.). 1979. The New Authoritarianism in
Latin America. Princeton, N.J.: Princeton University
Press.

Coppock, Joseph D. 1962. International Economic Instability: The Experience After World War II. New York:
McGraw-Hill.

Corbet, Hugh, and Paul Streeten. 1971. "Continuing World
Issues of Commonwealth Concern." In Commonwealth
Policy in a Global Context, eds. Paul Streeten and
Hugh Corbet, pp. 1-15. London: Frank Cass.

Cox, Robert W. 1979. "Ideologies and the New International Economic Order: Reflections on Some Recent
Literature." International Organization, Vol. 33, No.
2, pp. 257-67.

Crone, D. 1983. ASEAN States. Boulder, Colo.: Westview.

Deardorff, Alan V., Robert M. Stern, and Mark N. Greene. 1979. "The Implications of Alternative Trade Strategies for the United States." In The New International Economic Order: A U.S. Response, ed. David B. H. Denoon, pp. 78–108. New York: New York University Press.

Denoon, David B. H. 1979. "Facing the New International Economic Order." In The New International Economic Order: A U.S. Response, ed. David B. H. Denoon, pp. 3–31. New York: New York University Press.

Dernberger, Robert F. 1968. "Prices, the Exchange Rate, and Economic Efficiency in the Foreign Trade of Communist China." In International Trade and Central Planning: An Analysis of Economic Interactions, eds. Alan A. Brown and Egon Neuberger, pp. 202–45. Berkeley: University of California Press.

Destler, I. M. 1978. "United States Food Policy 1972–1976: Reconciling Domestic and International Objectives." In The Global Political Economy of Food, eds. Raymond F. Hopkins and Donald J. Puchala, pp. 41–77. Madison: University of Wisconsin Press.

Dolan, Michael B. 1978. "The Lomé Convention and Europe's Relationship with the Third World: A Critical Analysis." Journal of European Integration, Vol. 1, No. 3, pp. 369–94.

Dos Santos, Theotonio. 1971. "The Structure of Dependence." In Readings in U.S. Imperialism, eds. K. T. Fann and Donald C. Hodges, pp. 225–36. Boston: Porter Sargent.

Drysdale, Peter A. 1978. "An Organization for Pacific Trade, Aid and Development: Regional Arrangements and the Resource Trade." In Mineral Resources in the Pacific Area, Papers and Proceedings of the Ninth Pacific Trade and Development Conference, eds. Lawrence B. Krause and Hugh Patrick, pp. 611–61. San Francisco: Federal Reserve Bank.

_____. 1968. "Pacific Economic Integration: The Evolution of a New Approach to Regional Trade and Development Policies." Australia's Neighbors, October–December.

Drysdale, Peter A., and Hugh Patrick. 1979. Evaluation of a Proposed Asian-Pacific Regional Economic Organization." In An Asian-Pacific Organization: An Exploratory Concept Paper, U.S. Senate Committee on Foreign Relations, pp. 1–74. Washington, D.C.: U.S. Government Printing Office.

Duvall, Raymond D. 1978. "Dependence and Dependencia Theory: Notes Toward Precision of Concept and Argument." International Organization, Vol. 32, No. 1, pp. 51–78.

Duvall, Raymond D., and John R. Freeman. 1981. "The State and Dependent Capitalism." International Studies Quarterly, Vol. 25, No. 1, pp. 91–118.

Evans, Peter B. 1977. "Direct Investment and Industrial Concentration." Journal of Development Studies, Vol. 13, No. 4, pp. 720–38.

Evanson, Robert K., and James M. Lutz. 1983. "Soviet Economic Responses to Crises in Eastern Europe." Orbis, Vol. 27, No. 1, pp. 59–82.

Fagen, Richard G. 1978. "A Funny Thing Happened on the Way to the Market: Thoughts on Extending Dependency Ideas." International Organization, Vol. 32, No. 1, pp. 287–300.

Fallenbuch, Zbigniew M. 1981. "Policy Alternatives in Polish Foreign Economic Relations." In Background to Crisis: Policy and Politics in Gierek's Poland, eds. Maurice D. Simon and Roger E. Kanet, pp. 329–69. Boulder, Colo.: Westview.

FAO. 1982. FAO Trade Yearbook. Rome: Food and Agricultural Organization.

_____. 1977. FAO Trade Yearbook. Rome: Food and Agricultural Organization.

Feld, Werner J. 1976. The European Community in World Affairs: Economic Power and Political Influence. Alfred Publishing.

Fetherston, Martin, Barry Moore, and John Rhodes. 1979. "EEC Membership and UK Trade in Manufactures." Cambridge Journal of Economics, Vol. 3, No. 4, pp. 399–407.

Fishlow, Albert. 1978. "A New International Economic Order: What Kind?" In Rich and Poor Nations in the World Economy, 1980s Project/Council on Foreign Relations, eds. Alberg Fishlow, Carlos F. Díaz–Alejandro, Richard R. Fagen, and Roger G. Hansen, pp. 9–83. New York: McGraw-Hill.

Ford Foundation. 1982. Search for a New Economic Order. New York: Ford Foundation.

Fox, Annette Baker. 1971. "The Twenty and the One: Latin American Relations and the United States." In

Small States in International Relations, eds. August Schou and Arne Olav Brundtland, pp. 157–70. Stockholm: Almqvist & Wikesell.

Frank, Andre Gunder. 1982. "Asia's Exclusive Models." Far Eastern Economic Review (June 25), pp. 21–23.

————. 1970. "On the Mechanisms of Imperialism: The Case of Brazil." In Imperialism and Underdevelopment: A Reader, ed. Robert I. Rhodes, pp. 89–100. New York: Monthly Review.

Frank, Isaiah. 1975. "Introduction." In The Japanese Economy in International Perspective, ed. Isaiah Frank, pp. 1–16. Baltimore: Johns Hopkins University Press.

Franko, Lawrence G., and Sherry Stephenson. 1981. "French Export Behavior in Third World Markets." In World Trade Competition: Western Countries and Third World Markets, ed. Center for Strategic and International Studies, pp. 171–251. New York: Praeger.

Frey-Wouters, Ellen. 1980. The European Community and the Third World: The Lomé Convention and Its Impact. New York: Praeger.

Fukui, Haruhiro. 1975. "The Japanese Farmer and Politics." In The Japanese Economy in International Perspective, ed. Isaiah Frank, pp. 134–67. Baltimore: Johns Hopkins University Press.

Galtung, Johan. 1973. The European Community: A Superpower in the Making. London: Allen & Unwin.

————. 1971. "A Structural Theory of Imperialism." Journal of Peace Research, Vol. 8, No. 2, pp. 81–118.

Gantzel, Klaus Jürgen. 1973. "Dependency Structures as the Dominant Pattern in World Society." Journal of Peace Research, Vol. 10, No. 3, pp. 203–15.

Gerschenkron, Alexander. 1962. Economic Backwardness in Historical Perspective. Cambridge, Mass.: Harvard University Press.

Gilpin, Robert. 1971. "The Politics of Transnational Economic Relations." In Transnational Relations and World Politics, eds. Robert Keohane and Joseph S. Nye, Jr., pp. 48–69. Cambridge, Mass.: Harvard University Press.

Gosovic, Branislav. 1972. UNCTAD, Conflict and Compromise: The Third World's Quest for an Equitable World Economic Order Through the United Nations. Leiden: A. W. Sijthoff.

Gourevitch, Peter. 1978. "The Second Image Revisited: The International Sources of Domestic Politics." _International Organization_, Vol. 32, No. 4, pp. 881-912.

Graziani, Giovanni. 1981. "Dependency Structures in COMECON." _Review of Radical Political Economics_, Vol. 13, pp. 67-75.

Green, Reginold Herbold. 1980. "The Child of Lomé: Messiah, Monster or Mouse?" In _The Political Economy of EEC Relations with African, Caribbean and Pacific States: Contributions to the Understanding of the Lomé Convention on North-South Relations_, ed. Frank Long, pp. 3-31. Oxford: Pergamon.

Green, Robert T., and James M. Lutz. 1978. _The United States and World Trade: Changing Patterns and Dimensions_. New York: Praeger.

Griffin, Keith. 1978. _International Inequality and National Poverty_. New York: Holmes & Meier.

Grotewold, Andreas. 1979. _The Regional Theory of World Trade_. Grove City, Pa.: Ptolemy Press.

Gruber, William, Dileep Mehta, and Raymond Vernon. 1967. "The R&D Factor in International Trade and International Investment of United States Industries." _Journal of Political Economy_, Vol. 75, No. 1, pp. 20-37.

Hadley, Eleanor G. 1981. "Japan's Export Competitiveness in Third World Markets." In _World Trade Competition: Western Countries and Third World Markets_, ed. Center for Strategic and International Studies, pp. 253-330. New York: Praeger.

Harkness, Jon, and John F. Kyle. 1975. "Factors Influencing United States Comparative Advantage." _Journal of International Economics_, Vol. 5, No. 2, pp. 153-65.

Harrison, Selig S. 1977. _China, Oil, and Asia: Conflict Ahead?_ New York: Columbia University Press.

Hellmann, Donald C. 1975. "Changing American and Japanese Security Roles in Asia: Economic Implications." In _The Japanese Economy in International Perspective_, ed. Isaiah Frank, pp. 15-36. Baltimore: Johns Hopkins University Press.

Hirsch, Seev. 1972. "The United States Electronics Industry in International Trade." In _The Product Life Cycle and International Trade_, ed. Louis T. Wells, Jr., pp. 37-52. Boston: Division of Research, Graduate School of Business Administration, Harvard University.

Hirschman, Albert O. 1945 [1969]. National Power and the Structure of Foreign Trade. Berkeley: University of California Press.

Hofheinz, Roy, Jr., and Kent E. Calder. 1982. The Eastasia Edge. New York: Basic Books.

Hollerman, Leon. 1975. "Foreign Trade in Japan's Economic Transition." In The Japanese Economy in International Perspective, ed. Isaiah Frank, pp. 168-206. Baltimore: Johns Hopkins University Press.

Hollist, W. Ladd, and Thomas H. Johnson. 1979. "Political Consequences of International Economic Relations: Alternative Explanations of United States/Latin American Noncooperation." Journal of Politics, Vol. 41, No. 4, pp. 1125-55.

Holzman, Franklyn D. 1976. International Trade Under Communism--Politics and Economics. New York: Basic Books.

_____. 1968. "Soviet Central Planning and Its Impact on Foreign Trade Behavior and Adjustment Mechanisms." In International Trade and Central Planning: An Analysis of Economic Interactions, eds. Alan A. Brown and Egon Neuberger, pp. 280-305. Berkeley: University of California Press.

Hong, Wontack, and Lawrence B. Krause (eds.). 1981. Trade and Growth of the Advanced Developing Countries in the Pacific. Seoul: Korea Development Institute.

Hopkins, Raymond F., and Donald J. Puchala. 1978. "Perspectives on the International Relations of Food." In The Global Political Economy of Food, eds. Raymond F. Hopkins and Donald J. Puchala, pp. 3-38. Madison: University of Wisconsin Press.

Houston, David. 1967. "The Shift and Share Analyses of Regional Growth: A Critique." Southern Economic Journal, Vol. 33, No. 4, pp. 577-81.

Hudson, Michael. 1972. Super Imperialism: The Economic Strategy of American Empire. New York: Holt, Rinehart and Winston.

Huff, David L., and Lawrence A. Sherr. 1967. "Measure for Determining Differential Growth Rates of Markets." Journal of Marketing Research, Vol. 4, No. 4, pp. 391-95.

Hveem, Helge. 1973. "The Global Dominance System: Notes on a Theory of Global Political Economy." Journal of Peace Research, Vol. 10, No. 4, pp. 320-40.

International Monetary Fund and International Bank for
Reconstruction and Development. Various Years.
Direction of Trade. Washington, D.C.: International
Monetary Fund and International Bank for Reconstruc-
tion and Development.

JEI. 1982. Agricultural Protectionism, pamphlet detailing
interview with Dr. Fred Sanderson. Washington, D.C.:
Japanese Economic Institute.
JEI Report. Various Issues. Washington, D.C.: Japan
Economic Institute.
Jo, Yung-Hwan. 1968. "Regional Cooperation in Southeast
Asia and Japan's Role," Journal of Politics, Vol. 30,
No. 3, pp. 780-97.
Johnson, D. Gale. 1982. "The World Food Situation: De-
velopments During the 1970s and Prospects for the
1980s." In U.S.-Japanese Agricultural Trade Relations,
eds. Emery N. Castle and Kenzo Hemmi, pp. 15-57.
Washington, D.C.: Resources for the Future.
_____. 1978. "World Food Institutions: A 'Liberal' View."
In The Global Political Economy of Food, eds. Raymond
F. Hopkins and Donald J. Puchala, pp. 265-82. Madison:
University of Wisconsin Press.
Josling, Timothy E., and Scott R. Pearson. 1981. Develop-
ments in the Common Agricultural Policy of the European
Community, U.S. Department of Agriculture, Economic
Research Service, FA Report 172. Washington, D.C.:
U.S. Government Printing Office.

Kahn, Herman, with the Hudson Institute. 1979. World
Economic Development: 1979 and Beyond. Boulder,
Colo.: Westview.
Karunatilake, H. N. S. 1969. "The Impact of Import and
Exchange Controls and Bilateral Trade Agreements on
Trade and Production in Ceylon." In Economic Inter-
dependence in Southeast Asia, eds. Theodore Morgan
and Nyle Spoelstra, pp. 285-303. Madison: University
of Wisconsin Press.
Keesing, Donald B. 1979. "World Trade and Output of
Manufactures: Structural Trends and Developing Coun-
tries Exports." World Bank Staff Working Papers, No.
319.
Kennedy, Kieran A., and Brendan R. Dowling. 1975. Economic Growth in Ireland: The Experience Since 1947.
Dublin: Gill and Macmillan.

Keohane, Robert O. 1982. "The Demand for International Regimes." International Organization, Vol. 36, No. 2, pp. 325-55.

_____. 1980. "The Theory of Hegemonic Stability and Changes in International Economic Regimes, 1967-1977." In Change in the International System, eds. Ole R. Holsti, Randolph M. Siverson, and Alexander L. George, pp. 131-62. Boulder, Colo.: Westview.

Keohane, Robert O., and Joseph S. Nye. 1977. Power and Interdependence: World Politics in Transition. Boston Little, Brown.

Kojima, Kiyoshi. 1978. "Japan's Resource Security and Foreign Investment in the Pacific: A Case Study of Bilateral Devices Between Advanced Countries." In Mineral Resources in the Pacific Area, Papers and Proceedings of the Ninth Pacific Trade and Development Conference, eds. Lawrence B. Krause and Hugh Patrick, pp. 506-21. San Francisco: Federal Reserve Bank.

_____. 1971. Japan and a Pacific Free Trade Area. Berkeley: University of California Press.

_____. 1968. "Japan's Interest in Pacific Trade Expansion." In Pacific Trade and Development, ed. Kiyoshi Kojima, pp. 153-93. Tokyo: Japan Economic Research Center.

Krasner, Stephen D. 1982. "Structural Causes and Regime Consequences: Regimes as Intervening Variables." International Organization, Vol. 36, No. 2, pp. 185-205.

_____. 1981. "Transforming International Regimes: What the Third World Wants and Why." International Studies Quarterly, Vol. 25, No. 1, pp. 119-48.

_____. 1979. "The Tokyo Round: Particularistic Interests and Prospects for Stability in the Global Trading System." International Studies Quarterly, Vol. 23, No. 4, pp. 491-531.

_____. 1978. Defending the National Interest: Raw Materials Investments and U.S. Foreign Policy. Princeton, N.J.: Princeton University Press.

_____. 1976. "State Power and the Structure of International Trade." World Politics, Vol. 28, No. 3, pp. 317-47.

Krause, Lawrence B., and Hugh Patrick (eds.). 1978. Mineral Resources in the Pacific Area, Papers and Proceedings of the Ninth Pacific Trade and Development Conference. San Francisco: Federal Reserve Bank.

Krause, Lawrence B., and Sueo Sekiguchi. 1980a. "Economic Interaction in the Pacific Basin." In Economic Interaction in the Pacific Basin, eds. Lawrence B. Krause and Sueo Sekiguchi, pp. 219-42. Washington, D.C.: Brookings Institution.

_____. 1980b. "The End of U.S. Hegemony." In Economic Interaction in the Pacific Basin, eds. Lawrence B. Krause and Sueo Sekiguchi, pp. 23-50. Washington, D.C.: Brookings Institution.

_____. 1980c. "Japan's Emergence as an Economic Force." In Economic Interaction in the Pacific Basin, eds. Lawrence B. Krause and Sueo Sekiguchi, pp. 51-78. Washington, D.C.: Brookings Institution.

Kurth, James R. 1979. "The Political Consequences of the Product Cycle: Industrial History and Political Outcomes." International Organization, Vol. 33, No. 1, pp. 1-34.

Kuznets, Simon. 1964. "Quantitative Aspects of the Economic Growth of Nations. IX. Level and Structure of Foreign Trade: Comparisons for Recent Years." Economic Development and Cultural Change, Vol. 13, No. 1, pp. 1-106.

Lal, Deepak, with Martin Cace, Paul Hare, and Jeffrey Thompson. 1975. Appraising Foreign Investment in Developing Countries. New York: Heinemann.

Lall, Sanjaya. 1980. "Monopolistic Advantages and Foreign Involvement by U.S. Manufacturing Industry." Oxford Economic Papers, New Series, Vol. 32, No. 1, pp. 102-22.

_____. 1975. "Is 'Dependence' a Useful Concept in Analysing Underdevelopment?" World Development, Vol. 3, Nos. 11 & 12, pp. 799-810.

Levine, Herbert S. 1968. "The Effects of Foreign Trade on Soviet Planning Practices." In International Trade and Central Planning: An Analysis of Economic Interactions, eds. Alan A. Brown and Egon Neuberger, pp. 255-79. Berkeley: University of California Press.

Lewis, W. Arthur. 1978. The Evolution of the International Economic Order. Princeton, N.J.: Princeton University Press.

Lindblom, Charles. 1982. "Epilogue." In The New International Economy, Sage Studies in International Sociology, 26, eds. Harry Makler, Alberto Martinelli, and Neil Smelser, pp. 323-33. Beverly Hills, Calif.: Sage.

Lipson, Charles. 1982. "The Transformation of Trade: The Sources and Effects of Regime Change." International Organization, Vol. 36, No. 2, pp. 417-55.

Lockwood, W. W. 1954. The Economic Development of Japan. Princeton, N.J.: Princeton University Press.

Lowinger, Thomas C. 1975. "The Technology Factor and the Export Performance of U.S. Manufacturing Industries." Economic Inquiry, Vol. 13, No. 2, pp. 221-36.

Luke, Timothy W. 1983. "Dependent Development and the Arab OPEC States." Journal of Politics, Vol. 45, No. 4, pp. 979-1003.

Lutz, James M., and Robert T. Green. 1983. "The Product Life Cycle and the Export Position of the United States." Journal of International Business Studies, Vol. 14, No. 3, pp. 77-93.

McCullock, Rachel. 1978. "Commodity Power and the International Community." In The New Economics of the Less Developed Countries: Changing Perceptions in the North-South Dialogue, Westview Special Studies in Social, Political, and Economic Development, ed. Nake M. Kamrany, pp. 209-50. Boulder, Colo.: Westview.

McGowan, Patrick J., and Dale L. Smith. 1978. "Economic Dependency in Black Africa: An Analysis of Competing Theories." International Organization, Vol. 32, No. 1, pp. 179-235.

McGowan, Pat, and Stephen G. Walker. 1981. "Radical and Conventional Models of U.S. Foreign Economic Policy Making." World Politics, Vol. 33, No. 3, pp. 347-82.

McKeown, Timothy J. 1984. "Firms and Tariff Regime Changes: Explaining the Demand for Protection." World Politics, Vol. 36, No. 2, pp. 215-33.

Mah, Feng-hwa. 1971. The Foreign Trade of Mainland China. Chicago: Aldine-Atherton.

Mahler, Vincent A. 1981. "Britain, the European Community, and the Developing Commonwealth: Dependence, Interdependence, and the Political Economy of Sugar." International Organization, Vol. 35, No. 3, pp. 467-92.

_____. 1980. Dependency Approaches to International Political Economy: A Cross-National Study. New York: Columbia University Press.

Makler, Harry, Alberto Martinelli, and Neil Smelser. 1982. "Introduction." In The New International Economy, Sage Studies in International Sociology, 26, eds. Harry Makler, Alberto Martinelli, and Neil Smelser, pp. 3-33. Beverly Hills, Calif.: Sage.

Malmgren, Harald B. 1981. "Changing Forms of Competition and World Trade Rules." In World Trade Competition: Western Countries and Third World Markets, ed. Center for Strategic and International Studies, pp. 409-53. New York: Praeger.

Marer, Paul. 1979. "Eastern European Economies: Achievements, Problems, Prospects." In Communism in Eastern Europe, eds. Teresa Rakowska-Harmstone and Andrew Gyorgy, pp. 244-89. Bloomington: Indiana University Press.

Martinelli, Alberto. 1982. "The Political and Social Impact of Transnational Corporations." In The New International Economy, Sage Studies in International Sociology, 26, eds. Harry Makler, Alberto Martinelli, and Neil Smelser, pp. 79-115. Beverly Hills, Calif.: Sage.

Mathieson, John A. 1979. The ADCs: Emerging Actors in the World Economy, Development Paper 28. Washington, D.C.: Overseas Development Council.

Matthews, Jacqueline D. 1977. Association System of the European Community, Praeger Special Studies in International Business, Finance, and Trade. New York: Praeger.

Meier, Gerald M. 1974. "External Economic Relationships and the Process of Development: A Framework for Discussion." In Latin American-U.S. Economic Interactions: Conflict, Accommodation, and Policies for the Future, eds. Robert B. Williamson, William P. Glade, and Karl M. Schmitt, pp. 9-26. Washington, D.C.: American Enterprise Institute for Public Policy Research.

Meyer, F. V. 1978. International Trade Policy. New York: St. Martin's.

Michalet, Charles-Albert. 1982. "From International Trade to World Economy: A New Paradigm." In The New International Economy, Sage Studies in International Sociology, 26, eds. Harry Makler, Alberto Martinelli, and Neil Smelser, pp. 37-58. Beverly Hills, Calif.: Sage.

Mikdashi, Zuhayr. 1976. The International Politics of Natural Resources. Ithaca, N.Y.: Cornell University Press.

_____. 1974. "Cooperation Among Oil Exporting Countries with Special Reference to Arab Countries: A Political Economy Analysis." International Organization, Vol. 1, pp. 1-30.

Mikesell, Raymond F., and Mark G. Farah. 1981. "U.S. Export Competitiveness in Manufactures in Third World Markets." In World Trade Competition: Western Countries and Third World Markets, ed. Center for Strategic and International Studies, pp. 45-169. New York: Praeger.

Mingst, Karen A. 1980. "Process and Policy in U.S. Commodities: The Impact of the Liberal Economic Paradigm." Paper read at University of Nebraska, Fifth Annual Hendricks Symposium, April, Lincoln.

Mitchell, Daniel J. B. 1970. "The Occupational Structure of US Exports and Imports." Quarterly Review of Economics and Business, Vol. 10, No. 4, pp. 17-30.

Monroe, Wilbur F. 1975. International Trade Policy in Transition. Lexington, Mass.: Lexington Books.

Moran, Theodore H. 1974. Multinational Corporations and the Politics of Dependence: Copper in Chile. Princeton, N.J.: Princeton University Press.

Morrison, Thomas K. 1976. Manufactured Exports from Developing Countries, Praeger Special Studies in International Economics and Development. New York: Praeger.

Morton, Kathryn, and Peter Tulloch. 1977. Trade and Developing Countries. New York: Wiley.

Murphy, George G. S. 1966. Soviet Mongolia: A Study of the Oldest Political Satellite. Berkeley: University of California Press.

Murray, Tracy, and Ingo Walter. 1978. "Special and Differential Liberalization of Quantitative Restrictions on Imports from Developing Countries." In Trade Policies Toward Developing Countries: The Multilateral Trade Negotiations, ed. Lorenzo L. Perez, pp. 34-88. Washington, D.C.: Bureau for Intergovernmental and International Affairs, Agency for International Development.

Mutti, John H., and J. David Richardson. 1979. "Crucial Issues for Current International Trade Policy." In The New International Economic Order: A U.S. Response, ed. David B. H. Denoon, pp. 35-77. New York: New York University Press.

Mytelka, Lynn, and Michael Dolan. 1980. "The EEC and the ACP Countries." In Integration and Unequal Development: The Experience of the EEC, eds. Dudley Seers and Constantine Vaitsos with Marja-Liisa Kiljunen, pp. 237-60. New York: St. Martin's.

Nau, Henry R. 1978. "The Diplomacy of World Food: Goals, Capabilities, Issues, and Arenas." In The Global Political Economy of Food, eds. Raymond F. Hopkins and Donald J. Puchala, pp. 201-35. Madison: University of Wisconsin Press.

Nicholson, Norman K., and John D. Esseks. 1978. "The Politics of Food Scarcities in Developing Countries." In The Global Political Economy of Food, eds. Raymond F. Hopkins and Donald J. Puchala, pp. 103-43. Madison: University of Wisconsin Press.

Nicol, Davidson, Luis Escheverria, and Aurelio Peccei (eds.). 1981. Regionalism and the New International Economic Order. New York: Pergamon.

O'Donnell, Guillermo. 1973. Modernization and Bureaucratic Authoritarianism. Studies in South American Politics. Berkeley: Institute of International Studies, University of California.

OECD. 1979a. Facing the Future: Mastering the Probable and Managing the Unpredictable, Interfutures Project. Paris: OECD.

_____. 1979b. The Impact of the Newly Industrializing Countries on Production and Trade in Manufactures. Paris: OECD.

_____. 1972. Policy Perspectives for International Trade and Economic Relations, Report to the Secretary-General. Paris: OECD.

Okita, Saburo. 1979. "The Pacific Community Idea." In Three Dialogues with Saburo Okita, Occasional Paper, East Asia Program of the Woodrow Wilson International Center for Scholars, Princeton University.

Okumura, Ariyoshi. 1981. "Japan and East Asia." In The Political Economy of New and Old Industrial Countries, ed. Christopher Saunders, pp. 261-83. London: Butterworth.

Ouattara, Alassane D. 1973. "Trade Effects of the Association of African Countries with the European Economic Community." International Monetary Fund Staff Papers, Vol. 20, No. 2, pp. 499-543.

Ozawa, Terutomo. 1979. Multinationalism, Japanese Style. Princeton, N.J.: Princeton University Press.

_____. 1968. "Imitation, Innovation, and Japanese Exports." In The Open Economy: Essays on International Trade and Finance, Columbia Studies in Economics, 1, eds. Peter B. Kenen and Roger Lawrence, pp. 190-212. New York: Columbia University Press.

Paarlberg, Robert L. 1978. "Shifting and Sharing Adjustment Burdens: The Role of the Industrial Food Importing Nations." In The Global Political Economy of Food, eds. Raymond F. Hopkins and Donald J. Puchala, pp. 79-101. Madison: University of Wisconsin Press.

Paddock, William, and Paul Paddock. 1976. Time of Famines: America and the World Food Crisis. Boston: Little, Brown.

Page, S. A. B. 1981. "The Revival of Protectionism and Its Consequences for Europe." Journal of Common Market Studies, Vol. 20, No. 1, pp. 17-40.

Pazos, Felipe. 1973. "Regional Integration of Trade Among Less Developed Countries." World Development, Vol. 1, No. 7, pp. 1-12.

Persaud, Bishnodat. 1980. "Export Earnings Stabilisation in the ACP/EEC Convention." In The Political Economy of EEC Relations with African, Caribbean and Pacific States: Contributions to the Understanding of the Lomé Convention on North-South Relations, ed. Frank Long, pp. 99-106. Oxford: Pergamon.

Prebisch, Raul. 1959. "Commercial Policy in the Underdeveloped Countries." American Economic Review, Vol. 49, No. 2, pp. 251-73.

Rapp, William V. 1975. "Japan's Industrial Policy." In The Japanese Economy in International Perspective, ed. Isaiah Frank, pp. 37-66. Baltimore: Johns Hopkins University Press.

Ray, David. 1973. "The Dependency Model of Latin American Underdevelopment: Three Basic Fallacies." Journal of Interamerican Studies and World Affairs, Vol. 15, No. 1, pp. 4-20.

Ray, James Lee, and Thomas Webster. 1978. "Dependency and Economic Growth in Latin America." International Studies Quarterly, Vol. 22, No. 3, pp. 409-34.

Rehfeldt, Udo. 1980. "France." In Integration and Unequal Development: The Experience of the EEC, eds. Dudley Seers and Constantine Vaitsos with Marja-Liisa Kiljunen, pp. 155-75. New York: St. Martin's.

Richardson, J. David. 1971. "Some Sensitivity Tests for a 'Constant Market Shares' Analyses of Export Growth." Review of Economics and Statistics, Vol. 53, No. 3, pp. 300-04.

Ricks, David A., Michael R. Czinkota, and Gladys A. DeJesus. 1980. "A Note on 'The Great American Disadvantage: Fact or Fiction?'" Journal of International Business Studies, Vol. 11, No. 2, pp. 135-36.

Roe, Terry, and Mathew Shane. 1979. "Export Performance, Marketing Services, and the Technological Characteristics of the Malaysian Industrial Sector." Journal of Developing Areas, Vol. 13, No. 2, pp. 175-89.

Rothstein, Robert L. 1977. The Weak in the World of the Strong: The Developing Countries in the International System. New York: Columbia University Press.

Ruggie, John. 1982. "International Regimes, Transactions, and Change: Embedded Liberalism in the Postwar Economic Order." International Organization, Vol. 36, No. 2, pp. 379-415.

Russet, Bruce. 1981-82. "Security and the Resources Scramble: Will 1984 Be Like 1914?" International Affairs, Vol. 58, No. 1, pp. 42-58.

Sanderson, Fred H. 1978. Japan's Food Prospects and Policies. Washington, D.C.: Brookings Institution.

Sato, Seizaburo. 1977. "The Foundations of Modern Japanese Foreign Policy." In The Foreign Policy of Modern Japan, ed. Robert A. Scalapino, pp. 367-90. Berkeley: University of California Press.

Saunders, Christopher. 1981. "Introduction." In The Political Economy of New and Old Industrial Countries, ed. Christopher Saunders, pp. 1-24. London: Butterworth.

Sauvant, Karl P. 1981. "Preface." In Changing Priorities on the International Agenda: The NIEO, ed. Karl P. Sauvant, pp. xxiii-xxvi. New York: Pergamon.
_____. "Introduction." In The New International Economic Order: Confrontation or Cooperation Between North and South?, eds. Karl P. Sauvant and Hajo Hasenpflung, pp. 1-19. Boulder, Colo.: Westview.

Sauvant, Karl P., and Hajo Hasenpflung (eds.). 1977. The New International Economic Order: Confrontation or Cooperation Between North and South? Boulder, Colo.: Westview.

Saxonhouse, Gary R. 1977. "The World Economy and Japanese Economic Policy." In The Foreign Policy of Modern Japan, ed. Robert A. Scalapino, pp. 281-318. Berkeley: University of California Press.

Scalapino, Robert A. 1977. "Perspectives on Modern Japanese Foreign Policy." In The Foreign Policy of Modern Japan, ed. Robert A. Scalapino, pp. 391-412. Berkeley: University of California Press.

Seers, Dudley. 1980a. "Conclusions: The EEC and Unequal Development." In Integration and Unequal Development: The Experience of the EEC, eds. Dudley Seers and Constantine Vaitsos with Marja-Liisa Kiljunen, pp. 307-17. New York: St. Martin's.

_____. 1980b. "Theoretical Aspects of Unequal Development at Different Spatial Levels." In Integration and Unequal Development: The Experience of the EEC, eds. Dudley Seers and Constantine Vaitsos with Marja-Liisa Kiljunen, pp. 9-23. New York: St. Martin's.

Senghass, Dieter. 1975. "Multinational Corporations and the Third World: On the Problem of the Further Integration of Peripheries into the Given Structure of the International Economic System." Journal of Peace Research, Vol. 12, No. 4, pp. 257-74.

Senghass-Knoblock, Eva. 1975. "The Internationalization of Capital and the Process of Underdevelopment: The Case of Black Africa." Journal of Peace Research, Vol. 12, No. 4, pp. 275-92.

Serfaty, Simon. 1981. "The United States, Western Europe, and the Third World: Allies and Adversaries." In World Trade Competition: Western Countries and Third World Markets, ed. Center for Strategic and International Studies, pp. 1-44. New York: Praeger.

Simai, Mihály. 1981. "A Case Study of Economic Cooperation in Eastern Europe." In Regionalism and the New International Economic Order, Pergamon Policy Studies, eds. Davidson Nicol, Luis Echeverria, and Aurelio Peccei, pp. 122-37. New York: Pergamon.

Sklar, Richard L. 1975. Corporate Power in an African State: The Political Impact of Multinational Mining Companies in Zambia. Berkeley: University of California Press.

Smith, Glen Alden. 1973. Soviet Foreign Trade: Organization, Operations, and Policy, 1918-1971, Praeger Special Studies in International Economics and Development. New York: Praeger.

Smith, Gordon W. 1979. "U.S. Commodity Policy and the Tin Agreement." In The New International Economic Order: A U.S. Response, ed. David B. H. Denoon, pp. 184-208. New York: New York University Press.

Smith, Tony. 1979. "The Underdevelopment of Development Literature: The Case of Dependency Theory." World Politics, Vol. 31, No. 2, pp. 247–88.

Spero, Joan Edelman. 1977. The Politics of International Economic Relations. New York: St. Martin's.

Stallings, Barbara. 1982. "Euromarkets, Third World Countries and the International Political Economy." In The New International Economy, Sage Studies in International Sociology, 26, eds. Harry Makler, Alberto Martinelli, and Neil Smelser, pp. 193–230. Beverly Hills, Calif.: Sage.

_____. 1972. Economic Dependency in Africa and Latin America, Sage Professional Paper in Comparative Politics, Vol. 3, No. 01–031. Beverly Hills, Calif.: Sage.

Stehr, Uwe. 1977. "Unequal Development and Dependency Structures in COMECON." Journal of Peace Research, Vol. 14, No. 2, pp. 115–28.

Sternitzke, Donald L. 1980. "'The Great American Competitive Disadvantage: Fact or Fiction?' A Reply." Journal of International Business Studies, Vol. 11, No. 2, p. 137.

_____. 1979. "The Great American Competitive Disadvantage: Fact or Fiction?" Journal of International Business Studies, Vol. 10, No. 2, pp. 25–36.

Stockwell, Edward Grant, and Karen Anne Laidlaw. 1981. Third World Development: Problems and Prospects. Chicago: Nelson-Hall.

Strange, Susan. 1982. "Cave! hic Dragones: A Critique of Regime Analysis." International Organization, Vol. 36, No. 2, pp. 479–96.

Stryker, J. Dirck. 1968. "The Sources of Change in Export Performance: The United States and Canada." In The Open Economy: Essays on International Trade and Finance, Columbia Studies in Economics, 1, eds. Peter B. Kenen and Roger Lawrence, pp. 150–74. New York: Columbia University Press.

Sunkel, Osvaldo. 1973. "Transnational Capitalism and National Disintegration in Latin America." Social and Economic Studies, Vol. 22, No. 1, pp. 132–76.

_____. 1969. "National Development Policy and External Dependence in Latin America." Journal of Development Studies, Vol. 6, No. 1, pp. 23–48.

Szymanski, Albert. 1983. "The Socialist World-System." In Socialist States in the World-System, ed. Christopher K. Chase-Dunn, pp. 57–84. Beverly Hills, Calif.: Sage.

Talbot, Ross, and Young W. Kihl. 1982. "The Politics of Domestic and Foreign Policy Linkages in U.S.-Japanese Agricultural Policy Making." In U.S.-Japanese Agricultural Trade Relations, eds. Emery N. Castle and Kenzo Hemmi, pp. 275-340. Washington, D.C.: Resources for the Future.

Thompson, Seth B. 1981. "International Organizations and the Improbability of a Global Food Regime." In Food Politics: The Regional Conflict, eds. David N. Balaam and Michael J. Carey, pp. 191-206. Totowa, N.J.: Allanheld, Osmun.

Tironi, Ernesto. 1980. "A Case Study of Latin America." In Integration and Unequal Development: The Experiences of the EEC, eds. Dudley Seers and Constantine Vaitsos with Marja-Liisa Kiljunen, pp. 45-56. New York: St. Martin's.

Tokuyama, Jiro. 1981. "The New Pacific Era and Japan's Role." In Political Change and the Economic Future of East Asia, ed. Robert B. Hewett, pp. 53-63. Honolulu: Pacific Forum.

Toma, Peter A. 1979. "The Communist Party of Czechoslovakia." In The Communist Parties of Eastern Europe, ed. Stephen Fischer-Galati, pp. 87-165. New York: Columbia University Press.

Trade Policy Research Centre. 1983. In the Kingdom of the Blind: A Draft Report on Protectionism and the Asian-Pacific Region. London: Trade Policy Research Centre.

Tumlir, Jan. 1982. "International Economic Order: Can the Trend Be Reversed?" The World Economy (November), pp. 29-41.

Turpin, William Nelson. 1977. Soviet Foreign Trade: Purpose and Performance. Lexington, Mass.: Lexington Books.

Twitchett, Carol Cosgrove. 1980. "Patterns of ACP/EEC Trade." In The Political Economy of EEC Relations with African, Caribbean and Pacific States: Contributions to the Understanding of the Lomé Convention on North-South Relations, ed. Frank Long, pp. 145-81. Oxford: Pergamon.

Uri, Pierre. 1976. Development Without Dependence, Praeger Special Studies in International Economics and Development. New York: Praeger.

UNCTAD. 1977. Review of International Trade and Development. New York: United Nations.

United Nations Statistical Office. Various Years. Yearbook of International Trade Statistics. New York: United Nations.

UNITAR. 1976[?]. A New International Economic Order: Selected Documents, 1945-1975, UNITAR Document Service No. 1. New York: UNITAR.

UNIDO. 1975. "Lima Declaration and Plan of Action on Industrial Development and Cooperation." Adopted at the Second General Conference of UNIDO, Lima, March.

U.S. Congress, House of Representatives, Committee on Foreign Affairs. 1979. Hearings on the Pacific Community Idea Before the Subcommittee on Asian and Pacific Affairs. Washington, D.C.: U.S. Government Printing Office.

U.S. GAO. 1982. Industrial Policy: Japan's Flexible Approach. Washington, D.C.: General Accounting Office.

_____. 1979. United States-Japan Trade: Issues and Problems. Washington, D.C.: General Accounting Office.

Vaitsos, Constantine. 1982. "From the Ugly American to the Ugly European: The Role of Western Europe in North-South Relations." In The New International Economy, Sage Studies in International Sociology, 26, eds. Harry Makler, Alberto Martinelli, and Neil Smelser, pp. 167-90. Beverly Hills, Calif.: Sage.

_____. 1980. "Corporate Integration in World Production and Trade." In Integration and Unequal Development: The Experience of the EEC, eds. Dudley Seers and Constantine Vaitsos with Marja-Liisa Kiljunen, pp. 24-45. New York: St. Martin's.

Vastine, J. Robert. 1977. "United States International Commodity Policy." Law and Policy in International Business, Vol. 9, No. 2, pp. 401-76.

Vernon, Raymond. 1971. Sovereignty at Bay: The Multinational Spread of U.S. Enterprises. New York: Basic Books.

Walker, William B. 1979. Industrial Innovation and International Trading Performance, Contemporary Studies in Economic and Financial Analysis, Vol. 15. Greenwich, Conn.: JAI Press.

Walleri, R. Dan. 1978. "The Political Economy Literature on North-South Relations." International Studies Quarterly, Vol. 22, No. 4, pp. 587-624.

Wallis, W. Allen. 1984. "International Economic Issues." Current Policy, No. 545 (statement by W. Allen Wallis, Undersecretary for Economic Affairs before the Joint Economic Committee of the U.S. Congress). Washington, D.C.: U.S. Department of State Bureau of Public Affairs, February 7.

Whitman, Marina v. N. 1981. International Trade and Investment: Two Perspectives, Essays in International Finance, No. 143. Princeton, N.J.: Department of Economics, Princeton University.

Wilkenson, B. W. 1968. Canada's International Trade: An Analysis of Recent Trends and Patterns. Canadian Trade Commission.

Wionczek, Miguel S. 1980. "The Relations Between the European Community and Latin America in the Context of the International Economic Crisis." Journal of Common Market Studies, Vol. 19, No. 2, pp. 160-74.

Woods, Douglas W. 1979. "Current Price and Investment Trends in the World Aluminum/Bauxite Market: Their Effect on the U.S. Economy." In The New International Economic Order: A U.S. Response, ed. David B. H. Denoon, pp. 209-47. New York: New York University Press.

World Bank. 1982. World Development Report: 1982. New York: Oxford University Press.

_____. 1977. World Bank Atlas: Population, Per Capita Product, and Growth Rates. Washington, D.C.: World Bank.

_____. 1975. World Bank Atlas: Population, Per Capita Product, and Growth Rates. Washington, D.C.: World Bank.

_____. Various Years. World Bank Atlas: Population, Per Capita Product, and Growth Rates. Washington, D.C.: World Bank.

World Food Institute. 1982. World Food Trade and US Agriculture, 1960-81. Ames: Iowa State University Press.

Yamazawa, Ippei. 1981. "Adjusting to the ADCs in Face of Structurally Depressed Industries: The Case of Japan." In Trade and Growth of the Advanced Developing Countries in the Pacific, eds. Wontack Hong and

Lawrence B. Krause, pp. 435–75. Seoul: Korea Development Institute.

Yoffie, David B. 1981. "The Newly Industrializing Countries and the Political Economy of Protectionism." International Studies Quarterly, Vol. 25, No. 4, pp. 569–99.

Yoshino, M. Y. 1975. "Japanese Foreign Direct Investment." In The Japanese Economy in International Perspective, ed. Isaiah Frank, pp. 248–72. Baltimore: Johns Hopkins University Press.

Zartman, I. William. 1971. The Politics of Trade Negotiations Between Africa and the European Economic Community: The Weak Confront the Strong. Princeton, N.J.: Princeton University Press.

Index

About the Authors

Young Whan Kihl is professor of political science at Iowa State University, where he teaches international politics and comparative politics. He is the author of Conflict Issues and International Civil Aviation Decisions: Three Cases (1971), co-author of Party Politics and Elections in Korea (1976), and author of Politics and Policies in Divided Korea: Regimes in Contest (1984). Kihl has contributed a number of chapters to edited volumes, including U.S.-Japanese Agricultural Trade Relations (1982) edited by Emery Castle and Kenzo Hemmi. His articles have appeared in various journals, including the American Political Science Review, the Journal of Politics, the Journal of Developing Areas, Current History, Problems of Communism, Asian Survey, the Journal of Northeast Asian Studies, the Journal of Korean Studies, and Korea and World Affairs.

James M. Lutz is associate professor of political science at Indiana University-Purdue University at Fort Wayne. Among his interests are comparative politics, with particular reference to Western Europe and the developing countries and the international political economy. He has co-authored The United States and World Trade: Changing Patterns and Dimensions (1978) and contributed chapters to a number of edited volumes. He has authored or co-authored a number of articles in professional journals, including the Journal of International Business Studies, the Western Political Quarterly, Orbis, Economic Geography, the American Sociological Review, the Columbia Journal of World Business, and Energy and Development.